Instructional Techniques and Practice

ST(P) Handbooks for Further Education

Instructional Techniques and Practice

L WALKLIN
BA(Hons) MIPlantE CertEd

Stanley Thornes (Publishers) Ltd

First published in 1982 by
Stanley Thornes (Publishers) Ltd
Ellenborough House
Wellington Street
CHELTENHAM
Glos. GL50 1YD
United Kingdom

Reprinted 1987
Reprinted 1989 (twice)
Reprinted 1990
Revised and reprinted 1991
Reprinted 1994

British Library Cataloguing in Publication Data

Walklin, L.
    Instructional techniques and practice
    1. Teaching—Handbooks, manuals, etc.
    I. Title
    371.3   LB1025.2

    ISBN 0–85950–344–5

Typeset by Castle Colour Printers Limited, Berkeley, Glos.
Printed and bound in Hong Kong by The Dah Hua Printing Press Co. Ltd.

CONTENTS

Part 4 *PRACTICAL TEACHING*   *293*

10 TEACHING PRACTICE   295

Part 5 *APPENDICES*   *303*

SOLUTIONS TO PROBLEMS   370

INDEX   373

Foreword

Until relatively recently educational syllabuses were proscribed in descriptive terms by examining bodies, and teaching staff directly responsible for education and training in classroom and workshop tended to accept the descriptive subject lists provided from those central bodies as being sufficient to outline both the extent of educational intentions and, by implication, the teaching strategies to be used.

Such attitudes changed, indeed had to change abruptly with the new-found curricular freedoms heralded by the Industrial Training Boards, the Technician and Business Education Councils, and at senior levels, the Council for National Academic Awards. The freedom to be personally involved in detailed construction of curricula and to define their purposes more fully led in turn to a more intense and continuing interest in both the conceptual and practical aspects of the student–teacher relationship and to a concern for the identification of 'aims', 'objectives' and 'goals' specifying educational intent and the expected outcome of the communication processes.

With so varied a pattern of educational and training programmes there can be no uniformity of approach to the definition of educational objectives and to assessment procedures and patterns which purport to assess their value, for at the one extreme will be those defined by specifying the teaching activity and the teachers' instructional role, whilst at the other, those specifying the learning outcome and the learners' achievement.

It is in the context of these new developments that Leslie Walklin's book makes its contribution to the understanding of curriculum design and the associated teaching and learning practices, guiding the reader easily through the complex theoretical background and directing him firmly into the arena in which the practitioner needs to operate on a day-to-day basis.

For the experienced teacher, Mr Walklin's approach gives great food for thought and for the reappraisal of presently used methods; for the less experienced, it shows thoughtful pathways along which developments can proceed with infinite advantage to both instructor and student touching on the theoretical aspects of the teacher–learner relationship but concentrating on the practical realities of their interaction. It is just the approach to benefit teacher and student, instructor and trainee and to establish the clarity of understanding required of those participating in the communication process so that teaching may be at its most effective and learning at its most rewarding.

R Bailey BSc, PhD
Former Principal, Bournemouth and Poole
College of Further Education

Introduction

This book is written for supervisors and line managers whose jobs include roles such as communicating, handling human relations, training and vocational assessment. Backed by many years of experience gained while teaching on NEBSM and Advanced NEBSM programmes and supported by considerable skills trainer and teacher training work, the author demonstrates insight and understanding of planning and implementing practical training in business, industrial and educational settings.

Various reviews have acknowledged the 'easy to read and make sense of' qualities of the book, which may be dipped into whenever specific information is needed. This has proved to be a major advantage to readers overseas as well as in the United Kingdom.

Instructional Techniques and Practice is particularly suitable for supervisor and trainer training including **NEBSM** and and is useful when seeking background knowledge to support assessments for **TDLB Units** making up **Vocational Trainer, Assessor and C&G 730 FAETC** awards. The book's strength lies in the way it describes how people learn, why they learn and how readers may gain a clear understanding of the learning process. This is backed up with clear explanations of how to improve communication skills and plan, prepare, resource and deliver effective presentations.

The book aims to help improve the quality and relevance of training of those who will have responsibility for developing, coaching or otherwise helping other people to attain the knowledge, skills and attitudes needed to perform effectively in their chosen occupation.

Trainer development and **Investors in People** initiatives are key elements in the pursuit of excellence, and **trainer performance** is now recognised as being an essential factor in the success of many leading companies and training providers. This text seeks to provide a sufficient knowledge of the principles and methods of teaching and learning to enable those responsible to plan and facilitate high quality training.

Instructional Techniques and Practice is recommended reading for **NEBSM** students and people undertaking **NVQs in teaching, Cert. Ed (FE), JEB Teacher's Diploma Courses** and training qualifications such as the latest range of **workplace trainer and vocational assessor awards**.

NB: In recommending the text, the above bodies do not necessarily agree with every statement therein.

Format

The book is divided into five main parts.

Part 1 is concerned with communicating, testing and assessing, and includes information relating to writing and using behavioural objectives.

Part 2 relates to teaching and learning. It covers the important areas of perception, motivation, patterns of adolescent behaviour, lesson-planning and the many ways in which people learn. Industrial job instruction training and various teaching methods are also described in some depth.

Part 3 covers the purposes, preparation and uses of a wide range of audio-visual training aids with descriptions of their main features.

Part 4 is concerned with practical teaching and stresses the importance of the management of teaching and the deployment of resources.

Part 5 contains appendices, each of which includes much useful information on specific topics.

How to use the book

The book may be read from cover to cover, or 'dipped into' whenever information relating to a particular topic is required.

The text is numbered in chapters and sections, and each element may be read individually without necessarily referring to what has gone before.

A brief summary of content is provided at the end of each chapter, highlighting key information discussed more fully within the main text.

Case studies are provided where appropriate, and a set of review questions is to be found at the end of each chapter. The questions may be used either for group discussion or as self-tests.

The chapters have been numbered in accordance with objectives set out in the BTEC unit DOR/058 (see page 360); many of these unit objectives may be taught in any preferred sequence.

Acknowledgements

The Author and Publishers wish to thank the following for permission to reproduce illustrations appearing in this book:

Anchor Foods Ltd
Bell and Howell Ltd
British Leyland Cars Ltd
British Standards Institution
City and Guilds of London Institute
Education and Training, ABE Publications
Engineering Industry Training Board
Hodder and Stoughton (London)
Mr Lance Nation
The Open University
Pitman Books Ltd
The Principal, South Thames College
Rank Aldis Ltd
The Controller of Her Majesty's Stationery Office
Warner-Lambert (UK) Ltd
Warner Swasey Turning Machines Ltd

Acknowledgement is also due to the following:

Addison-Wesley Publishing Co Inc for 'Flanders Interaction Analysis Categories' (FIAC) from *Analysing Teaching Behaviour* by N Flanders

R Bailey BSc, PhD, MBIM, Former Principal, Bournemouth and Poole College of Further Education, for permission to reproduce drawings by Mr Brian Snape

Bell and Howell A-V Ltd for information relating to: 'The Preparation of Slide/Tape Programmes'

The British Standards Institute for extracts from BS 3138:1969

Mr G Chamberlain and the Institution of Plant Engineers for the article 'Fault Analysis'

The City and Guilds of London Institute for extracts from their 'Manual of Objective Testing'

The Controller of Her Majesty's Stationery Office for extracts from 'Training Advisory Leaflet No. 2' (SHW 12)

Fearon Publishers for a quotation from *Preparing Educational Objectives* by R F Mager

Peter J M Finney for source material relating to participative learning

Granada Publishing Ltd for a quotation from *Class, Equality and Political Order* by Frank Parkin

A Greer and G W Taylor for diagrams from *BTEC First-Mathematics for Technicians* published by Stanley Thornes (Publishers) Ltd

Guild Sound and Vision Ltd for descriptions of film and video programmes that may be hired

Harcourt Brace Jovanovich for references from *Introduction to Psychology* by E Hilgard, R C Atkinson and R L Atkinson

Steven Keeping for cartoons

K G Lavender BSc(Hons), CEng, MIEE, MInstW, Principal, South Thames College, London, for extracts from handbook 'The Overhead Projector'

Longman Group Ltd and David McKay Co Ltd for references from *Taxonomy of Educational Objectives* by B Bloom, D Krathwohl *et al*

John McCafferty for the algorithm from his article 'Innovation and Education' (*Education and Training*, Volume 22 No. 9)

Methuen Ltd for references from *Social Interaction* by Professor M Argyle

Mirror Group Newspapers for the Daily Mirror Mirrorgrams (in issues of 20 and 25 January 1982)

Mouton Press for references from *Current Trends in Linguistics* ed. A S Abramson

The Open University for: extracts from 'Intervening in the Learning Process'—course E281, unit 16, by D Moseley
A quotation from Professor Derek Wright's television programme 'Naughty Things'—course D305
Instructions given in 'Communication'—course D305, block 11, by J Greene
'Trial and Error Learning Activity'—course E281

Penguin Books Ltd for permission to reprint the 'Chart for Bales's Interaction Process Analysis' adapted from W P Robinson: *Language and Social Behaviour* (Penguin Education, 1972) figure 1, page 44; and for quotations from *Asylums*, by E Goffman

Pitman Books Ltd for diagrams from *Production Technology for Technicians*, by H H Marshall

Staedtler UK Limited for information relating to: 'Preparing Overhead Projector Transparencies'

Quartet Books Ltd for references from *The State in a Capitalist Society* by Ralph Miliband

Professor M D Stephens for a quotation from *Teaching Techniques in Adult Education*

The Sun, New Group Newspapers Ltd for the 'Sun Mindbender Number 222'

The Business & Technician Education Council for BTEC unit DOR/058 and extracts from BTEC unit U76/056

Christine Ward for an extract from *Designing a Scheme of Assessment* published by Stanley Thornes (Publishers) Ltd

Warner-Lambert (UK), for photograph of Sloans Liniment

Roy Whitlow, Bristol Polytechnic, for extracts from: 'Notes for Guidance —provision of BTEC courses in Construction Assessment System for Technician Certificate'

John Wiley & Sons Ltd, for an extract from *Exploration in Personality* by H A Murray

James Winthorpe, Bournemouth and Poole College of Further Education, for photographs of magnetic aids

David Whitby for examples of 'doodlings'

Paul Yeandle, Bournemouth and Poole College of Further Education, for extracts from Micro No 2, March 1982

I would like to thank Roy Hall, Head of the Department of Social and Community Studies, Bournemouth and Poole College of Further Education, for reading the manuscript and for his constructive comments.

Thanks are due to Malcolm Welchman of the Department of Educational Resources, South Thames College, for providing valuable information relating to the preparation of overhead projector transparencies.

Special thanks are due to Miss Trudy Hayter for her goodwill and infinite patience in typing the manuscript during time which could have been spent much more pleasurably.

The characters named in case studies in this book have no existence outside the imagination of the Author and have no relation whatsoever with any company or person bearing the same name or names. They are not even distantly inspired by any individual known or unknown to the author, and all incidents are pure invention.

Part 1
Communicating, Testing and Assessing

1
Developing the techniques of communication

Communication is the art of successfully conveying one's meaning to others by means of an interchange of experience. The important word is *successfully*, which implies that desired behaviour change results when the receiver takes in the message.

During a lesson the instructor could transmit information for the whole period, but there is no guarantee that any of the information would be received and retained by the learner.

The learner will need to be motivated before attention is paid to what the instructor is saying. Motivation comes in many forms. Learners must be aware of the importance of learning to themselves and their future careers, or they must have some other psychological need to learn, if they are to learn anything.

Instructing involves two-way communication, contrary to the commonly held view that it is one-way and achieved simply by passing information from instructor to learner. Although the instructor is responsible for presenting audio and visual stimuli, and for maintaining attention, communication forms the link along which information, concepts, opinions and attitudes flow, and this requires active participation on the part of the trainee. Poor communication leads to mistakes, misunderstandings and time-wasting, so that constant effort is required from all concerned to ensure that the flow of communication is maintained.

Poor communications can have a drastic effect on individual relationships, leading to general feelings of dissatisfaction which spread throughout the group and result in poor co-operation. The ability of an instructor to establish rapport goes a long way towards providing an atmosphere compatible with effective communication and learning, thereby enhancing relationships.

3

Instructors must be able to assess problems of understanding, embarrassment and confusion in their learners. They should accordingly pitch instruction at a level commensurate with the learner's previous knowledge, especially when introducing abstract concepts and technical terms. Simple words should be used wherever possible.

Both verbal and non-verbal signals play important parts in the communication process, while facial expressions and gestures substitute for and reinforce other forms of communication.

1.1 Psychological needs which motivate people to work

Frederick Winslow (Speedy) Taylor was one of the first to apply psychology to problems relating to inefficient working methods and worker performance in the first half of the twentieth century.

As Chief Engineer at the Midvale Iron Works in the United States of America, he found that the existing traditional way of working was often inefficient. He knew that inefficiency cost the company money, and that if he could find a means of improving efficiency, a higher output per worker could be obtained and this would result in increased productivity and greater profitability for the company. With this in mind, he set about studying groups of workers and reorganising work along 'scientific' lines—work was simplified, and efficient working methods employing the most economical movements were developed.

Later, at the Bethlehem Steel Company, as Management Consultant in the field of engineering, he focused his attention on a gang of seventy-five labourers loading railway wagons at the works. On average, each man was observed to load $12\frac{1}{2}$ tons of pig-iron per day. He decided that this could be improved, and that a target of 48 tons per day could be achieved by an efficient, trained worker. After discussions with management, he set up an experiment to justify his assumptions. His strategy was based on three key factors:
(a) selecting the best workers for the task;
(b) instructing them in the most efficient methods of working;
(c) giving incentives by way of bonuses for high individual output.

Taylor chose a strong, thrifty and industrious Dutch labourer, carefully trained him and then put him to work. Soon he was able to load $47\frac{1}{2}$ tons of pig-iron in a day, and what is more, he maintained this rate consistently over the next three years. For his efforts the man was paid a bonus of 60 per cent on his base rate of pay. Other men received similar training and the outcome of the experiment was that a reduction of 72 per cent in the labour force needed to load the wagons was achieved. This saved the company 75 000 dollars a year, while the remaining loaders were a good deal better off financially.

Taylor spent a great deal of his working life armed with stop-watch, developing a form of method study combined with time and motion techniques. He became unpopular, being seen by the workmen as a tool of management bent upon exploitation of the work-force, and interested only in increasing productivity, with little concern for the well-being of the exploited.

The work of Taylor described above is representative of the view then commonly held by employers: that most people are lazy, find work distasteful, are motivated by fear or greed and do as little as possible when at the works. Other possible reasons for improving output tended to be overlooked or dismissed out of hand.

However, the work of Elton Mayo brought to light other hidden factors which greatly affect the performance of a work-force.

In 1923 Elton Mayo, a professor at the Harvard Graduate School of Business, investigated the causes of high labour turnover at a textile works near Philadelphia. The work of the department concerned was unskilled and monotonous. Noise from the machines made conversation impossible. Mayo instituted rest periods for a group consisting of one-third of the shop work force. Labour turnover decreased, output rose, and bonus was earned, not only by the selected group, but also by the two-thirds who continued to work without breaks.

Later a rush order was received and the supervisors stopped rest breaks, believing that longer hours of work would produce increased output. Within a few days, output had slumped to the pre-experiment level, with a significant increase in absenteeism.

The supervisors brought back the rest periods on an earned basis. The workers did not respond; output remained low.

Mayo then invited the president of the company, who was popular with the employees, to take personal charge of operations in the shop. He ordered all textile machinery to be shut down during the breaks so that both supervisors and workers could rest without background noise.

Soon, productivity reached the high level attained after the rest breaks had first been implemented, morale improved and absenteeism once again decreased.

Again, the Hawthorne investigations carried out at the General Electric Company works in Chicago, between 1924 and 1927, provide a good example of how individual and group behaviour can yield confusing results, even in a most carefully controlled experiment.

The investigations were set up because even though the company (described by Mayo as 'a company definitely committed to justice and humanity in dealing with its workers') provided good material conditions and fringe benefits, there was a good deal of dissatisfaction amongst the 30 000 employees.

A team of efficiency experts was called in to examine ergonomics at the workplace and lighting in particular. Rest periods were also varied in both duration and frequency, for it was known that fatigue and toxic matter in the bloodstream could be eliminated by refreshment and rest breaks. It was hoped that the outcome of changes recommended by the team would be a reduction in stress and tension, which management thought might have been generated by environmental factors and existing patterns of working hours.

For one of the lighting experiments, the shop staff was divided between two groups—a control group and a test group. The control group's lighting was maintained at the existing level whilst the test group's lighting brilliance was increased. The test group's output rose as was expected, but so did that of the control group.

Light for the test group was then, with their knowledge, decreased below that of the control group and yet again its output rose as did the control group's.

Management was baffled. Clearly the results had made a nonsense of their scientific expectations. Something more than the changes made in the working environment had caused the rise in output and morale of both groups.

What factors do you think contributed to the improvements in output and morale outlined in the cases described?

A check-list of factors affecting output and morale is given in Appendix 1.

Why do people work?

One commonly held view is that 'economic man' is an individual, motivated to work only by greed or fear of dismissal—the 'carrot and stick' concept. It is further held that when at work he does as little as possible for as much as he can get for his labour. No one can deny that for a large majority of the work-force, paid work is a basic necessity for existence, and so, to some extent, it must be true that money is an important motivator. But this does not account for the fact that football pools winners and the like often opt to continue working, generally in the same type of employment. Why then do people continue to work if there is no pressing financial necessity to do so?

The question 'Why do you work?' has often been put to groups. The initial response to the question is generally: 'For money, why else?' 'Can't live without money so I have to work.' 'To support myself and my family.'

After a while other reasons are given, such as:
'I'd be bored if I didn't go to work.'
'I've always worked.'
'It's traditional to go to work.'
'I'm interested in my job.'
'I'd miss my workmates.'
'I find the work challenging.'
'I've got power at work.'
'I have a laugh at work.'
'Mine's a responsible job.'
'I enjoy my work, really.'
'My boss respects me for my skill on the tools.'
'I'd work even if I were paid for doing nothing.'

The conclusion to be drawn from such discussions is that work is a social activity and that, while money is important, there are many other reasons for working.

The drive reduction concept of motivation

Homeostasis is a self-regulating process in which the biological conditions necessary for a man's survival are kept within safe limits. If his body needs replenishing with food and water, homeostatic mechanisms make him feel hungry or thirsty. Hunger and thirst are examples of primary drives, while the acquisition of food and drink become primary goals. The primary biological needs for survival are: food, water, air, sleep and propagation of the species. (See figure 1.1.)

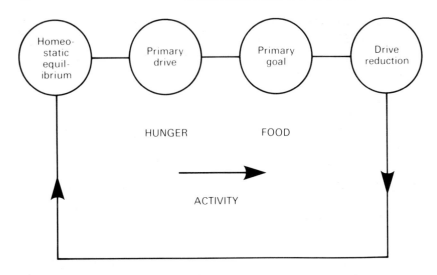

FIG. 1.1

Drive is the motivational force causing behaviour—the man feels hungry, he seeks food, finds food, consumes it and no longer feels hungry. Drive reduction has occurred and he has reached homeostatic equilibrium.

Primary drives are essential to survival but there are also secondary drives which can be acquired through learning. It is the latter which form the basis for understanding a person's behaviour, both at work and in his social world outside working hours.

Murray's list of 'psychogenic' needs is given in Appendix 2. The reader may like to peruse the list and consider those factors which relate to the need of an individual to work.

Details of audio-visual aids which relate to motivation and which may be hired are given in Appendix 3.

1.2   Why people need to communicate

Man is an information processor and as such is constantly handling information which he receives from his environment.

Communication is the imparting or exchanging of information by message or otherwise, and the effectiveness of this process is measured by observing its results.

Person-to-person relationships depend upon how well the communication is received and how the message it contains is perceived. This perception will be influenced by a person's social experience and knowledge of similiar communications previously acquired.

Language itself plays a major role in communication and serves to transmit knowledge from one person to another. Man is fortunate in being able to acquire knowledge through language, this ability being a genetically determined characteristic which gives him superiority over other species. He is able to decide what to say, when to say it and how to say it with most effect.

The modern industrial environment has created a need for both managers and instructors to communicate effectively, and the success of an enterprise depends largely on how well they cope with day-to-day interactions with the work-force.

In the instructional situation, communication is used to convey an instructor's thoughts to others. He states facts, poses problems and discusses solutions. Communication is therefore necessary in order to give and to receive information, to elicit responses and hence to influence others in one way or another.

1.3 How communication aims at behaviour change

Behaviour occurs as a response to stimuli, and when related to human beings it could be defined as those activities of a person that can be observed by others.

Behavioural science is a branch of psychology or sociology which is concerned with the behaviour of both human beings and other organisms. *Behavioural scientists* are interested in areas such as the effect of communication upon behaviour.

Individuals and groups are constantly being bombarded by stimuli, some of which result from written and verbal communications received from mass media sources. Banner headlines attract attention; politicians hold meetings and make speeches; radio and television blast out advertising slogans, news and current affairs; and, at the workplace, supervisors communicate.

News is news. Most people are intrinsically curious and feel the need to keep abreast of events, both national and world-wide. With certain broadcast propaganda, as with advertising and political speeches, the interest of the originator lies in the extent to which the listener's morale, attitudes, beliefs and opinions are modified by exposure to the communication.

In the case of persuasive communications, those who originate the communication often carry out surveys designed to measure opinion or behaviour change. Two main methods are employed: the 'before and after' survey and the 'control group/experimental group' survey. In the first method, surveys prepared in order to evaluate opinion and behaviour are administered both before and after receiving the communication, the difference giving a measure of change. The second method utilises two randomly selected groups—an experimental group which is exposed to the communication and a control group which is not. Again, the difference in results gives a measure of change.

In the instructional situation then, the purpose of communication is to promote a change in behaviour. The aim is to cause a change to occur, either in the amount of knowledge held by a trainee in a given topic area, or in his ability to perform certain tasks.

The effectiveness of the instruction will depend not only on adequate preparation of subject-matter, but also on the way trainees evaluate the communicator. If the instructor is seen to be credible, that is, to be reliable and qualified by his experience and ability in the task area, then there should be a significant change in behaviour. On the other hand, if the instructor professes to be an expert and is seen by the trainees to lack this expertise, a discrepancy will be noted and little, if any, positive behaviour change will occur.

1.4   The importance of non-verbal signals to the instructor

People spend a good deal of time interacting with others. They meet at work, in the classroom and during leisure activities. During these meetings, communication takes place. At first, it would appear that face-to-face communication consists of taking it in turns to speak. While one is speaking the other is expected to listen. However, upon closer examination it can be seen that people resort to a variety of verbal and non-verbal behaviour in order to maintain a smooth flow of communication. Such behaviour includes head nods, smiles, frowns, bodily contact, eye movements, laughter, body posture, language and many other things.

Non-verbal cues play an important part in regulating and maintaining conversations. During a meeting, speech is backed up by an intricate network of gestures which affect the meaning attached to what is said.

In a teaching situation, the instructor will be continuously moving his head, body and hands while delivering the lesson. These movements are coordinated with speech to make up the total communication. Some movements will be unplanned and perhaps carried out quite unconsciously. Such movements are known as mannerisms, and if repeated frequently, they will be noticed and will provide a source of amusement for the group, who will probably mimic the unfortunate instructor.

The facial expression of group members provides feedback on their reaction to the instructor. Glazed or down-turned eyes indicate boredom or disinterest, as does fidgeting. Fully raised eyebrows signal disbelief and half-raised indicate puzzlement. Bodily posture adopted by group members provides a means by which their attitude to the instructor may be judged and acts as a pointer to their mood during the lesson.

Control of the group demands that the instructor should be sensitive to the non-verbal signals being transmitted by individual members. Their faces usually give a good indication of how they feel, and a working knowledge of the meaning of non-verbal signals will prove invaluable to the instructor.

TASK

1. Make a list of the non-verbal signals being transmitted by:
   (a) a bored class;
   (b) an interested class.

2. Make a list of non-verbal signals which may:
   (a) aid an instructor's communications;
   (b) hinder an instructor's communications.

1.5 The reasons for nervousness in an instructor and how to overcome it

All speakers, no matter how experienced, feel slight nervousness before they start to talk. Nervousness can be an asset. It is bottled up energy. Once a speaker gets into his talk, gets excited and animated, this nervousness releases itself in effective energy.

Dale Carnegie

Many people get the shakes when asked to stand up in front of a group for the first time and deliver a talk. Actors get stage fright and even experienced lecturers tend to be nervous on occasions, but they usually manage to conceal their nervousness. For the novice, the prospect of standing alone exposed to the group can take on nightmarish proportions. There are three main reasons for this nervousness:
(a) lack of knowledge of the subject-matter;
(b) lack of preparation before delivering the talk;
(c) lack of confidence due to inexperience in presenting talks.

Nervous speaker performing

How to overcome nervousness

Having suggested reasons for nervousness, the next step is to decide how to overcome the problem. Some preliminary thinking is called for.

Ask yourself:
(a) What is the nature of my audience? Are they laymen? Are they technically equal to myself? Why are they attending the talk? What do they expect of me?
(b) What are my objectives?
    What do I hope to achieve?
    What exactly do I wish to convey to the audience?
(c) Where will the talk take place?
    How long will it last?
    Will I need visual or audio-visual aids?
    Will I need handouts?

KNOWLEDGE

Once you have written down your objectives, research and revision of subject-matter relating to the objectives can be carried out. Even if you are an expert in the subject, the same procedure should be adopted, because it is easy to find yourself unable to recall critical information due to lack of use. It pays to refresh your memory.

The next step is detailed preparation of the subject-matter. Gather information. Check it for accuracy. Check old notes and ensure that information is up to date. Has that British Standard been superseded? Is your data metricated? Has new legislation been introduced? Sort the information. List important points under separate headings and sub-headings. Arrange in correct sequence.

The actual talk should be arranged in three parts:
(a) introduction;
(b) main body;
(c) conclusion.

The introduction should focus attention upon the subject of the talk or pose a problem. It should serve as a lead-in. Start with a story, anecdote, alarming fact or a quotation.

The main body should contain the facts, arguments and supporting evidence.

The conclusion should summarise and reinforce the key facts and preferably contain a punchline or final appeal.

Many speakers like to write out the whole talk in full beforehand and use this for rehearsal, but few speakers would read this draft to an audience. The audience would soon become bored and disinterested, especially if the speaker continually lost his place after looking up. It is much better to draft the talk and then use this to prepare a set of file cards with headings or key words printed in large letters in correct sequence as lecture notes. If you have invested sufficient effort in preparation, these key words will be enough to trigger your thought processes and the talk will flow easily. Any visual aids required should be designed and prepared well in advance. It is better to use stencils or Letraset to produce printing on overhead projector transparencies rather than resorting to handwriting—which can be illegible and is often too small to be read at a distance. Or use a desk-top publisher to produce really professional aids.

PRESENTATION

Before delivering your talk, number the cue cards and visual aids, and make sure that they are in the correct sequence. It pays to rehearse the whole talk in front of a mirror. Don't try to hide the cue cards, just glance down, read the cue and then turn the card face down on a separate pile. The audience will appreciate the effort you have made in coming adequately prepared.

Talking 'off the cuff' can be readily identified, and only a relatively few experienced speakers can get away with it.

Arrive at the venue early. Set up your equipment. Check the microphone, lay out the cue cards and aids. If you arrive at the last minute, ill-prepared, you may as well go home.

Before you start speaking, you will probably be introduced to the audience. Give the introducer a few background details about yourself in advance; he will probably wish to state your name, relevant qualifications and the title of your talk. Then he will retire and you will be on your own.

Try to stand in a comfortable relaxed manner and, above all, try to project a friendly, sincere image. If you can do this, the audience will soon warm to you. The first few minutes are important so try to relate your introduction to familiar things and to the audience's own experiences. Get them on your side, then after a few minutes you will forget your anxiety and, as Carnegie predicts, your nervous energy will be translated into useful energy and enthusiasm.

When speaking, look at each member of the audience in turn. Share yourself around and avoid fixing your gaze on one or two especially sympathetic listeners. Vary the pitch and tone of voice and do not gabble or mumble. Avoid a monotone and adjust the rate of speaking to the importance and complexity of the information you are imparting. Key facts and statements should be put over slowly while less important detail and anecdotes may be delivered at a faster rate. Statistics and quotations should be read in full from cue cards so as to avoid the risk of inaccuracy. Never go beyond the facts available. If you do, you will run the risk of being challenged during question time.

Non-verbal signals are an important part of the communication process. Unpleasant and distracting mannerisms are undesirable, and you may find that the audience concentrates on watching these, rather than listening to your talk. Other gestures can actually help to convey meaning to the audience and may serve to brighten up the talk. Remember, stiffness and formality are barriers to effective communication.

Check-list—giving a talk

A check-list of suggested Do's and Do Not's is provided in the hope that it may help the reader to achieve a skilled performance in public speaking.

DO

Know your subject.
Research books, newspapers and periodicals.
Check your references and evidence.
Check latest legislation.
Check British Standards.
Ensure authorities quoted are reliable.
Metricate your data.
Define specialised vocabulary.
Write out key facts and statements in full and read these during delivery.
Check time, date and place of talk.
Use cue cards.
Present information clearly in simple direct language and in logical
    sequence or chronological order.
Repeat important information in several ways.
Use concrete examples and stories relating to your theme.
Emphasise important information.
Arouse curiosity.
Avoid ambiguity.
Use visual aids wherever possible.
Vary pitch, tone and rate of delivery.
Share yourself out among the audience.
Be friendly, polite and sincere.
Be dynamic and make a dramatic opening.
Check your appearance before the talk.
Stand in a comfortable and relaxed manner.
Determine level of language expected.
Resist verbosity—long words, long-winded exposition.
Rehearse the talk.
Use useful non-verbal signals.
Avoid confrontations with the audience.

DO NOT

Arrive late.
Rush your talk.
Mumble.
Speak in a monotone.
Read the talk in its entirety.
Apologise for lack of experience.
Fidget, toss chalk, jingle keys, etc.

Fix your gaze on few individuals.
Make wisecracks or jokes unless they are relevant and really good.
Go beyond your facts.
Make sarcastic remarks.
Show off.
Ridicule individuals during question time.

Training films and video tapes available

An outline of the content of some resources dealing with presentation skills is given in Appendix 4. Films and video tapes may be hired from Guild Training.

1.6   Typical mannerisms associated with nervousness

Fear of embarrassment is accompanied by nervousness and can lead to disorganisation and lack of control. The inexperienced speaker feels like running away. His heart-rate increases, he begins to tremble and his palms sweat. These are the symptoms of nervous anxiety brought about by intense stimulation.

Somehow or another the novice manages to get started but soon finds that he has forgotten his lines. He blushes, stutters, becomes tongue-tied or freezes. If he manages to keep going, his speech becomes irregular, jerky and too fast. He gabbles, and the ums and ers fall thick and fast, sometimes interspersed with bouts of nervous laughter.

Mannerisms associated with nervousness are often the source of audience annoyance or displeasure. Typical mannerisms include frequent removal and replacement of spectacles, and high-speed polishing of the spectacles on coat or shirt-front. Pen-tapping, chalk-tossing, fumbling, winding of watches, ear-lobe tugging, foot-tapping and jingling coins in pockets—these are all frequently observed signs of nervousness.

Fortunately, with adequate preparation, rehearsal and hard-won practical experience, many of the mannerisms described above will disappear. Rest assured that many polished speakers have had to overcome these same nervous mannerisms in order to attain their refined technique.

1.7   Use of video in controlling non-verbal signals

Video is a powerful resource medium which can be employed for training in a wide field of activities. Its main advantage is its immediacy. Events can be transmitted as they occur, and at the same time a videotape may be recorded for replay and analysis later.

Video is invaluable when undertaking microtraining exercises in controlling mannerisms and non-verbal signals. The instructor presents a piece of instruction to a group while another person records his performance. The videotape so produced can then be examined and appraised in terms of both what is done and what non-verbal aspects are employed. Undesirable mannerisms can be isolated and steps taken to eliminate them.

1.8 Characteristics which establish rapport

Student–teacher relationships in the classroom are one of the most important factors in the learning process. Little or no learning can take place unless the students want to learn. The general assumption is that the majority of students enter a classroom with a desire to learn something, this being an intrinsic characteristic of the human race. The outcome depends largely upon the teacher, who can make or mar the lesson by his apparent attitude towards the students. Similarly, if the students cannot identify themselves with the teacher, the result can be disastrous.

The ability to establish rapport rests upon the teacher's demonstration of a sympathetic attitude towards the group and on its showing willingness to follow the teacher's lead. Mutual co-operation and support is the keystone of success.

Rapport is a difficult concept to describe and involves many facets, such as respect, regard, concern, harmony, solidarity and affiliation. If rapport can be established, the group will see eye to eye and a bond of union will be forged. This will result in the group acquiring a sense of belonging, a team spirit and good relations. A smooth pattern of interaction should then follow.

A teacher's personality traits govern, to some extent, his ability to encourage rapport; but a trait is yet another elusive concept. One school of thought holds that a personality trait is a mental structure based upon consistent behaviour in a large number of different situations. This would suggest that a teacher is always easy-going or aggressive, or persevering, with every group, every lesson. Another theory suggests that there is no constant trait but that behaviour depends upon past experiences with different groups.

It may be that teacher plus group A are very compatible and rapport is well established, but teacher plus group B just cannot make headway due to an inability to establish rapport. The difference between the two groups will certainly be shown up when educational attainment is compared.

Possibly the best means of establishing rapport is to exhibit a firm, fair, warm and friendly attitude and to show empathy towards the group. Attention should be paid to making eye contact with each member of the group and speaking in a pleasant tone of voice. The members of the group should be treated as equals, within limits, and attempts made to break down social barriers. A keen interest should be taken in listening carefully to responses from the group when accepting answers, and if an incorrect response is received, anxiety should be reduced by preserving the respondent's self-esteem.

1.9 Responses required of trainees in order that spoken communication may take place

In order that communication may take place, the communicator must gain the attention of the person with whom he wishes to communicate. If this can be done, a response should be forthcoming.

A *response* is the behavioural result of stimulation brought about by exposure to verbal or non-verbal signals from the environment which impinge on the recipient. A stimulus produces a response in a living organism. It may also rouse a person to action, or increased action. Stimuli are important in gaining attention. The most signficant properties are intensity, size, contrast, colour and movement.

When a stimulus attracts our attention we respond by performing certain body movements that improve our reception of the stimulation. 'Orienting reflexes' result. If we hear our name, we look toward the speaker. If an intense light flashes, we look in its direction. In the classroom situation we pay attention when the instructor speaks. If he writes on the chalkboard or switches on the overhead projector, we read what is written.

The main problem in gaining attention is that people are usually pre-occupied with messages circulating in their inner systems. These messages may result from having received stimuli from the surroundings or from thought processes. While these take precedence, little or no effective communication can take place. To gain full attention, irrelevant sensory inputs must be filtered out so that the trainee concentrates only on those directed to him by the instructor. The trainee must therefore respond by concentrating on what the instructor says or does.

Attention involves motivation while personality factors and the nature of the task are strong influences on the trainee's behaviour in the classroom. The main aims of the instructor are to transmit to the trainee words, ideas and concepts. Therefore, for successful communication the trainee must be interested in what is being transmitted, and having received the message he must decode it in terms of previously known information. What is perceived and the meaning attached to it is determined to some extent by the trainee's needs and values, and this perception must coincide with the instructor's intended communication in order to be effective.

1.10 Instruction is the art of causing desired responses to happen

No learning can take place without active responses from the trainee. A training situation can be said to have been successful if the instructor's actions result in a desired change in trainee behaviour. Throughout the training session the instructor's role is that of enabler. He should provide a framework within which the desired responses are made to occur.

Attention peaks at the beginning of a lesson. This is the time to outline the ground to be covered and to fuel the imagination and interest of the trainees. Instructional objectives should be spelled out, and overall direction indicated. The expected terminal behaviour resulting from the instruction should be made known to the trainees, and if evaluative tests are to be included, this fact should be indicated before instruction commences.

The instructor should analyse the material to be taught in terms of previously learned material and material to be learned. The means of obtaining the necessary responses from the trainees follow the usual form: introduce stimuli, elicit response and obtain feedback. Verbal material used should be meaningful to the trainee and should progress from the known to the unknown and from the familiar to the unfamiliar. Ample opportunities should be provided for the trainee to make the necessary responses, and practice on a massed or distributed basis should be scheduled.

Correct responses should be rewarded, and knowledge of test results or performance on a task should be fed back to the trainee as quickly as possible. Increased motivation can often be obtained by relating material to the work situation or real world and by indicating the benefit to the trainee of successfully mastering the work.

1.11 The three elements of communication

Words or phrases uttered may have different meanings in different situations, so that a communication must be interpreted both in terms of the message and the nature of the situation in which it occurs.

A communication comprises three elements: a measure of the communicator's feelings, the form or style of the message and an indication of the desired behaviour or response. The feelings expressed may include those of sincerity, hostility, irony, humour or sadness. The style may be technical or non-technical and the message may be formed in such a way as to produce a specific response.

The communication channel is opened by attracting the receiver's attention and maintained by verbal utterances backed up with non-verbal signals. Both verbal and non-verbal signals combine to convey the three elements of communication, and the way in which the total communication is perceived governs its effectiveness.

1.12 The distinction between one-way and two-way communication

Information is not merely transmitted and received; it is also interpreted. The message is frequently distorted as it passes through barriers to communication, while an individual's interpretation of the content may be affected by previous experience or personal values. How the message is perceived and what meaning is ascribed to it will govern the receiver's behaviour.

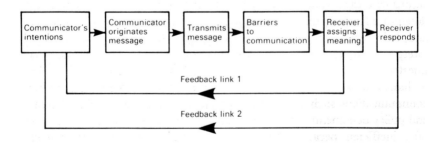

FIG. 1.2 **Communication system**

Effective communication results when a receiver's response corresponds with a communicator's intentions. Communication failure results when a communicator's intention and a receiver's response are incompatible.

In order to avoid misunderstandings due to ambiguity, complexity or sheer volume of message content, feedback should be provided between the receiver and the communicator before the receiver responds. It is too late to shut the gate when the horse has bolted. A second feedback link enables the receiver's response to be compared with the communicator's intentions. This is particularly necessary in the workplace as a means of checking that orders or instructions have been carried out effectively.

Barriers to communication

Barriers to effective communication take two forms: *extrinsic* and *intrinsic*. Extrinsic barriers relate to external influences bearing on the communication, and include noise, code of language used and the environment in general. Intrinsic barriers are set up within the receiver, and include attitudes based upon past exprience, feelings, emotions and internal thought processes relating to both the communicator and message content. All of these factors affect the receiver's perception of the communication.

One-way communication

'One-way' communication means precisely what it says: the communicator decides on the nature of the message he wishes to convey, chooses the means of communicating and sends the message. There is no face-to-face inter-action or discussion; therefore the receiver responds according to the meaning he derives from the communication.

Administrative communications are designed to elicit certain responses. However, terminal behaviour exhibited by the receiver may not always accord with the response intended by the communicator. Communications downward from top management are easy to word in unambiguous language and, being of an authoritative nature, leave little room for judgement or interpretation. Unfortunately, management seldom make provision for interference or other contingencies, and no allowance for subjective opinion or individual attitude is considered. Public address systems and written communications such as bulletin board notices, staff handbooks, circulars and policy documents are examples of one-way communication. These are often inefficient because a large number of staff never read notices, while others either do not understand, or misconstrue the meaning or choose to disbelieve it.

Two-way communication

Face-to-face 'two-way' communication is a better means of ensuring that sources of error are reduced or eliminated. Situational factors may be allowed for and distortion minimised. In two-way communication immediate responses to the message may be obtained. The communicator is able to listen to the receiver's point of view and is in a position to correct any misunderstanding. Questions may be asked by either party and detailed explanations given to clarify technical points or other areas of difficulty.

Clearly, face-to-face communication is not practical in every situation, especially where large numbers of staff are involved, but it remains one of the most effective ways of communicating. The unofficial 'grapevine' is the fastest means of communication, but content is not always accurate!

1.13   Exercises involving one-way and two-way communication

One-way communication exercises

1   You are a supervisor in charge of a workshop and stores in factory A. You need to have stores transferred from your workshop to a location in factory B. Write a memo which fully covers your requirements. When you have finished writing the memo, pass it to another person who will check it for completeness.

2   Write a report covering a training need which you have identified within your department. Outline the area of work involved, the number and type of employees concerned, the nature of the training required and any other factor which you consider to be relevant. Suggest how the training might best be carried out.

When you have finished the report, pass it to the person on your left, who will mark and evaluate it in terms of its completeness and clarity. The person will award up to ten marks for your work.

Now mark and précis into one half of the total number of words the report you have received from the person on your right. When you have finished, pass the précis to the person on your left for marking and evaluation. The person will check the précis, compare it with the original full report and award up to ten marks.

After this has been completed you will receive your own report plus the précis. Compare the précis with your original report. Could you have conveyed all that you wanted to in fewer words than in your original report?

Participation in this type of exercise will give an insight into the effectiveness of one-way written communication.

3   Draft a one-way verbal communication relating to any subject of your choice. Tape-record the communication and take it in turns to play back the tape to the whole group. Allow the group to discuss the effectiveness of your communication.

Two-way communication exercises

Role-playing exercises provide a valuable means of gaining experience in man management and interviewing. In some cases a detailed brief is provided for both players although many exercises are designed to be fairly open-ended. For successful role-play the actors must behave in a serious manner and try to adopt a real-life approach; the object of the exercise being to obtain a solution to the problem which is acceptable to both sides. The observers often learn more about human relations than the actors, and constructive criticism after each role-play is a valuable part of the learning process.

Case studies

1   TWO-WAY COMMUNICATION

1   It is Christmas Eve. John Walker is driving his coach, laden with passengers, from London to Salisbury Coach Station. Just before reaching his destination he passes a stationary tour coach filled with passengers. John drops his load at the coach station and, thinking that it is an unusual place for a tour coach to stop, walks back to it.

The tour driver tells John that he has broken down on his way to a Bournemouth hotel where the holiday-makers are booked in for dinner. John offers to take them to the hotel. The tour driver accepts. The passengers are transferred to John's coach and taken to Bournemouth in time for dinner. John later reports the matter to his traffic office.

You, as traffic manager, hear of the incident and decide to interview John. On the one hand you wish to commend John for his initiative, but on the other hand you need to discuss with him the problems of insurance and the need to keep the traffic department informed at all times.

2 John Walker is an experienced continental tour driver who has been with your company for only a short time. The company has a considerable continental tour commitment, but the work is normally carried out by a number of drivers who have been with the company for many years. There is considerable prestige attached to continental tour work and the existing tour drivers insist on sharing the work between themselves.

It is an unwritten law that new staff undertake school runs, contracts and local work. John soon becomes dissatisfied and wishes to join the elite group of continental drivers. He asks the dispatcher to detail him for some continental work. The dispatcher tells him that he has no chance, and that if he did detail John there would be hell to play.

John requests an interview with you, the traffic manager, in order to state his request officially.

3 John Walker has been detailed to report to a Bournemouth hotel for an afternoon tour of local beauty spots. He loads his passengers and drives off. After a short time the party organiser asks him why he is not giving a commentary. John tells him that his public address system is not working.

The organiser becomes irate and tells John that he specifically requested a commentary when he placed his order for the coach. Words are exchanged and tempers flare.

Upon returning to the hotel the organiser phones you complaining about the incident and demands a considerable reduction in his bill.

A notice is displayed in each of the company vehicles stating that the microphone must not be used while the coach is in motion. This is ignored by the drivers, many of whom possess a small microphone which may be clipped to their tie and which does not interfere with their driving. It is common practice for the driver to give a commentary during local tours but John's work ticket makes no mention of a request for a commentary.

You, as traffic manager, decide to interview John regarding his public address system and alleged behaviour.

4 You are the traffic manager and have received the following accident report. Read the report and interview both Owboy and Walker. Decide what action to take and call Owboy back to make known your decision.

CONFIDENTIAL

Traffic Manager
Bournemouth

Statement—Traffic Accident—20 July 1991

At about 11.15 hours on 20 July 1991, I was travelling as a passenger on a coach driven by C Owboy from Lymington to the depot. There were no other passengers aboard.

At a point between Downton and Everton on the A337 we had just passed a very narrow part of the road near a culvert when the road curved to the left. From my position in the second seat adjacent to the offside window, I saw a heavy gravel lorry approaching from the opposite direction.

Owboy's speed at the time was about 40 mph, the coach being about half a metre from the nearside grass verge. Owboy braked heavily, the front wheels locked and the vehicle veered sharply to the offside, moving over the white line by about a metre. The vehicles collided, the main impact being with the centre of the gravel lorry body. The coach rebounded off the lorry and came to rest close to the grass verge on its nearside.

At the time of impact, I was thrown from my seat across the coach to the nearside, ending up on the floor. A piece of metal about 5 cm square and 1 metre long struck the top of my head and I was showered by glass from the broken windows.

I picked myself up from the floor and saw that Owboy was all right except for minor cuts.

On leaving the coach, I looked at the skid marks on the road. Only the front wheels had locked, both producing skid marks about 50 metres long (the police took exact measurements later). There is no doubt that the vehicle veered to the right, as borne out by the skid marks, which commenced at a point just to the nearside of the central white line, crossed the line by a metre and then went back to the left. I noticed that the front wheels were on a left-hand lock and that the skid marks continued until the vehicle came to rest.

Several possibilities occurred to me:

(a) The front brakes had grabbed, pulling the vehicle sharply over to the right.

(b) With the front wheels locked by excessive braking, the momentum of the coach caused the vehicle to move in a straight line from its approach position. (Owboy should have released the brakes to get the wheels rolling again.)

(c) The rear brakes were not working efficiently—no skid marks from the rear wheels were seen.

The road was about 6 metres wide at this point, with little space for the vehicles to pass, and I attribute the accident to three factors:

(a) Approach speed too fast.
(b) Brakes locking and pulling vehicle to the offside.
(c) Very narrow road being used by heavy vehicles.

I personally avoid using this road because of the difficult driving conditions. It is a very narrow road in places, with many severe bends, and I prefer to use the Milford-on-Sea road.

I later attended Lymington Hospital for examination, clean-up and tetanus injection, and then continued my duties.

My injuries were slight, consisting of a bump and cut on the top of my head and several small facial cuts.

Mr Owboy was neither smoking nor talking at the time of the accident.

John Walker (Driver)

5   You are the manager and have received an incident report from driver Walker. Company regulations state: 'In the event of serious illness or death of a passenger while travelling on a company vehicle, the driver will:

(a) stop the vehicle;

(b) call an ambulance;

(c) advise the police;

(d) report position and circumstances to traffic control.'

24 December 1991

Traffic Manager
Bournemouth

Incident Report

At about 13.00 hours, while approaching Frockton, Gloucestershire, I was advised that a female passenger was feeling unwell.

I stopped the coach and found that she was unable to move her hands or feet. I suspected that she might be suffering a stroke. As I was very close to Frockton I decided to take her to a doctor or hospital and deviated from my route, taking her to Frockton Cottage Hospital. I placed her in the care of the Nursing Sister.

Her luggage was at the front of a fully loaded boot so I decided to drive on in order to make the 14.30 connections. I left her luggage at the lost property office.

Her name is Miss Trust, of 10 Railway Cottages, Woking, Surrey.

I reported the incident to Station Control on arrival.

John Walker (Driver)

6   Jack Adams is the foreman of the engine shop. He is an autocratic supervisor. He has been with the company for ten years and thinks he knows it all. He is supervising the lifting of a brand new Leyland engine when it suddenly crashes to the floor, smashing the crankcase and trapping a fitter by the leg.

The lifting equipment being used was designed to lift the much lighter Bedford engine. Jack knew this but had chosen to ignore the load limit having got away with it in the past.

After studying the accident report, you, the chief engineer, call Jack Adams to your office for an explanation.

Face-to-face communications between supervisors, training officers and staff serve to strengthen working relationships. If an employee has a grievance, learn to listen to him. Let him do most of the talking. What he has to say will be important to him, so encourage him to suggest his own solution to the problem.

2 DISHONOURED PROMISES

Ted Aiken is a mechanical engineer working for a company specialising in
the manufacture of electro-mechanical devices. His immediate superior is
leaving the company to take up a senior position in an overseas company.
Ted thinks that he will be promoted to fill the vacancy. He is well qualified
and well thought of. He does an excellent job of work.

Due to the growing importance of the silicon chip, the Director of
Technology decides to take the vacancy out of the establishment for the
mechanical side of the company and create a new post in the electronics
section for which Ted is unqualified.

When the vacancy is advertised, Ted and several other mechanical
engineers are up in arms. Ted has fallen victim of 'carrot-dangling' and
asks for an interview with the director in order to discuss why the
company hasn't honoured its promises.

1.14   Appraising a videotaped presentation in terms of its non-verbal support

Non-verbal signals play an important part in two-way communications, and
a description of some of the ways in which these signals affect human social
behaviour has been given in section 1.4.

A videotape programme or television interview may be used to illustrate the
widespread use of non-verbal signalling to maintain interaction. The sound
should be turned down and each occurrence of non-verbal signalling scored
on an appraisal sheet. A group interaction involves so many signals that it is
unlikely that an inexperienced observer without special equipment would
be able to score each participant effectively. Begin with a two-person interaction, or decide on which two members of a group you wish to observe, and
complete the appraisal sheet given in figure 1.3.

The appraisal is designed to increase the reader's awareness of the frequency
and variety of non-verbal signals during any interaction. Detailed analysis
of verbal and non-verbal communication may be found in Michael Argyle's
excellent book, *The Psychology of Interpersonal Behaviour,* published by
Penguin Books.

FIG. 1.3   **Non-verbal signals—appraisal sheet**

SIGNAL	FREQUENCY	
	Interactor A	Interactor B
Nods head	| | | |	⊬⊬ | |
Nods rapidly	| |	|
Smiles	|	| | | |
Laughs	| |	|
Frowns		
Scowls		
Pouts		
Purses lips		
Wrinkles nose		
Gazes		
Raises eyebrows		
Winks		
Perspires		
Clenches fists		
Wrings hands		
Trembles		
Points finger		
Wags forefinger		
Claps hands		
Shakes hands		
Drums fingers		
Sits:		
Head on		
Side by side		
At right angles		
Moves closer		
Backs away		
Sits upright		

(cont.)

SIGNAL	FREQUENCY	
	Interactor A	Interactor B
Lounges		
Shrugs shoulders		
Nudges		
Taps foot		

1.15   Microtraining—establishing rapport

Instructors are faced with problems of communication and control whenever they commence lessons, and this is particularly true when meeting groups for the first time. It is common knowledge that, in any social context, first impressions are important in the development of an interaction. In every walk of life people tend to form subjective opinions about others on the basis of very little evidence. In the classroom instructors and their trainees are constantly trying to interpret each other's actions, so that the atmosphere created depends largely upon how they see one another. The development of a healthy rapport is, therefore, based upon the trainee's perceptions of the instructor and vice versa.

The aim of a *microtraining* session in establishing rapport is to record an instructor's attempts to establish a friendly democratic relationship with the group, so that the intentions and expectations of the group coincide with those of the instructor.

The videotape recording may be played back after the microtraining session and discussed with the tutor.

Microtraining is further discussed in sections 8.3 and 8.4.

SUMMARY

- Psychological needs may be either intrinsic or extrinsic. People do not work for bread alone. Work is a social activity.

- Man is an information processor. Language plays an important role in communications.

- Behaviour may be defined as those activities of an organism that can be observed by others. Communication involves the sharing of experiences, which in the instructional situation promotes learning or observable changes in behaviour.

- Non-verbal signals include gestures, smiles, head nods, frowns, bodily contact, eye movements, body posture and laughter. Non-verbal signals help to regulate and maintain conversation and social interactions. An instructor should be sensitive to non-verbal signals.

- Speakers tend to feel nervous before giving a talk. Nervousness may be due to lack of knowledge, lack of preparation or lack of confidence.

- Nervousness is evidenced by increased heart-rate, perspiring, blushing, stuttering, gabbling and annoying mannerisms.

- CCTV and video-recordings show both desirable and undesirable mannerisms.

- Rapport is essential to good classroom interaction. It involves respect, concern, sympathy and empathy. It results in team spirit, good relations and high morale.

- In order for communication to take place, the listener must attend, concentrate and respond.

"Give the man a fair hearing"

- Instructing is the art of causing desired responses to happen. Successful instructing results in a relatively permanent change in behaviour, known as learning.

- A communication comprises: communicator's intention; method of transmission; receiver's behaviour or response to message.

- One-way communication—no immediate interaction between transmitter and receiver. Public address, notices, media. Two-way communication—face to face. Allows for discussion, clarification and repetition.

- Videotaped presentations may be analysed using non-verbal appraisal skills.

- Microtraining sessions may be employed to develop the technique of establishing rapport.

QUESTIONS

1. Write down the reasons why you, personally, work.

2. What is communication? Why do people need to communicate?

3. Communication in an instructional situation aims at behaviour change. How is the effect of behaviour change measured?

4. List commonly used non-verbal signals and describe how they help to maintain communication.

5. Many speakers feel nervous before delivering a talk. Give three reasons for this and suggest ways of overcoming the problem.

6. Mannerisms are associated with nervousness. List examples of nervous mannerisms and state the effect of these upon the audience.

7. Observe a talk which is being broadcast on TV and make a note of the mannerisms and non-verbal signals exhibited by the speaker.

8. Explain the importance of rapport in the instructional situation.

9. How does an instructor cause desired responses to be made?

10. List the three main elements of communication and differentiate between 'one-way' and 'two-way' communications.

2
Using behavioural objectives

Before instructing someone to do something for us, we first have to sort out in our minds exactly what has to be done. Then we determine standards of work and completion dates. The instruction is given and we later follow up by checking that the work has been done to our satisfaction.

Unfortunately, not everyone thinks in these terms. Orders are vague and often ambiguous. We are too busy to check up, and from time to time things go wrong. If morale is low, or we have rubbed someone up the wrong way, they will deliberately interpret an instruction in a manner other than that originally intended. Think of the consequences of the following: 'When I nod my head, hit it,' or 'If the baby doesn't thrive on milk, boil it.'

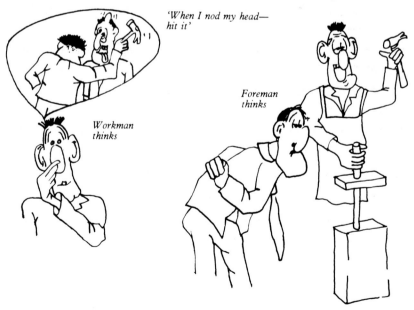

'When I nod my head— hit it'

Workman thinks

Foreman thinks

Nurse thinks

Mother thinks

'If the baby doesn't thrive on milk—boil it'

If we are involved in training, we cannot afford to be slapdash. We must first define carefully the goals to be achieved by the trainee at or before the end of the programme. Then, select the means of achieving these goals and, finally, decide on the method of evaluating the trainee's performance relative to the goals set.

The programme is best designed around a set of aims and behavioural objectives, with test criteria built in to measure the effectiveness of the instruction. Alternatively, performance criteria may be specified.

The importance of classifying, writing and evaluating educational objectives in the field of curriculum development has been recognised for over 60 years. During that period many have suggested methods of stating aims and behavioural objectives with a view to increasing the efficiency of teaching and learning.

Dr Ralph Tyler proposed that objectives should be stated in the form that makes them most helpful in selecting learning experiences and in guiding learning. From this, it follows that statements of specific objectives should be written in terms of what the student should be able to do at the end of a course rather than in terms of what the teacher intends to lecture on. This leads to the requirement that curricula should be developed which enable the student to exhibit the exact behaviour required to confirm that the objectives have been met.

In order to create the necessary framework in which effective learning may take place, the teacher must himself be aware of exactly what he is doing. To meet this requirement D R Krathwohl† has suggested that objectives be defined at three levels: broad statements of course aims; specific behavioural objectives and lesson plans specifying precisely how the objectives will be attained. Armed with these statements, teaching materials and sequences may be developed and criterion tests produced.

The Taxonomy of Educational Objectives†† was written so as to provide a framework for curriculum development. It describes and classifies all kinds of educational objectives and is divided into three *domains; cognitive, affective* and *psychomotor* (see section 2.3). The *taxonomy*, or classification, is used as a reference against which educational objectives may be compared and analysed when developing the curriculum. Its use facilitates the classification of goals, increases the reliability of communication of intent and provides a system for describing test items and course evaluation.

Another book, entitled *Preparing Instructional Objectives*, by R F Mager††† was written in order to provide specific instruction in the writing of statements of objectives. The preface contains a fable, the moral of which is that if you are not sure of where you are going at the onset, then you are liable to end up elsewhere and not even be aware of it. Mager insists that before you prepare instruction, before you choose material, machine or method, it is important to state clearly what your goals are. The book sets out to demonstrate the form of usefully stated objectives. Its purpose is to help readers to specify and communicate educational intent; for as Mager says, 'until you describe what the learner will be doing when demonstrating that he "understands" or "appreciates" you have described very little at all'. Throughout the book, Mager offers very sound practical advice on the writing of objectives, and the book is highly recommended to anyone interested in transmitting skills and knowledge to others.

†Krathwohl D R et al *Taxonomy of Educational Objectives: Handbook 2 Affective Domain* (Longman, London 1964).

††Bloom B S (ed) *Taxonomy of Educational Objectives: Handbook 1 Cognitive Domain* (David McKay, New York 1956).

†††Mager R F *Preparing Educational Objectives* (Fearon Publishers, Belmont, California 1962).

2.1 Aims and objectives defined

An *aim* is a broad statement of intent and is the first step in planning a programme. It is a non-specific guideline and relates to overall policy or strategy rather than to detailed specifications.

In military terms an aim might be to capture the town of Bloggsville, while an *objective* is more specific and describes definite activities, such as:

Support Company, Mortar Section, will bombard and destroy the enemy barracks at map reference 073 824. Bombardment to commence at 0700 hours and cease at 0730 hours.

Number 1 Company will advance at 0715 hours with fixed bayonets and clear the barracks of surviving enemy troops. The Company Commander will report by radio to Battalion Headquarters when objective is secured.

Number 2 Company will stand by from 0700 hours and will, when ordered to do so, move off, pass through Number 1 Company area and occupy the radio station at map reference 073 862.

Notice that in each of the three objectives above, *terminal behaviour* has been specified. Support Company will have destroyed the enemy barracks. Number 1 Company will have cleared the barracks of enemy troops. Number 2 Company will have occupied the radio station.

In expressing terminal behaviour in the writing of objectives, words that do not define behaviour clearly or are open to wide interpretation should be avoided.

More detailed objectives could have been written which included times by which objectives should be attained and limits on casualty levels.

The advantages of stating objectives in behavioural or activity terms are that they:

(a) help in planning both in choice of target and weapons;
(b) emphasise the troops' activities;
(c) provide a means of evaluating the attack.

Applying the writing of aims and objectives to a training programme relating to the use of micrometers, the aim might be: 'The trainee will become proficient in measuring diameters using a micrometer.'

The relevant learning objectives might be: 'The expected learning outcome is that the trainee will be able to:

(a) explain the markings on both the barrel and thimble of a 0-25 mm metric micrometer;
(b) measure the diameter of six specimen round bars, supplied, correct to within 0.01 mm;
(c) demonstrate how a 0-25 mm metric micrometer should be checked for accuracy over its full range with the aid of a set of metric slip gauges.'

Notice that each of the objectives specifies exactly what the trainee is required to do in order to satisfy the aim. Again, words that do not define behaviour clearly should be avoided. Such phrases as 'to know', 'to understand', 'to appreciate', 'to believe' fall into this category—they cannot be used accurately to measure the outcome of behaviour. Such phrases as 'to describe', 'to explain', 'to select', 'to compare', 'to calculate', 'to construct', 'to solve' are recommended, because terminal behaviour can be measured in terms of what the trainee is able to do on completion of the instruction.

From the trainee's point of view, the main advantages of writing strict behavioural objectives is that he knows exactly what is expected of him and he can evaluate his own progress against the specified objectives.

2.2 Writing aims

Aims may be specified by any member of the company hierarchy from the managing director to a leading hand on the shop floor. The content and breadth of the aim may vary from directing overall company policy to re-organising working methods on the drilling section.

Examples of aims

(a) To investigate the feasibility of transferring gearbox production from the Oxford plant to a new plant located in Cardiff.
(b) To develop improved labour relations throughout the company.
(c) To institute induction courses for new employees so as to accelerate settling-in processes.
(d) To review company organisation with a view to improving communications.
(e) To improve information dissemination throughout the company.
(f) To improve customer relations by co-ordinating the work of service departments.
(g) To reduce labour turnover in the plating department.
(h) To reduce scrap rates in the horizontal boring shop.
(i) To improve productivity in the relay assembly shop.

(j) To improve ventilation in factory A.

(k) To retrain horizontal millers as jig-borer operators.

Each of the aims listed above can be broken down into detailed specific objectives so that the broad outlines of the aim may be satisfied.

Imprecisely stated aims relating to training can be vague and open to many interpretations. Badly written aims are of little use to the instructor concerned. Aims prefaced with ambiguous statements such as, 'at the end of the training programme, the trainee will have a sound knowledge of...' should be avoided because the words 'sound knowledge of' could be interpreted in many ways. Who could say exactly what 'sound' meant? It would therefore be impossible to evaluate the trainee's performance against such aims.

2.3 Terminology

Educational or instructional objectives have been classified by Bloom† and others into three *domains,* or spheres:

(a) *affective*—feeling or valuing;

(b) *cognitive*—knowing or thinking;

(c) *psychomotor*—practical or physical skills.

The affective domain

This relates to the feelings, attitudes, emotions and values of the trainee. According to Krathwohl†† the organising principle is that of 'internalisation'. He suggests that the process of internalisation appears to describe the process of learning and growth in the affective field.

Internalisation is a characteristic quality pertaining to the inner nature or feelings; and describes the act of incorporating, within oneself, values, attitudes and interests. Internalisation occurs in stages similar to Piaget's stages of moral development described in Appendix 10, and in some ways resembles the process of socialisation.

Inner growth of affective characteristics commences as the trainee becomes aware of some stimulus and directs his attention to it. This is followed by responses brought about by conforming to the instructions of some external

---

†*Taxonomy of Educational Objectives.*
††*Taxonomy of Educational Objectives Handbook 2 Affective Domain,* chapter 3.

authority such as the teacher. Finally, the trainee's inner control causes responses to occur in the absence of the teacher or other person in a position of power. The trainee becomes capable of making value judgements according to codes of conduct and principles which he has internalised over a period of time.

Krathwohl† produced five main categories in the taxonomy structure:

(a) *Receiving* (attending)
Awareness
Willingness to receive
Controlled or selected attention

(b) *Responding*
Aquiescence in responding
Willingness to respond
Satisfaction in response

(c) *Valuing*
Acceptance of a value
Preference for a value
Commitment

(d) *Organisation*
Conceptualisation of a value
Organisation of a value system

(e) *Characterisation by a value or value complex*
Generalised set
Characterisation

Behaviour within the five categories listed ranges from, at the lowest level (a), receiving or attending, where the trainee's role is passive and limited to taking in information rather like a sponge, with little personal concern, up to, at the highest level (e), the integration of concepts and subject-matter into his own life-world.

The cognitive domain

In the writing of objectives, stress is placed on one or more of the following, each involving a different degree of complexity of thinking:

†*Taxonomy of Educational Objectives Handbook 2 Affective Domain*, chapter 3.

(a) *Simple recall of knowledge*
Emphasis placed upon remembering facts or terminology without the need to understand that which is recalled.

(b) *Comprehension*
Elementary level of understanding. The trainee should be able to explain what he is doing when using recalled information.

(c) *Application*
Having comprehended the meaning of a given concept, the trainee is able to relate the knowledge to other different situations. He should be able to generalise, using basic principles.

(d) *Analysis*
The breaking down of a statement or operation into its basic components and the relating of each component to the remainder.

(e) *Synthesis*
The assembling of a variety of concepts or elements so as to form a new arrangement.

(f) *Evaluation*
Making value judgements about arrangements, arguments or methods. Highlighting strengths and weaknesses in arguments and assessing the points for and against.

COGNITION

Behavioural objectives relating to the cognitive domain are concerned with information and knowledge. Cognition is the name given to mental processes such as sensation, perception and thinking by which knowledge may be apprehended.

Thinking is a complex behaviour involving mental activity such as reasoning, where thought is characterised by symbol reference. Thinking involves the internal representation of events and may be applied to arithmetical activities and problem-solving.

Language is an important source of symbols, while symbols acquire meaning and convey information. L S Vygotsky, a Russian psychologist, studied the importance of language in the formation of concepts. He exposed learners to situations in which they could acquire concepts and simultaneously learn related verbal symbols. By the process of word association (see 'Verbal association', section 7.6) a physical object can be linked with a word. When the word is heard later, an image of the object or concept can be visualised in the mind. Symbolic representation of the object may be recalled by the process of thinking.

Given a problem, a learner will begin to think about it. He will turn the problem over in his mind using symbols which represent real objects. When verbalising the problem, words—another form of symbol—will represent the objects involved. At an elementary level, practical problems may be solved using images alone while facts and terminology may be recalled and used to solve academic problems. Higher levels in the cognitive domain require a greater complexity of thinking, and linking of concepts or principles by means of appropriate language.

By classifying levels of cognition, Bloom has provided a guideline by which the degree of complexity of thought involved in a task may be reflected in the construction of learning objectives.

INVENTIVENESS

The cognitive domain is divided into a number of levels of mental performance ranging from simple recall at the most elementary level to evaluation at the highest level.

Bloom's top three categories, i.e. analysis, synthesis and evaluation, are grouped together into one known as 'invention'. The learner demonstrates inventiveness by breaking down information into parts, identifying the parts, determining relationships, recognising principles and detecting fallacies. He then proceeds to synthesise, that is, to combine the elements or parts into a whole. The outcome is an arrangement that did not exist before. Planning or proposing methods and procedures, collating information from several sources and developing abstract relationships, also fall within the process of synthesis. The remaining category, that of evaluation, involves making judgements as to the value or worth of material for a given purpose. Such judgements may take the form of appraisals, comparisons, or contrasts, and the learning outcomes of this category tend to contain elements of all others, combined with the need to make value judgements.

The psychomotor domain

This area is concerned with the learning of muscular and motor skills and is by its very nature concerned with the acquisition of such abilities as hand skills in the workshop, typing, manipulation of equipment and the assembling of apparatus. At the lower level of performance, behaviour will be characterised by slow, clumsy and hesitant movements, probably with frequent errors. After following a well-designed training programme, and

FIG. 2.2 **Identification of skills involved in producing stepped shaft**

OPERATION	SKILL ELEMENT
Chuck blank: locate in collet chuck with correct projection	Reading steel rule Clamping in collet using correct force
Centre-drill end	Visually checking condition of centre drill Locating centre-drill in correct position Clamping centre-drill in drill chuck using correct force Advancing tailstock to correct operating position Locking tailstock to bed Feeding centre-drill using correct force and at a suitable rate (feel) Peck drilling
Remove drill chuck	Withdrawing tailstock Ejecting drill chuck from tailstock
Locate centre	Cleaning taper Fitting centre Advancing tailstock to operating position Locking tailstock to bed Adjusting contact between blank and centre to correct pressure Locking quill
Turn to diameter and length	Setting stops to length using slip gauges Indexing depth of cut Starting machine Engaging feed Disengaging feed Stopping machine Using micrometer to measure diameters Checking lengths with steel rule
Unload	Releasing tailstock centre Withdrawing tailstock Releasing collet Removing blank from collet

2.6 Writing aims and objectives for a training programme

Situation

The effectiveness of communications within the company is below par. You as training officer, have been requested to put forward, for discussion by higher management, a set of aims and objectives for a course aimed at improving matters. The group selected for training consists of senior supervision.

First decide the broad aims of the course and from these write down a set of objectives written in behavioural terms. The exact detail of content and conditional aspects of the objectives can be finalised after the draft has been accepted.

TITLE

Training programme for senior supervisors.

SUBJECT

Communications.

AIMS

To improve the effectiveness of communications within the company by improving the senior supervisors' ability to speak, write, listen, record and observe.

OBJECTIVES

Each of the objectives listed should be preceded by the words: 'The expected learning outcome is that the supervisor will be able to:'

present information graphically;
record data in tabular form;
construct a 'break even' chart;
design a safety poster;
draft a bulletin board notice;
draft written orders and instructions;
write an order for spare parts;
complete a stores requisition;
reply to a letter of complaint;
reply to a letter of enquiry;
draft a letter of enquiry;
prepare a technical report;
write a comprehensive memorandum;
précis articles;
recall principles of interviewing;
prepare the structure for an interview;
conduct an interview;

prepare and present a short talk;
prepare and deliver a job instruction;
prepare visual aids;
chair: a discussion;
      an informal meeting;
      a formal meeting;
take comprehensive notes at a meeting;
give verbal orders unambiguously;
achieve a higher reading rate with adequate recall of information;
use a dictionary effectively;
demonstrate clear thinking;
reason logically;
interpret the meaning of non-verbal signals.

2.7   Writing behavioural objectives for a short talk

Situation

You are a member of the training department and are required to give a short talk forming part of a course covering 'The Abrasive Wheel Regulations, 1970'. The subject allocated to you is: 'Advice on the mounting of abrasive wheels' and the particular type of wheel to be discussed is a straight-sided wheel exceeding 250 mm in diameter.

PREPARATION

First, obtain from the Health and Safety Executive, H M Factory Inspectorate, a copy of 'Training Advisory Leaflet No. 2, reference number SHW 12'. Using the leaflet, prepare a list of important elements which will form the basis of the talk.

ELEMENTS FORMING THE TALK

(a) Examination of wheels before mounting
(b) Grinding machine spindles
(c) Flanges
(d) Washers
(e) Securing the wheel
(f) Starting up new wheels
(g) Plain (straight-sided) wheels with small holes
(h) Plain (straight-sided) wheels with large holes

WRITING THE BEHAVIOURAL OBJECTIVES

For the purposes of this example, no practical training will be described. The objectives will be set on 'knowledge' to be derived from the talk and will be written around the desired outcome of the talk.†

OBJECTIVES

After the talk, members of the audience will be able to:

(a) recall that before mounting a wheel it should be cleaned by brushing and examined for damage in transit;
specify the method of checking a wheel for cracks by suspending it vertically and tapping it with a light non-metallic implement;
identify a cracked wheel by observing a dead sound when the wheel is struck;

(b) recall that a wheel should fit easily, but not loosely, on the spindle;
indicate the result of mounting a wheel that fits too tightly on the spindle;
specify the direction of tightening of the securing nut relative to the direction of rotation of the spindle;
determine the action to be taken in the event of discovering worn bearings on the machine;
match the speed of the wheel to speed of the spindle;

(c) specify the correct flange diameter to wheel diameter ratio;
give reasons for fitting flanges with recesses, recessed side next to the wheel;
describe means of securing the inner driving flange to the spindle;
specify materials suitable for the manufacture of flanges;
list defects in flange bearing surfaces which cannot be tolerated and specify remedial action;

(d) describe materials, dimensions and applications of washers used in the mounting of grinding wheels;

(e) list the methods of securing outer clamping flanges;
describe means of applying correct tightening pressures;

(f) list procedures for correctly adjusting guards and work-rest;
apply correct procedures for running new wheels;
adopt safety precautions for staff in the vicinity of the machine when starting up;

---

†The main body of the talk and the elements on which it is based were derived from an extract taken from Leaflet SHW 12. See section 3.7, 'Preparing an objective test to measure the effectiveness of a talk'.

(g) list correct procedures for mounting plain (straight-sided) wheels with small holes;
list unacceptable practices when mounting plain (straight-sided) wheels with small holes;

(h) state that flanges for wheels with large holes should not be recessed, but that corners of the wheel seatings should be undercut.

2.8   Concluding a talk

The conclusion should be planned and not dreamed up on the spur of the moment. It should summarise, restate and reinforce what has already been said. Threads of the argument should be drawn together and re-emphasised using a clear, firm voice which should convey to the audience an impression of urgency or the need for action or caution.

A weak, apologetic finish will undermine the effectiveness of the whole talk, so be positive. Think of a dramatic conclusion containing a 'plug line', emotional appeal or fact that the audience will remember or at least think about.

Examples of closing sentences

'And please remember, when you are starting up the wheel, stand clear. They have been known to explode!'

'The lad had long hair. Now he's bald at eighteen. Why? The grinding machine won. Didn't wear his safety cap!'

'Rules are made to be broken, or so he thought until he removed the guard. Now he wears mittens. No fingers!'

2.9   Analysing other instructors' presentations with reference to objectives stated

Each member of the group should be asked to:

(a) choose a topic for a short talk;
(b) write down the elements forming the talk;
(c) write a set of objectives on which the talk will be based;
(d) prepare an assessment test designed to check the effectiveness of the talk;
(e) give the talk;
(f) apply the test;
(g) evaluate the responses.

After each instructor or trainee has presented his talk and evaluated the responses, he should be asked to outline the strengths and weaknesses of his presentation. The group should then be asked to discuss how well the stated objectives were met.

SUMMARY

- *The Taxonomy of Educational Objectives* classifies educational objectives and is divided into three domains: cognitive, affective and psychomotor.

- The affective domain relates to the feelings, attitudes, emotions and values of the learner. The cognitive domain involves knowledge and thinking ranging from simple recall to evaluation. The psychomotor domain involves motor skills, sensory perception, responding and the development of complex skills in written, verbal and manual forms.

- R F Mager's book, *Preparing Instructional Objectives* was written to provide instruction in the writing of statements of objectives.

- An aim is a broad statement of intent.

- An objective describes precisely what the learner is expected to be able to do in order to demonstrate learning. In the writing of objectives, words open to wide interpretation should be avoided. Action verbs are favoured.

- A behavioural objective contains: an indication of terminal behaviour expected, important conditions under which it will occur (if any) and a standard of acceptable performance.

- Skills involved in a list of objectives may be categorised as: knowledge type or motor type.

- The conclusion to a talk should be planned. It should summarise, restate and reinforce. Dramatic conclusions are very effective.

QUESTIONS

1. Define:
   (a) an aim
   (b) a behavioural objective

2. Write an aim covering:
   (a) the topic for a discussion
   (b) a piece of instruction

3. Give two examples of each of the following categories of knowledge:
    (a) specific facts
    (b) terminology
    (c) conventions
    (d) trends or sequences
    (e) classifications or categories
    (f) test criteria
    (g) methodology of enquiry
    (h) principles
    (j) theories
    (k) ways of dealing with problems

4. Give two examples of each of the following *intellectual abilities* or skills:
    (a) comprehension of communicated information
    (b) translation of verbal statements into symbolic statements
    (c) interpretation of communicated information
    (d) extrapolation beyond given data

5. Give two examples of the *application* of principles to specific situations.

6. Give two examples of:
    (a) the analysis of a communication
    (b) the synthesis of a number of statements
    (c) the evaluation of material or methods

7. Discuss the importance and value of the use of specific objectives in the areas of:
    (a) developing learning aids
    (b) teaching subject-matter
    (c) learning

8. Write a list of twenty action verbs which might be used in the writing of behavioural objectives.

9. Write a behavioural objective and identify its component parts.

10. Write down the type of skills involved in each of the following objectives:
    'The student will be able to:'
    (a) name the component parts of a Bloggs Model 20A cigarette lighter
    (b) solve a quadratic equation of the form $y = ax^2 + bx + c$

(c) locate and rectify a single fault in a Bloggs Model 2C radio, given a component diagram and comprehensive repair kit

(d) tighten a 14 mm sparking plug to a specified torque reading

11. Write examples of behavioural objectives for each of the categories of knowledge listed in Question 3.

12. Choose a topic for a short piece of instruction and write a set of aims and objectives covering the content.

13. 'Behavioural objectives stifle creativity.' Discuss.

14. Are behavioural goals appropriate to all subjects?

15. What are the advantages of writing strict behavioural objectives from the point of view of:
(a) the trainee
(b) the instructor?

3

The value of testing and the design of tests

Two important areas of testing may be identified: employment testing and educational testing. Testing is undertaken for a good many reasons, and the design of certain types of test and their subsequent assessment is a complex business.

The aim of this section of work is to outline some common types of test and to discuss matters relating to testing and assessing. Specialist books such as *Designing a Scheme of Assessment,* by Christine Ward†, deal in depth with the task of designing and operating schemes of assessment.

Employment testing

Employment tests take the form of a set of questions or exercises or other means by which a person's suitability for a particular job may be measured. They are also used to assess a person's appropriateness for a particular occupation or employment within a particular area or organisation.

Aptitude tests

An *aptitude* is the inherent natural ability to acquire a skill or particular type of knowledge. An aptitude test is a test of a person's ability to learn a task or of potential ability to perform a task. This type of test is sometimes called a proficiency test which measures how well a person can perform a given task.

Performance tests

Performance testing is a procedure for measuring what a person can do. Such tests may be applied during selection of staff for both skilled and unskilled vacancies, and often take the form of trade tests or tests of hand/eye co-ordination. For unskilled workers, tests are designed to indicate manual

†Ward C *Designing a Scheme of Assessment* (Stanley Thornes (Publishers), Cheltenham 1980).

52

dexterity and accident proneness. The ability to co-ordinate hand and eye movements well goes a long way towards accident prevention.

E G Chambers† reported a case in which 128 applicants for London bus-driver vacancies were given hand/eye co-ordination tests at selection. Their progress was followed over the next five years. During that period there were 1052 road traffic accidents involving the sample group. Fourteen of these drivers were involved in nearly 25 per cent of these accidents. Of these fourteen drivers, five could have been rejected at selection on the evidence of their co-ordination test results. Such evidence supports the use of this type of test.

Phase testing a form of trade testing, is used extensively by the Industrial Training Boards. In the case of the Engineering Industrial Training Board (EITB) a series of modules has been produced covering various types of training for engineering craftsmen.

At the end of the instructional period, phase tests are administered. The purpose of the tests is to measure the progress of trainees who have taken the module. Elements of the test include dimensional accuracy, quality and time allowed (which approximates to the time a skilled craftsman would normally take to complete the task). Similar tests would be suitable for selecting skilled craftsmen.

Personality tests

Personality testing is a procedure for measuring aspects of a person's psychological, intellectual or emotional characteristics. It is used to help in predicting their ability to fit in with others; or to indicate likely behaviour in times of stress or boredom; or where the ability to make decisions is important.

This type of test is also used to discover whether a person has the special attributes required in order to perform a particular job. It is helpful when selecting staff to fill vacancies within a team or existing group, reducing the risk of incorrect placements thereby eliminating 'misfits'.

Educational testing

Testing is an essential part of the educational process. Tests are used to assess the overall efficacy of teaching and learning and to measure the attainment of objectives. Tests are most commonly used to evaluate knowledge of particular objectives following appropriate instruction and

†Chambers E G *Memorandum on Accident Proneness amongst Drivers of Road Vehicles* (Medical Research Council, Unit of Applied Psychology, Cambridge University, Report 47/385, 1946).

later to assess knowledge of the whole syllabus, or, in the case of some BTEC courses, the whole unit.

A number of other types of test are used. *Selection* or *prerequisite* tests may be used to assess a person's suitability for admission to a particular course, while *diagnostic tests* are used to detect weaknesses and to highlight difficulties experienced in specific subject areas. *Attainment tests* are applied to large numbers of students with similar backgrounds in a single subject area, so that average performance, or a *standardised norm*, may be obtained. This may then be reliably used as a norm for smaller classes following the same type of course. *Pre-tests* may be used to find out existing knowledge of unit objectives before instruction, while *post-tests* may be applied at intervals following instruction.

Assessment may be made using internal, external, continuous assessment or terminal tests. BTEC continuous assessments often amount to 70 per cent of the marks allocated followed by a 30 per cent terminal test, although test specifications for units vary.

Tests: purposes and types

Tests are set for a variety of reasons and can take many forms. There are also many different types of item format available to test constructors.

In his informative paper 'Notes for Guidance', Roy Whitlow, a Senior Lecturer at Bristol Polytechnic, has produced a number of tables. The tables, given in figures 3.1, 3.2 and 3.3, are an excellent guide to test constructors, in that for each category of test a note is given of what the test will indicate and of any requirements in terms of pre-testing, sampling and the like. Examples of the various types of test item are also clearly laid out.

Examinations

There are many arguments both for and against using formal examinations to assess educational achievement, and much argument as to whether or not their use should continue. The debate is likely to continue for some time yet and for many practising teachers there will be no alternative but to comply with current regulations.

For those who have a choice in the matter, some of the factors both for and against the use of examinations are given in figure 3.4.

Continuous assessment

Assessment in the form of negotiating what the outcomes of training have been is carried out during debriefings and reviews. Democratically agreed outcomes of learning are then recorded on *profiles* or *competence checklists*. *Continuous assessment* of learner achievement is ongoing throughout training, in contrast to *terminal assessment* that takes place only at the conclusion. Its purpose is to involve and motivate, to monitor progress and provide feedback that will help learners set future targets. The instructor's aim is to provide learners with records of assessment that range over training objectives attempted or in the case of learning to drive, all the manoeuvres, skills and knowledge to drive competently. Reference to a record gives a better picture of overall performance. It indicates what the learner "can do" or "has done" rather than what the learner knows how to do.

Profiling

Profiling is a means of recording *achievement* and *competence* and it plays an important role in the many vocational training courses that are offered. The *profile* or *record produced contains details of formative assessments* made during training and a *summative statement of achievement* recorded on completion of the course or training.

Content of profiles

The content of profiles should include a list of *performance criteria* forming the basis of the assessment. The criteria would specify the skills and standards together with a means of indicating the level and context of performance attained. With each assessment an indication of the evidence used to support achievement should be provided. This evidence is often ignored although it is vital to indicate the context in which a skill is assessed if its validity and value is to be recognised. The level of performance for each criterion should also be indicated. There are a number of different style profiles in use but it may be necessary for instructors to design their own to suit needs of clients.

Formative and summative assessments

Formal assessment is the customary impersonal testing or measuring of learning which often leads to awards. It is not necessarily a terminal test or examination, since it may occur within a course in the form of continuous assessment.

Informal assessment provides feedback learners need to assess their own performance. Included would be knowledge about strengths and weaknesses and what they will need to do next in order to achieve the competences that are important to them in a particular occupational area.

Formative assessment or *evaluation* is a process designed to improve the training system by feeding-back information from tests or negotiations that can be used to justify training methods used or to identify learning difficulties. The process is ongoing so that if regular assessments of progress are made, the system can be modified to overcome problems identified. (It is no good waiting until the learner fails the Driving Test to put matters right!)

Periodic assessment measures levels of attainment reached at pre-determined stages throughout the course.

Summative assessment is made at the end of the programme in order to determine the overall effectiveness of training and learning outcomes. This type of assessment can also be made at the conclusion of or at any break point in course activity to evaluate its effectiveness. It can also be used for certification purposes.

In order to provide systematic formative and summative assessments, trainers must be able to explain the purpose of initial assessment or "control" lessons and be clear of their own role in the process. Criteria upon which performance standards are set and suitable assessment methods should be identified and used to measure learners' performance. Learners when carrying out self-appraisal may also refer to the criteria. A recording and reviewing system based on initial and ongoing formative assessment should be devised and used.

Purpose of initial assessment

Initial assessment is intended to influence decisions concerning a learner's placement and progress. It is no use trying to fit a square peg into a round hole.

Trainability testing is often used to get an idea of a learner's suitability for training in given competences. Tests that measure job aptitude and training potential are applied before or during induction. The tests are practical, involving specific job-related tasks for which learners have been given prior instruction. The number of errors made is noted and a performance rating allocated. After the test, individual performance is discussed with learners and a mutual decision made as to whether they will be likely to benefit from training in the skills needed to perform the job. This could well be the first negotiating experience for some learners, so great care should be exercised to make it a pleasant one.

The instructor's role during initial assessment is to make the learners feel at home, to conduct assessments fairly and efficiently and to encourage them to reflect on their past experiences. Negotiation then follows, during which the learners' competences and strengths are identified and recorded.

Throughout training, formal assessments can be made against performance criteria. The candidate will pass if performance meets the criteria. This system of assessment depends to some extent on the instructor adopting a modular approach to training where successful completion of one learning step leads on to the next. Informal assessments may also be made and these involve negotiating with learners or carrying out trainee-centred reviewing.

FIG. 3.1   Tests: **Purposes, indications, requirements**

PURPOSE	*will indicate*	*will require*
1. Evaluation of instruction	effectiveness of an instructional sequence or procedure when applied to particular group	pre-test/post-test systems to consider group achievements in terms of overall objectives and skill enhancement
2. Comparison of instruction	comparative effectiveness of instructional sequences or procedures, or instructors	pre-test/post-test systems in terms of group achieve-ments either cross-sequence or cross-group based
3. Assessment of individuals (a) for awards	level of graduation to be accorded, or suggested pass/fail decision	sampling of all the individual's work considered relevant, using mainly content-standard test scores
(b) to determine transfer to higher grade	suitability, or otherwise, of individual for transfer to the next (higher) part of a course	sampling of all work at present grade using mainly content-standard tests
(c) to measure progress	degree of mastery of specified objectives and skills	specific objective-related tests (criterion-referenced) of a progressive nature
(d) to predict future achievement levels and success expectancy	a prognosis relating the level of achievement that may be anticipated to that required for success, i.e. pass/fail, graduation	criterion-referenced tests that can be interpreted in probabilistic terms
(e) diagnosis of weaknesses and difficulties	areas of weakness or misunderstanding in specific subjects; indi-vidual ability problems, e.g. language, reading difficulty	structured and graded criterion-referenced test in limited areas of study as part of feedback-correction procedures

(cont.)

PURPOSE	will indicate	will require
(f) self criticism reward by individual	to the individual some of the aspects of 3(c), 3(d), 3(e) and provides a measure of reward either in terms of the score or in progress to the next item	structured criterion-referenced tests with in-built success pattern, e.g. programmed-learning text
4. Consolidation of learning	usually very little except that those completing the test have made the effort and have therefore added to what had been previously taught	exercises which extend the individuals beyond the levels already achieved; usually with subjective assessment (e.g. essays) or short-scale content-standard tests

(Source: *Notes for Guidance* R Whitlow, Bristol Polytechnic)

FIG. 3.2   **Types of test items**

TYPE/DESCRIPTION	EXAMPLES
MULTIPLE-CHOICE *Type M* Test items requiring less than 3 minutes for answering or completion.	1. Multi-choice recall 2. Associative recall 3. Completion, e.g. of sentence, diagram 4. Matching and association 5. Analogies, sets, lists, etc. 6. Alternative response e.g. true/false, yes/no 7. Rank-ordering, arrangements 8. Reaction and association including physical stimulus/cognitive reasoning e.g. picture association, verbal reaction, tactile reaction, etc.)

(cont.)

TYPE/DESCRIPTION	EXAMPLES
SHORT ANSWER *Type S* Test items requiring from 3 to 40 minutes for answering or completion.	1. Short essay (associative or critical) 2. Short essay (descriptive) 3. Comparative listings, tabulations, classifications. 4. Annotated sketches and diagrams, illustrated definitions, descriptions, etc. 5. Creative short essays and/or sketching 6. Computations, problem-solving and analytical exercises.
LONG ANSWER *Type L* Test items requiring more than 40 minutes for answering or completion.	1. Long essays (descriptive or imitative) 2. Long essays (creative) 3. Problem-solving or long analytical exercises 4. Long computation exercises.
PRACTICAL WORK *Type P* Items essentially designed to test psychomotor skills.	1. Laboratory work including language laboratory, audio/visual exercises, radio/TV exercises and other creative/discovery exercises 2. Workshop exercises 3. Exercises in the field, e.g. surveying, site investigation 4. Technical and/or geometrical drawing 5. Model-making 6. Fine art exercises 7. Community and social activities 8. Physical education activites.
COURSEWORK *Type C* Test items integrated into coursework and the learning process.	1. Reports of laboratory and other practical work 2. Reports of projects 3. Reports of visits, industrial training, etc. 4. Commentaries on events 5. Verbal reports, interviews, etc. 6. Group activity assessments, e.g. discussions, seminars 7. Tutor observations of specific objective attainment.

(Source: *Notes for Guidance* R Whitlow, Bristol Polytechnic)

FIG. 3.3   **Application of test items**

TYPE/DESCRIPTION	APPLICATION
MULTIPLE-CHOICE Consisting entirely of Type M items.	Mainly skill areas I.C.A.F. (in order of decreasing suitability). Intermittent and short stage test, basic abilities grading tests, pre-/post-testing, formative testing, tests associated with programmed and/or package learning.
SHORT ANSWER Consisting entirely of Type S items	All skill areas generally. Stage tests, terminal tests, both formative and summative, in-class testing, private-study testing. More useful than M for expressive and creative work.
LONG ANSWER Consisting of one or more Type L items.	All skill areas generally. More useful than M or S for expressive and creative work, of limited use in terminal testing, well suited to private-study testing.
PRACTICAL TEST Consisting essentially of Type P items.	Specifically to test psychomotor skills, with or without associated intellectual skills.
COURSEWORK Consisting of items integrated within coursework.	That portion of coursework functioning as a test, whether formative or summative, that is to be incorporated in the overall assessment.
ORAL TEST Test question and response given orally.	May include written, visual, aural or tactile stimuli, but strictly oral question and response. Particularly useful for testing level and type of response.
TERMINAL TEST Test given at the end of the learning process related to a unit or part.	Usually a timed, unseen examination demanding written and/or graphic response, with or without study aids (e.g. course notes, texts, information sheets, etc.)

Note: Skills Area   I = Invention
                     C = Comprehension
                     A = Application
                     F = Factual recall

(Source: *Notes for Guidance* R Whitlow, Bristol Polytechnic)

FIG. 3.4

Case for examinations

Examinations:
  provide an overall aim for the teacher;
  provide a goal for and motivate students;
  measure progress and attainment of objectives;
  test ability to discriminate, reason and work at speed;
  reveal weaknesses in teaching and learning;
  provide feedback to employers.

Case against examinations

Examinations:
  bind teacher strictly to syllabus;
  limit exploration;
  control curricula;
  stress recall and memory;
  emphasise speed;
  promote rote learning, preparation of model answers and
    concentration on banker questions.

Advantages to the learner

Provide:
  a goal;
  motivation;
  competition;
  reinforcement;
  a sense of advancement.

Advantages to the teacher

Provide:
  assessment of student knowledge;
  evaluation and validation of course content;
  feedback.

Measure:
  effectiveness of teaching.

Reveal:
  weaknesses in instructional techniques.

Enable:
  teaching methods to be compared.

3.1 Monitoring progress and measuring the terminal effect of training

Testing monitors the trainee's progress and measures the terminal effect of the training given.

The effect of a training programme on a trainee can only truly be assessed if the trainee takes a criterion test both before and after training. If a criterion test is applied only after the training programme has been completed, no account will have been taken of how much the trainee knew about the subject before training commenced, and a false evaluation of the programme may be obtained.

Before the training programme can be devised and implemented, the instructor must be able to specify precisely what learning will take place. If he cannot do this, he will be unable to evaluate the outcome of the learning. There is, therefore, a need to plan the training carefully and to write test assessments based upon the desired behavioural objectives set. The test programme should then accurately measure how well the trainee has achieved the objectives.

Recording criterion test scores

A criterion test is based on the desired outcome of the training programme. The trainees are tested before training commences and results for the pre-test are recorded. After completing the training programme the criterion test is applied and, once again, results are recorded. The difference between scores obtained before and after training is a measure of the effectiveness of the training programme. Another advantage is that gain scores for each trainee may be determined by comparing 'before' and 'after' scores.

Figure 3.5 shows a graph on which both pre-test and terminal test scores are plotted. Individual gain scores are calculated by deducting pre-test scores from terminal test scores.

3.2 Before writing a test

Before sitting down to write a test, it is necessary to consider the purpose of the test and to decide what use can be made of the results. One of the main outcomes of evaluation by means of a criterion test is that it measures changes in trainees' behaviour against course objectives—it measures competence against objectives set. However, other valuable information can be extracted from a set of test results.

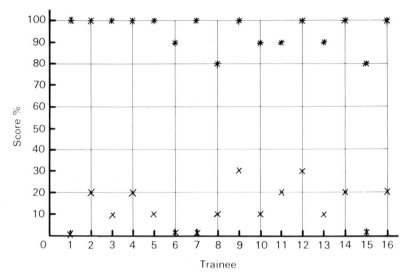

X = Pre-test scores

✳ = Terminal test scores

FIG. 3.5   **Criterion test scores for sixteen trainees**

The marks can be listed and trainees ranked in order of success in attaining course objectives. This would in itself identify regular high achievers who might subsequently be considered for upgrading or training in other specialised fields. Similarly, low achievers could be singled out and necessary remedial action taken to bring them up to satisfactory standards.

From the instructor's standpoint, the test results would show up strengths and weaknesses in the course design. Where objectives had not been met, the course could be modified to overcome weaknesses and, if necessary, additional resources employed to remedy shortcomings in performance.

The terminal test results will provide valuable feedback to manpower planners, in that they will know exactly what the trainees should be capable of doing in a production situation.

Different types of test can be designed to serve a variety of needs. A *prerequisite test* would be set in order to determine the suitability of an applicant to undertake the course of training under consideration. This type of test is not specifically related to theory or detailed knowledge of a given process, but is designed to test the suitability of an applicant to undergo a course of training within a given area. Such abilities as manual dexterity, spatial ability, literacy or numeracy might form the basis of a prerequisite test.

A *pre-test* is designed to find out what, if anything, the trainee already knows about the content of the proposed training programme. This enables the instructor to start the trainee at the correct point in the programme and allows the percentage gain to be calculated at the end of training.

A *post-test* should be given as soon as possible after instruction and practice ends, whether this be at the end of a lesson or at the end of the course.

A *retention test* is given later and is designed to show just how much of the information previously learned can be recalled or demonstrated. If the subject-matter or behaviour is not reinforced by subsequent repetition, there will in general be a marked difference between post-test and retention test results.

When constructing a test, one should decide what is:
(a) critical;
(b) important;
(c) relevant.

Critical material is that which the trainee *must know* in order to achieve programme objectives.

Important material is that which *should* be known but is not essential to successful attainment of specific objectives.

Relevant material is concerned with the matter in hand and *could* be known. It is pertinent to the subject but not so important for attaining the immediate objective.

The test should contain questions based on the critical material and be structured so as to satisfy the criteria laid down in the programme for demonstrating terminal behaviour. A proportion of questions set on important and relevant material could also be included, but these should be weighted accordingly.

3.3   Tests should be valid and reliable

When designing tests we must ensure that the test content covers what we actually intend to test. It is easy to construct a test which unintentionally includes items other than those written into the course as objectives. Such additional items would be invalid in terms of course content, learning experiences and evaluation.

Another feature of any satisfactory test is reliability. Subjective marking and assessment unavoidably involves value judgements, opinion and bias on the part of the examiner, especially when the trainees are known personally by the marker. Depending on the nature of the test, one examiner might award a fail grade, while another would come down in favour of a credit or even a distinction. Similar performance by several trainees should yield the same grade in any reliable test, and similar results should be obtained by groups of comparable trainees using the same test on other occasions, even when marked by a different examiner.

3.4 Validity and reliability defined

Validity is inextricably linked with course objectives, so that three important criteria must be fulfilled in order that the complete learning package may be validated. These are:
(a) course content;
(b) learning experiences;
(c) testing.

If we take, for example, the following objective relating to the use of a micrometer, the three criteria listed above may be identified.

'The trainee will be able to measure to within ±0.1 mm the outside diameter of a parallel round bar supplied using a 0-25 mm micrometer'.

Valid *course content* might include instruction on the interpretation of measuring scales provided on the micrometer, or the use of the ratchet to overcome problems of 'feel' when taking measurements.

Invalid content would be comparing the principle of measurement employed by the micrometer with that of using a Vernier calliper to make the measurement.

A valid *learning experience* might involve the trainee in using a micrometer to measure the outside diameter of a variety of round bars.

An invalid learning experience would be using an inside micrometer to measure the bores of round bars.

A valid test would be based upon the desired outcome of the learning, i.e. the trainee could be provided with a parallel round bar and asked to measure it. His result would be compared by the examiner to the known value and hence the outcome of the training evaluated.

An invalid test would involve the trainee in using a calliper or comparator and slip gauges to measure the diameter.

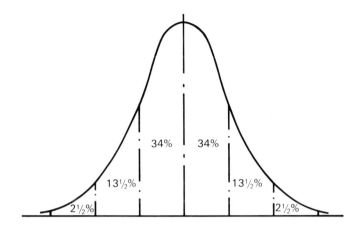

FIG. 3.6   **Normal curve of distribution**

99.7% of the population. The approximate percentage of the population located in each section of the curve is shown on the sketch. The area under the curve between the mean and ±1 standard deviation is 68% per cent; between the mean and ±2 standard deviations is about 95% of the total area. Whenever any data are obtained by measuring large numbers of components or sizes, a curve which is approximately normal is obtained; unless abnormal factors distort the process being measured.

The standard deviation is a measure of dispersion or scatter. If the standard deviation is small then the population will be grouped closely either side of the mean, if it is large then the population will be relatively widely spread.

The *range* is the difference between the smallest observation and the largest observation. If the population is normally distributed, a rough value for the standard deviation may be obtained by finding the range of the data and dividing it by six.

Interpreting graphs of test results

Figure 3.7 shows graph of test results.

Graph A is negatively skewed; that is, a high proportion of candidates scored high marks. The graph indicates that the test was too easy.

Graph B is positively skewed; that is, a high proportion of candidates scored low marks. The graph indicates that the test was too difficult.

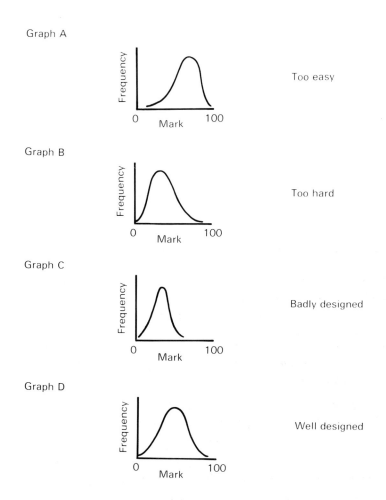

Graph A

Too easy

Graph B

Too hard

Graph C

Badly designed

Graph D

Well designed

FIG. 3.7 **Graphs showing examples of test results (Not applicable to criterion post-tests)**

Graph C shows the results clustered closely about a certain mark. The spread of marks is small. The central value may be located anywhere along the base line (mark axis). The graph indicates a badly designed test.

Graph D shows an approximately normal curve of distribution with a wide spread of marks. The graph indicates a well-designed test.

Calculating the mean and standard deviation of examination results

EXAMPLE

Two hundred candidates sat an examination. The results are given in the table below. Draw a frequency polygon (see figure 3.10) to represent these results.

Calculate:
(a) The mean mark achieved;
(b) The standard deviation.

Mark	1-10	11-20	21-30	31-40	41-50	51-60	61-70	71-80	81-90	91-100
Mid point (x)	5.5	15.5	25.5	35.5	45.5	55.5	65.5	75.5	85.5	95.5
Frequency (f)	4	10	20	27	40	41	29	16	9	4

Let standard deviation = s Arithmetic mean = x

Then

x	f	fx	$(x-x)$	$(x-x)^2$	$f(x-x)^2$
5.5	4	22	-44.5	1980.25	7921
15.5	10	155	-34.5	1190.25	11902.5
25.5	20	510	-24.5	600.25	12005
35.5	27	958.5	-14.5	210.25	5676.75
45.5	40	1820	- 4.5	20.25	810
55.5	41	2275.5	5.5	30.25	1240.25
65.5	29	1899.5	15.5	240.25	6967.25
75.5	16	1208	25.5	650.25	10404
85.5	9	769.5	35.5	1260.25	11342.25
95.5	4	382	45.5	2070.25	8281
	200	10000			76550
	$\sum f$	$\sum fx$			$\sum f(x - \bar{x})^2$

$$x = \frac{10000}{200} = 50$$

The average mark = 50

$$s = \frac{76550}{200} = 382.75 = \underline{19.564}$$

The standard deviation = 19.564 marks

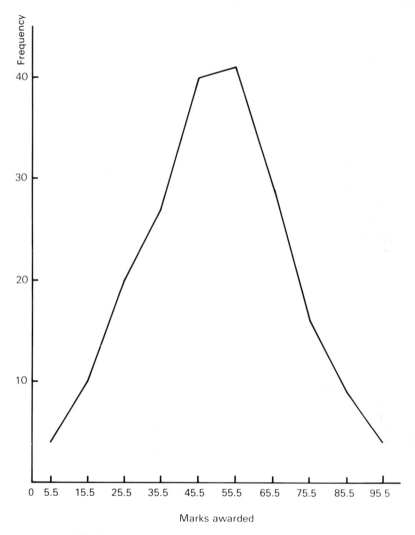

FIG. 3.8 **Frequency polygon showing examination results**

Calculating the range of examination results

The marks awarded to candidates were as follows:

%	25	30	40	42	51	53	55	57	62	70	81

Calculate the range.

Range = Highest mark – Lowest mark
      = 81 – 25 marks
      = <u>56 marks</u>

Test results

National educational tests and examination scores tend to be normally distributed as do pre-tests applied before training commences. On the other hand, local criterion terminal tests tend to be biased towards the high end of the marking scale. This is because criterion tests are designed to measure specific performance and are formulated directly from a limited number of objectives.

A properly designed training programme based upon specific objectives should result in the normally distributed pre-test scores being replaced at the end of training by a 90/90 criterion; that is, 90 per cent of the trainees should achieve a mark of 90 per cent or over in the terminal test.

Evaluation of test scores

There is a wide tange of test statistics which can be used in the evaluation of learning. The statistical analysis of test results is a specialised subject-area and the selection of test statistics to be employed in analysing the data requires expert knowledge. Interested readers are therefore recommended to consult books such as *Designing a Scheme of Assessment*, by C M Ward†, and *Fundamental Statistics in Psychology and Education*, by J P Guilford††, for in-depth treatment of the subject-area.

Pass or fail?

If the test results produce a normal curve of distribution, the mean and standard deviation can be calculated. Having considered the job for which the trainees have been trained, it might be deemed necessary for the trainee to obtain at least the average score. Obviously 50 per cent of the trainees would pass and the other 50 per cent would fail. Alternatively, a rule of thumb might be to pass those with a mark equivalent to or greater than the mean minus one standard deviation, which would yield a pass rate of 84 per

†Ward C M *Designing a Scheme of Assessment* (Stanley Thornes (Publishers), Cheltenham 1980).
††Guilford J P *Fundamental Statistics in Psychology and Education* 4th edn (McGraw-Hill, New York 1965).

cent of trainees tested. If the minimum acceptable mark was the mean minus one-half of a standard deviation, the pass rate would be about 69 per cent. *Statistical Tables,*† by Murdoch and Barnes, gives values of the 'areas in tail of the normal distribution' in terms of units of standard deviation.

For the sample calculation given, the mean mark calculated was 50 with a standard deviation of, say, 20 marks. Pass marks could therefore be calculated:

PASS CRITERIA	PASS MARK
Mean	50
Mean —0.5s	40
Mean —1.0s	30

In her book *Designing a Scheme of Assessment* Christine Ward writes: 'A typical value of standard deviation for a written paper is 13%, with up to 20% for a calculations paper; an objective paper may have a standard deviation as low as 10%.'

Ward goes on to illustrate the effect of standard deviation on pass rate by means of the two curves given below:

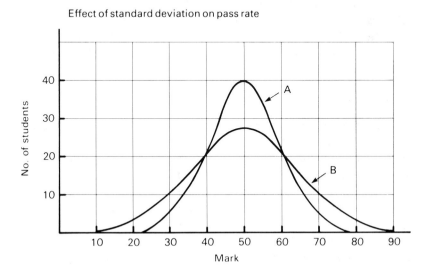

Effect of standard deviation on pass rate

†Murdoch J and Barnes J A *Statistical Tables* (Macmillan, London 1968) page 13.

The area beneath each of the curves A and B represents a population of 1000 examinees. The mean mark for both sets of results is 50 with a standard deviation of 10 for curve A and 15 for curve B.

Ward interprets the curves as follows: 'It can be seen that below 40 there are far more B students than A students, so that if the pass mark were set at 40, more B students than A students would fail (in fact 84% of A students would pass and 75% of B students). However, if the credit or merit level were set at 60 or 65, more B students than A students would receive the higher award.'

Guesswork

Instructions for completing multiple choice type tests often include the words: 'Do not ring answers to questions for which you do not know the answer,' the aim being to reduce the probability of candidates guessing the answer. When marking the paper, the examiner applies the formula given below, so that a candidate who ignores the instruction and makes wild incorrect guesses is penalised, while the mark obtained by those who abide by the instruction is unaffected.

$$\text{Final score} = \text{Number correct} - \frac{\text{Number incorrect}}{\text{Number of choices} - 1}$$

The following examples illustrate the method:

Number:
of questions set	100
of alternative answers	4
correct	64
incorrect	30
not attempted	6

$$\text{Final score} = 64 - \frac{30}{3} = 54\%$$

Suppose the same candidate had incorrectly guessed answers to the six questions not attempted in the previous example. His score would now be:

$$\text{Final score} = 64 - \frac{36}{3} = 52\%$$

Had he answered only those questions in which he was absolutely sure of the answers his score would have been:

$$\text{Final score} = 64 - \frac{0}{3} = 64\%$$

3.7 Preparing an objective test to measure the effectiveness of a talk

Before they get up they do not know what they are going to say; when they are speaking, they do not know what they are saying; and when they sit down, they do not know what they have said.

Sir Winston S Churchill

Before preparing a talk, a set of objectives is produced covering the subject to be discussed. It is then a fairly straightforward matter to devise a set of objective-type questions based upon these objectives.

The talk entitled 'Advice on the mounting of abrasive wheels' (see below) was based upon a set of objectives. A method of evaluating the effectiveness of the talk is by the subsequent application of an objective test, the advantages of this type of test being absence of subjectivity and speed of marking, there being only one correct answer.

The preparation and presentation of a short talk has already been discussed in section 1.5, while the writing of objectives upon which the talk will be based has been covered in section 2.7.

After drafting a suitable introduction, the bulk of knowledge to be imparted will be given in the main body of the talk. The main body should contain the important facts and information relating to the subject of the talk. The talk should be concluded with a summary of key points, after which an assessment test or questionnaire may be applied (see section 3.8).

An example covering the main body of a talk entitled 'Advice on the mounting of abrasive wheels' is given below. The text, together with figure 3.9 (a and b), has been reproduced from 'SHW 12 Training Advisory leaflet No. 2'.† Reference to the use of visual aids has been omitted.

†With the permission of the Controller of Her Majesty's Stationery Office.

Examination

Immediately before mounting, clean the wheel with a brush and examine it for possible damage in transit. The soundness of a vitrified wheel can be further checked by suspending it vertically and tapping it with a light non-metallic implement. Do not use the wheel if it sounds dead (cracked).

Spindles

Do not mount the wheel on a machine for which it is not intended.

The wheel should fit easily, but not loosely, on the spindle. Do not attempt to mount a wheel that fits tightly on the spindle; the heat of operation could cause the spindle to expand and possibly crack the wheel.

Before mounting the wheel check that the speed of the spindle does not exceed the maximum permissible speed marked on the wheel.

When the wheel is secured by means of a single central spindle nut the thread should be such that the direction of tightening the nut is opposite to the direction of rotation of the wheel.

The spindle should be checked for wear in the bearings. Bearings which are unduly worn should be renewed.

Flanges

With certain exceptions, which I shall deal with later, every abrasive wheel must be mounted between suitable flanges which should be not less than one-third the diameter of the wheel. The flanges should be recessed on the side next to the wheel to ensure that clamping pressure is not exerted near the hole. Flanges for wheels with large holes should not be recessed but the corners of the wheel seatings should be undercut so that the corners of the wheels will not be subjected to pressure. The inner (driving) flange should be keyed, screwed, shrunk or otherwise secured to the spindle, and the flange bearing surface should run true with the spindle.

Flanges should be of mild steel or other material of equal or greater strength and rigidity. Ordinary cast iron is not suitable. Both flanges fitted to a particular wheel should be of the same diameter and have equal bearing surface. The flange-bearing surfaces should be machined true and there should be no exposed rough edges or surfaces. If the bearing surfaces become damaged, they should be retrued, and the recess recut, care being taken to maintain the original diameter and depth of recess.

Washers

Except as indicated, washers (blotters) of compressible material, usually paper, as supplied by the wheel maker, should be used between the wheels and their flanges. Washers should be slightly larger than the flanges. Washers should not, however, be used with tapered wheels, threaded hole wheels or on the hub section of depressed centre wheels.

Securing the wheel

In the case of a single central spindle nut, tighten the nut only sufficiently to ensure that the flanges drive the wheel and prevent slip. If the tightening torque recommended by the maker is known, a torque wrench should be used. Otherwise tighten by hand pressure on a spanner. Excessive clamping pressure applied, for example, by using an extension to a spanner or by hammering, may damage the wheel.

When the flanges are clamped by a series of screws, take care to tighten them uniformly. First screw them home with the fingers and then tighten in a diametrical sequence.

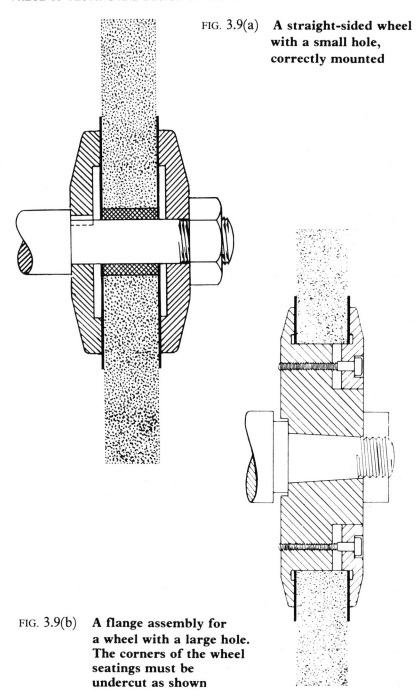

FIG. 3.9(a) **A straight-sided wheel with a small hole, correctly mounted**

FIG. 3.9(b) **A flange assembly for a wheel with a large hole. The corners of the wheel seatings must be undercut as shown**

Starting new wheels

Before running the wheel make sure the guard is in proper adjustment.

If the machine is fitted with a work-rest, adjust this as close as possible to the surface of the wheel; rotate the wheel by hand to make sure it is clear all the way round.

New wheels should be run free at full operating speed for a short period before they are used; during the trial run everyone should stand clear.

Plain (straight-sided) wheels with small holes

Figure 3.11(a) shows a wheel correctly mounted. The wheel is gripped between flanges of equal diameter. The inner flange is keyed on the spindle and pressure is exerted on the outer one by a nut on the threaded spindle. Each flange has an equal recess and the washers are slightly larger than the flanges.

In contrast, the following *unacceptable practices* increase the liability of the wheel to fracture because they result in excessive stress concentrated near the hole:
(a) paper washers not used between the wheel and the flanges;
(b) flanges not recessed;
(c) flanges unmatched in outside diameter and diameter of recess;
(d) one flange omitted and the nut tightened directly against the wheel;
(e) the use of an ordinary steel washer as a substitute for a properly recessed flange.

Plain wheels with large holes

Figure 3.11(b) shows a plain wheel with a large hole, mounted correctly on adapter or hub-type flanges. The corners of the wheel seatings are undercut to prevent pressure being exerted on the corners of the wheel.

A typical objective-type test based upon the content of the talk follows.

Read through the main body of the talk and attempt the following selection of questions based upon the objectives given on page 47.

OBJECTIVE TEST—MOUNTING OF ABRASIVE WHEEL

Tick correct answer:

1. An abrasive wheel should be tested for cracks by:
    (a) non-magnetic testing
    (b) dye-penetrant testing
    (c) tapping with a non-metallic object
    (d) rotating wheel on knife edge

2. The recommended fit between wheel and spindle should be:
   (a) a transition fit
   (b) an interference fit
   (c) loose running fit
   (d) a close clearance fit

3. The correct flange diameter to wheel diameter ratio is:
   (a) 1:1
   (b) 1:3
   (c) 1:4
   (d) 1:5

4. A suitable material for the manufacture of wheel flanges is:
   (a) cardboard
   (b) cast iron
   (c) copper
   (d) mild steel

5. The wheel should be secured by tightening the nut with a:
   (a) box spanner with extension
   (b) spanner 0.5 metres long
   (c) stilson wrench
   (d) torque wrench

6. New wheels should be tested by running under:
   (a) no load
   (b) light load
   (c) medium load
   (d) heavy load

7. The corners of wheel seatings for plain wheels with large holes are:
   (a) chamfered
   (b) radiused
   (c) undercut
   (d) fluted

8. The speed marked on a grinding wheel is:
   (a) the minimum safe operating speed
   (b) the maximum safe operating speed
   (c) used when reordering from manufacturer
   (d) the recommended speed for efficient cutting

9. A cracked wheel must not be operated because it may:
   (a) set up vibrations when running
   (b) cause chatter marks on work surfaces
   (c) disintegrate
   (d) not cut efficiently

10. A wheel rotating in a clockwise direction towards the work-rest should be secured to the spindle by a nut with a:
    (a) tapered thread
    (b) two-start thread
    (c) right-hand thread
    (d) left-hand thread

3.8 Checking the effectiveness of a talk by means of assessment test

Very often the group may be described as a 'captive audience'. They are present only because they have been told to attend. Under such circumstances the amount of information retained after the talk may be very little. If, however, the group is told that an assessment test will follow the talk, more attention will be paid to what is said. In any event, an assessment test or questionnaire presented after a talk provides the speaker with feedback as to the effectiveness of his talk.

The following assessment test has been written to check the effectiveness of the talk entitled: 'Advice on the mounting of abrasive wheels' (see section 3.7). Notice that each question refers to the actual content of the talk. Wherever possible, the questions should relate directly to the objectives upon which the talk is based.

ASSESSMENT TEST

1. State two important checks to be carried out during the examination of wheels prior to mounting.
2. Describe the type of fit recommended between wheel and spindle.
3. How is the maximum permissible speed of the wheel determined?
4. What could result if a wheel is mounted that fits too tightly on a spindle?
5. What action should be taken if worn bearings are discovered?
6. If a wheel rotates clockwise, in which direction should the nut be tightened?

7. What is the minimum flange diameter to wheel diameter ratio?

8. Why are flanges with recesses assembled with recessed side next to wheel?

9. State three methods of securing the inner driving flange to the spindle.

10. Name two materials from which flanges may be safely produced. Name one unsuitable material.

11. State two common defects found in old used flanges.

12. Outline remedial action to be taken in order to reclaim defective flanges.

13. From what material are washers made? Where are the washers fitted?

14. State three types of wheel where washers should not be fitted.

15. State two methods of clamping flanges.

16. Describe two methods of applying correct tightening pressures.

17. Describe two adjustments which should be made after fitting a new wheel and before running.

18. State two safety precautions to be implemented before putting the wheel to work.

19. List five unacceptable practices when mounting plain straight-sided wheels with small holes.

20. Why are the corners of wheel seatings for plain wheels with large holes undercut?

3.9 Review and rating

After the talk, make a note of the strengths and weaknesses in your performance. Record questions raised and be prepared to insert or delete information if the talk is to be repeated. If the talk can be videotaped or tape-recorded and reviewed later, so much the better. During group training, talks can be rated by group members on a five-point scale and the rating used as a basis for constructive criticism and improvement of technique.

Evaluating the rating score

For the example given, the number of aspects rated was sixteen. Therefore the highest possible number of points awarded would be $16 \times 5 = 80$ and the lowest possible number of points awarded would be $16 \times 1 = 16$.

The speaker in the example was awarded 41 points out of a possible 80, therefore his rating was:

$$\frac{41}{80} \times 100\% = 51.25\%$$

FIG. 3.12   **Example of rating sheet**

ASPECT OF TALK	RATING				
	Low			High	
	1	2	3	4	5
Introduction			★		
Main body – Content				★	
Sequence				★	
Relevance					★
Intelligibility					★
Interest				★	
Conclusion				★	
Use of aids		★			
Personal appearance			★		
Stance		★			
Clarity of delivery				★	
Enthusiasm		★			
Useful non-verbal signals		★			
Absence of distracting mannerisms		★			
Contact with audience			★		
Attention from audience				★	
	4	8	12	12	5

Rating $\% = \dfrac{41}{80} \times 100\%$

$= 51.25\%$

Total points awarded 41
Maximum points possible 80

Looking at the rating sheet given in figure 3.12, it would appear that the preparation was a little above average whereas the presentation was poor. An expert speaker would obtain a rating of near 100 per cent, while the lowest acceptable performance might be in the region of 60 per cent. Clearly, our speaker needs to concentrate on his presentation and delivery.

A better assessment of the speaker's performance would be obtained if he were rated by all members of a training group. Their individual scores would be totalled and an average rating determined. The following example based upon twenty ratings illustrates the method of obtaining a group assessment.

Individual	60	35	38	56	52	38	51	39	41	51
Ratings	48	43	39	43	41	41	43	43	41	39

Maximum possible points = 80
  Sum of individual ratings = 882 points
  Number of ratings = 20
  Average rating = $\dfrac{882}{20}$ = 44.1

Average % rating = $\dfrac{44.1}{80} \times 100\% = 55.125\%$

SUMMARY

- Testing monitors progress and measures the terminal effect of training.

- Test performances may be scored and the scores used to compare individual differences.

- A criterion test is based upon the desired outcome of a training programme. The test measures changes of trainees' behaviour against course objectives.

- A prerequisite test is used to determine the suitability of an applicant for a course of training.

- A pre-test is designed to find out what a trainee already knows about the content of a training programme.

- A post-test is given immediately after instruction.

- A retention test is administered some time after training ends to show how much of the course content can be remembered.

- Before constructing tests, decide what is: critical, important, relevant.

- Tests should be both valid and reliable.

- Validity is defined as: the degree to which a test measures what it is intended to test.

- Reliability is defined as: the degree to which a test consistently measures what it is intended to measure.

- Test questions may take the following forms: objective items, statements with key words missing, short answer written tests and essay-type questions. Oral examinations are used as part of the assessment procedure in languages and supervisory management courses.

- A curve of normal distribution is bell-shaped. The area under the curve between the mean and ±3 standard deviations represents about 99.7 per cent of the population. Standard deviation is a measure of scatter or dispersion. Range is the difference between the largest mark and the smallest mark.

- Talks may be based on a set of objectives. An objective test may be used to measure the effectiveness of a talk; alternatively a verbal or written questionnaire may be used.

- Talks may be rated on a number of aspects using a five- or seven-point scale. The rating may be used to identify weaknesses in both preparation and presentation.

- Talks are made up of an introduction, main body and conclusion.

QUESTIONS

1. (a) Using the table showing 'Criterion test scores for sixteen trainees' (figure 3.7), identify those trainees with
    (i)   the *highest* gain;
    (ii) the *lowest* gain.
    (b) What is the average gain for the whole group?

2. Choose an objective from a BTEC unit and write test items covering each of the following classes of knowledge. Each question should relate to attainment of the objective:
    (a) critical;
    (b) important;
    (c) relevant.

3. *Objective*
    'The desired outcome is that the trainee will be able to calculate the area of a triangle.'

    Test question

    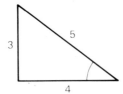

    'Determine the area of the triangle shown in the sketch.'

Both the objective and the test question are ambiguous because the work involved can be performed in a variety of ways. Identify the reasons for the ambiguity and rewrite the objective and test question so that specific performance may be qualified.

4. For any BTEC unit:
    (a) Write a list of test questions which you consider to be valid in terms of unit content.
    (b) Write examples of questions which would be invalid for test purposes, but which are connected with the subject in some way. Explain why the questions would be invalid.

5. List the advantages and disadvantages of using the following types of question to evaluate knowledge:
    (a) essay;
    (b) short answer written;
    (c) objective.

6. In an oral examination relating to a 'design and manufacture' project a student scored very high marks, but in written assessments for other BTEC units he did badly. What are possible explanations for this?

7. Select a topic for a short talk and write an objective test to measure the effectiveness of the talk.

8. Choose a topic for a talk. Write down a set of objectives based upon the desired outcome of your talk. Prepare an introduction. Write out a set of cue cards covering the main points you hope to cover. Prepare a conclusion. Prepare rating sheets for the talk including as many aspects as you think necessary. Ask someone to rate your performance. Deliver the talk and analyse your ratings.

9. One hundred students sat an examination. The results are given in the table below. Draw a frequency polygon to represent the results. Calculate:
    (a) The mean mark   (Answer $\bar{x} = 53.2$)
    (b) The standard deviation   (Answer $s = 13.47$)

What do you consider would be the minimum acceptable pass mark? Give reasons for your decision.

Mark	Frequency	Mark	Frequency
1-10	1	51-60	37
11-20	1	61-70	12
21-30	2	71-80	4
31-40	3	81-90	2
41-50	36	91-100	2

10. During a talk, 10 ratings of 18 aspects on a 5-point scale were obtained:
    72, 63, 65, 75, 61, 58, 67, 73, 76, 80.
    Determine:
    (a) the average number of points awarded;
    (b) the percentage rating.
    Answer:
    (a) 67   (b) 74.44%

A set of questions based upon the U75/004 Physical Science I unit follows.
Attempt the questions and comment upon this type of test format. The solution
is given on page 370.

Select a letter which represents the correct answer from the list provided
on page 93. Write the letter in the box provided.

QUESTIONS

1. Current flows due to the existence of .... between two points in an electrical conductor	
2. Small currents can be measured by	
3. A light bulb is an example of a .... resistor	
4. The ratio of the voltage across a resistor to the current through it is the definition of	
5. Some non-metallic conductors and electrolytic conductors obey	
6. The sum of the voltages in a .... is equal to the total applied voltage	
7. The voltage is the same across resistors in	
8. The property of a conductor that limits current is	
9. The sum of currents in resistors connected in .... is equal to the total current flowing into the network	
10. The current is the same in all parts of a .... circuit	
11. The resistance of a metal conductor increases with .... and can be allowed for in calculations by using the formula $R_T = R_0 (1 + xT)$	

(cont.)

12. The .... is used to deflect an electron beam in a television set	
13. Volts × amps = ...	
14. A current carrying conductor produces	

Note: The following may be prefixed by the words 'a', 'an' or 'the':

A   Series circuit
B   Parallel circuit
C   Parallel network
D   Parallel
E   Series
F   Temperature
G   Ohm's law
H   Kirchhoff's law
J   Newton's law of proportionality
K   Fleming's constant temperature law
L   Non-linear
M   Linear
N   Parabolic
P   Potential difference
Q   Resistance
R   Volt drop
S   Galvanometer
T   Watts
U   Joules
V   Coulombs
W   Magnetic field
X   Field force
Y   Voltage surge
Z   Voltmeter
AA Length
AB C.S.A.
AC Volume
AD Magnetic effect of a current
AE Polar effect of a current
AF Electromagnetic effect of a current
AG Farads

4

Managing a discussion

In his article 'Discussion Methods†, Derek Legge outlines some important features of a discussion. Under the heading 'What is a "discussion"?' he writes:

The important distinguishing characteristics of discussion lie in its purposes and in the manner in which the activity is carried out. Thus the word describes not any group of human beings talking together, but a group seeking to put together their knowledge, ideas and opinions about one subject in a co-operative endeavour to learn from each other. Instead of the destructive rivalry of a debate, a discussion seeks to be constructive, to encourage members to speculate freely, to withdraw or amend earlier statements and to make adjustments to their opinions without fear or loss of status. In a real discussion people try to listen to each other, to learn from each other, and by working together to reach a little nearer to the truth or to the solution of the problem or to whatever other educational objective they have in mind.

The discussion method is a valuable teaching technique. It involves active student participation and provides a vehicle by which individuals may develop social skills and effect attitudinal changes. The teacher's contribution to a discussion is considerable, in that very careful preparation and guidance are essential requirements of this mode of instruction.

4.1 Distinguishing a discussion from a debate

A group discussion is a planned meeting with a specific purpose or goal. Members are brought together to discuss some controversial issue or matter of company policy and are encouraged to actively participate in the proceedings. There is no formal sequence of speakers and each member may speak at will.

A discussion is intended to provide a framework within which the participants may freely air opinions while the remainder listen. The main

†Legge D, in *Teaching Techniques in Adult Education* Stephens M D and Roderick G W (eds) (David & Charles (publishers) Newton Abbot 1971) page 76. Reprinted by kind permission of Professor M D Stephens.

94

point about a discussion is that it should be constructive with those present pulling towards a common goal.

A debate differs from a discussion in that it is a somewhat destructive procedure. There are generally two sides, each with opposing views. A question or proposition is put forward and each side takes it in turn to speak for or against the motion. The participants are mainly concerned with destroying one another's arguments or putting forward opposing inter- pretations of evidence under review during the debate.

The debate is formally organised with the proposer of the motion, usually a person of high standing, speaking first. The opposer of similarly high standing, follows directly. After the opening speeches the seconder to the proposer speaks, followed by the seconder to the opposer. Then follows the general debate, after which the main opposition speaker sums up the case for the opposition followed by the proposer.

4.2 The feelings which prompt responses in a discussion situation

People attending discussions often arrive with fixed ideas regarding a subject and the statements which they make usually reflect their opinions. In a properly organised discussion the instructor should remain silent for most of the time, allowing the group to explore the subject in their own way.

Unfortunately, things do not always run smoothly, and members display feelings of hostility, anxiety, resentment and self-pity. Some experience feelings of inadequacy, some are afraid to speak, some ridicule statements made by others, and some make sarcastic remarks. Emotions such as anger or fear result from oversensitivity to remarks made. These are the factors which prompt various kinds of responses in a discussion situation.

Clearly, the aim of a discussion is to allow people to re-examine and modify their attitudes in an atmosphere without threat, and to bring about a change in behaviour in a desired direction. The instructor must therefore ensure that control is maintained and that tension, friction and personal threats are not allowed to develop. He must, however, avoid becoming the central figure through whom all points are made and must not allow his personal views to influence the discussion.

4.3 Influences

Throughout a discussion, group members may be affected by a variety of influences which serve to constrain their contributions.

The status of other members relative to their own standing within the group may affect their willingness to make suggestions or volunteer information. The risk of exposure in making an unguarded incorrect statement or the fear of appearing incompetent may cause a person to clam up. There is safety in silence. The size of a group, the presence of strangers and the venue may overwhelm a person who feels out of his depth. Length of discussion, jargon and specialised knowledge required can inhibit participation as can the presence of senior management.

Some discussions are used as a platform for attaining political ends or personal gain. Speakers monopolise the meeting and attempt to manipulate others or to convert them to their own beliefs. Bias may be introduced by the chairman attempting to guide the discussion to a conclusion in line with his own beliefs.

Such influences have a detrimental effect on what might otherwise prove to be a healthy discussion.

4.4   Responsibility for other members

A discussion should be managed so that each member feels a personal responsibility for every other member. Each group contains a network of relationships between members and only remains intact when each person plays the part expected of him. Group interaction should be directed towards agreement and the establishment of a pleasant friendly atmosphere. Behaviour likely to promote tension should be discouraged and mutual reinforcement encouraged.

Good relationships are essential to efficient working. Efficient groups are happy groups and each member should be prepared to listen to and learn from others. All should be made to feel equally important and the scene should be set for individuals to modify their attitudes and opinions without threat or loss of face.

In large groups there is less opportunity for all to participate in the discussion. Moreover, feelings of inhibition increase with group size. Sub-groups form, especially if the group is made up of staff with different disciplines and status, and it is often difficult to reach consensus without arguments. It is the duty of the discussion leader to ensure that the goals of such sub-groups are relevant to the discussion subject, and to give guidance whenever it is needed.

4.5 The purpose of discussions

The main aim of a discussion group is to endeavour collectively to put together ideas, knowledge and opinions relating to the subject for discussion, in a spirit of co-operation.

A discussion is used to examine a problem, to seek information or to enquire into a matter. The subject is introduced or the question posed by the discussion leader. The business on hand is then thrown open for group members to examine in detail. Opinions are aired, information is exchanged, questions are asked and the matter is probed from all angles. Members are encouraged to speculate freely and all are encouraged to participate. Often during the discussion, new ideas are formulated, accepted, modified or rejected, while many aspects previously overlooked are brought into focus and reviewed.

The desired outcome of the discussion is to work towards a solution to the problem or question originally propounded.

4.6 Leaderless discussion groups

In the absence of effective leadership, groups lack direction and individual personal behaviour takes over which tends to dominate the discussion. Often group activity is fragmentory and more attention is paid to satisfying individual needs than to task-orientated behaviour. Individuals wishing to dominate the discussion in order to gain self-satisfaction tend to speak more and to adopt extreme positions. Several compete for the leadership while others with more moderate views control the situation by promoting compromise and directing discussion towards the task. This enables those vying for leadership to preserve self-esteem while gaining some satisfaction. In such circumstances the unofficial leadership role passes around the group, changing with group needs at a given instant.

Deliberate use may be made of leaderless group discussions in the field of attitudinal and communication training. The participants can talk as equals and develop the ability of self-expression in an unstructured trainee-centred atmosphere. Absence of authority in the form of an official leader encourages problem-solving through mutual participation and criticism. Emotions are allowed to run free and individuals receive both group reinforcement and sanctions in the form of reward or punishment for behaviour exhibited. Differences between an individual's self-image and the group's perception of him are highlighted, allowing him to modify his attitudes if he so chooses.

Sound leadership unifies group activity and creates within the group an awareness of the need for cohesive behaviour in order for effective discussion to take place. The leader directs and steers group thinking and prevents the discussion degenerating into a free-for-all shouting match. In Appendix 7 two main theories of leadership are discussed under the heading, 'Leadership is not a personal quality, it is a contingent role'.

4.7 The value of a discussion plan

The function of a discussion leader is to prepare a plan, to introduce the topic, to direct, control and evaluate contributions made and to conclude the discussion.

If a discussion is to be used in order to evaluate learning, it should take place towards the end of a lesson, the lesson plan being used as a basis for the discussion. If, however, a discussion is to be used as a teaching method, the teacher should ensure that he does not do all of the talking and should avoid answering his own questions. This type of discussion is best designed around a plan based upon a specific purpose or goal. The plan should not be too rigid and should be sufficiently open-ended to allow the group to explore ideas.

The use of a plan enables the discussion to be steered in the desired direction and prevents the group from rambling and deviating too far from the topic.

4.8 Preparing the plan

The discussion method involves the instructor in a good deal more preparation work than does a lesson. A lesson can be controlled by the instructor as far as content is concerned, especially if he is constrained by a tight syllabus.

A topic for discussion is often more open-ended and throws up a wider range of ideas and information. To cope with this, the instructor must be well prepared and be in a position to correct untrue or misleading statements. He must also be able to impart missing information if the discussion grinds to a halt.

A suitable plan for discussing motorway driving is given below:

Discussion Topic: Motorway driving

1. Brief introduction to motorway driving.
2. Joining a motorway.
3. Changing lanes and lane discipline.

4. Braking and overtaking.
5. Leaving a motorway.
6. Summary.

4.9   Procedure for discussions

Visual material, sets of discussion documents and any other aids should be prepared before the group assembles. To save time and interruptions, sets of paperwork should be placed on the table ready for use by the group. Nameplates or stiff cardboard and felt-tip pens should be available to each member for identification purposes.

The discussion should commence with an introduction—leaders often forget to introduce themselves. After putting the group at ease, the leader should give a brief introduction to the topic, followed by a broad general question such as 'What is a motorway?' This should get things going, although there may be a short period of silence before a response is heard.

During the main discussion the leader should act as a referee, speaking only when necessary. He should note key points made by the group and summarise these at intervals throughout the discussion in order to qualify and condense progress made. When the topic has been well and truly aired, and before enthusiasm flags, the discussion should be brought to a close.

The discussion leader should then sum up important aspects of the discussion and assess how well the group has answered the questions posed. Any central principle not brought out by the group should be outlined and linked to group conclusions.

A follow-up to the discussion may take the form of a written report or action along the lines of group recommendations.

4.10   Opening a discussion

Discussion topic: 'Brakes and braking'

The instructor opens the discussion by briefly outlining the purpose and scope of the content to be covered.

'Right Martine, I think now would be a good time to talk a little bit more about stopping the car. I was pleased to see that you checked your pedal and handbrake before beginning to drive. You also tested your brakes to see that they were working properly soon after moving off. These checks are most important. On the road you stopped without hazard to other road users. Good. How did you feel about stopping? (*Here the learner would have chance to respond to the instructor's assessment ask questions and clarify points . . .*)

Proper use of the brakes is an essential part of good safe driving. All drivers must be able to stop their cars smoothly and maintain control at all times when braking. Nowadays, cars have efficient braking systems but remember—they're only as good as the drivers who use them.

I'd like to spend the next five minutes discussing with you things like deciding where to stop, braking distances, progressive braking, downhill braking, emergency drill, skidding and anything else you'd like to talk about. I'm not sure how much you already know about the brakes but I feel that the more you understand how and why things work the quicker you will learn to use the controls and master their use. Would you like to get to know more? . . .'

TASK

Instructors should prepare and present learners a discussion topic paying particular attention to the opening sentences.

4.11   Analysing a discussion
After a training session instructors should complete a rating sheet (see figure 3.10) for each presentation in order to evaluate the openings. Each opening should be assessed in terms of clarity of presentation, amount and relevance of information supplied, interest generated and whether or not discussion aims were clearly spelled out.

The ratings should be used by the instructor as a basis for constructive self-criticism although it is better if instructors can discuss together one another's presentations. Criticism by an authority figure can be embarrassing and instructors appear to accept comments more readily from their peers.

4.12   Value of a video-taped discussion
Groups of instructors participate in discussions in front of a videotape recorder for about ten minutes. The tape produced is replayed and analysed. This facility shows instructors where their weak and strong points are and enables them to observe the effect of non-verbal signals on behaviour.

Using the tape, a Bale's type interactional analysis can be carried out (see figure 4.1). The twelve categories into which group behaviour is classified may be identified and the various roles exhibited by members observed.

4.13   Leading a discussion
A discussion incorporates questions, answers, statements and comments, and can be a very effective method of learning. It is of particular value as a

follow-up to individual learning but it can also be used in a wide variety of situations including academic studies and management training.

The role of the discussion leader is to open the discussion and thereafter to keep it going by posing questions, clarifying trainees' answers, encouraging group members and generally controlling the procedure. The leader should keep a sharp look-out for non-verbal signals indicating the way members are feeling and should encourage the quieter ones while restraining the over-talkative.

The quality of a discussion is largely the responsibility of the leader or chair person, although no attempt should be made to impose personal views upon the learner or group. If the discussion is such that comments and ideas are addressed to a chairperson, they should be accepted and acknowledged. Where it is due discussion details should be reinforced and main points summarised.

TASK

Prepare a plan and lead a fifteen-minute discussion.

Case studies

RISKY SHIFT PHENOMENON†

USED CAR DILEMMA

Read through the information given below and select the minimum odds you would accept and still advise Miss G to purchase the newer car. Do not discuss your decision with anyone at this stage. Write your odds down on a piece of paper and fold it up.

Miss G is eighteen years old and is scanning the newspaper advertisements looking for a used car. She spots two Ford Escort 1300 cc cars at the same price. One of the cars is privately owned. The other car, offered for sale by a reputable garage is one year older.

The privately owned car is being sold 'as seen', while the older car carries a twelve-month parts and labour guarantee. Miss G has little mechanical knowledge.

†After: Kogan N and Wallach M A, *New directions in psychology III* (Holt, Rhinehart and Winston, New York 1967).

FIG. 4.1　**Chart for Bales's interaction process analysis**

Adapted from W P Robinson, *Language and Social Behaviour* (Penguin 1972). Fig 1 page 44. Copyright © W P Robinson, 1972. Reprinted by permission of Penguin Books Ltd.

Socio-emotional area: A
positive reactions

Task area: B
attempted answers

Task area C:
questions

Socio-emotional area: D
negative reactions

1	2	3	4	5	6	7	8	9	10	11	12

								No.	Description
								12	shows antagonism; deflates other's status; defends or asserts self
								11	shows tension; asks for help; withdraws out of field
								10	disagrees; shows passive rejection, formality; withholds help
								9	asks for suggestion, direction; possible ways of action
								8	asks for opinion, evaluation, analysis; expression of feeling
								7	asks for orientation, information repetition, confirmation
								6	gives orientation, information; repeats; clarifies; confirms
								5	gives opinion, evaluation; analysis; expresses feeling; wish
								4	gives suggestion, direction; implying autonomy for other
								3	agrees; shows passive acceptance; understands; concurs; complies
								2	shows tension release; jokes; laughs; shows satisfaction
								1	shows solidarity; raises other's status; gives help; reward.

Instructions

Use the chart to observe the group behaviour. Try scoring each occurrence of the twelve categories of interactions in the columns on the chart. You will find it near impossible to score all the participants so first pick one person and score his or her responses. There would be likely to be more responses in the 'TASK' area if you ask the group to discuss some problem, like how unemployment could be reduced. Alternatively, you could try doing this exercise when observing a discussion going on in a TV programme.

Instructions source: J Greene *Communication*, Social Psychology Course D305 Block 11 — The Open University page 50.

Miss G must decide whether it would be best to purchase from the garage where she could feel secure, knowing that any repairs required would be carried out entirely free of charge; or, on the other hand, to take the risk and buy the newer car, which would save her £300 at current garage prices but which would cost her large sums of money if it proved unreliable.

Imagine you are advising Miss G. Select from the following list (a-f) the lowest probability that you would consider acceptable for the risk to be taken, and write down your choice.

(a) Miss G should not risk purchasing the privately owned car whatever the chances are of it breaking down.

Chances that the car will break down:
(b) 9 in 10
(c) 7 in 10
(d) 5 in 10
(e) 3 in 10
(f) 1 in 10

Now break up into small groups. Appoint a leader. Hand your folded papers to him. No one should look at the papers yet. Discuss the same problem and make a collective decision on the minimum odds the whole group would accept and still advise Miss G to purchase the newer car.

Work out an average minimum odds for the group, using the folded papers. Compare the average odds with the group decision and with your own original decision.

What conclusions do you draw from the results?

2 THE INSPECTOR'S DILEMMA

A coach company operates a daily service from Bournemouth to Cheltenham which returns the same day. Tickets for the journey, which includes sixteen stops, may be purchased from travel agents and booking offices along the route. The company uses a charting system whereby bookings reported by the booking agents are collated and entered on a chart at Bournemouth for the outward journey and at Cheltenham for the return journey. The system is unreliable and the number of passengers waiting to board the coach at stops seldom agrees with the number charted. Sometimes there are more, sometimes less. Company rules state that if a person holds a ticket he is guaranteed a seat on a coach regardless of his point of departure. No standing passengers are allowed.

On one occasion the duty inspector at Bournemouth has loaded the Cheltenham coach and finds that only four empty seats remain shortly before the scheduled time of departure. He checks the chart and finds that if all goes well the number of passengers joining the coach along the route will be offset by those leaving it. The inspector is concerned that the four empty seats leave a very small margin for errors in charting.

If uncharted passengers exceed four, the driver will be unable to abide by the company's guarantee of a seat and the ticket holders would be left at the stop. If the driver hires in a private coach en route, the cost will be double that incurred by using a company coach and would involve serious delays, with the risk of passengers missing connections for outward journeys from Cheltenham.

If the inspector orders a relief coach to start from Bournemouth and it is not utilised on the journey to and from Cheltenham, he will involve the company in a good deal of unnecessary expense and will also prevent the coach being used to generate additional revenue in Bournemouth.

Imagine that you are advising the inspector. Decide the lowest probability (a–f) you would accept for the inspector to send the coach without a relief, and write down your choice.

(a) The inspector should send a relief whatever the chances are of the coach being filled.

Chances that the number of ticket holders will never exceed the number of seats:
(b) 9 in 10
(c) 7 in 10
(d) 5 in 10
(e) 3 in 10
(f) 1 in 10

Repeat the procedure given at the end of Case Study 1.

SUMMARY

- A discussion should be constructive rather than destructive. Participants may modify their attitudes without threat.

- A debate can be a somewhat destructive procedure. There are generally two sides, each with opposing views.

- Jargon, status, size of group, venue and the presence of strangers may influence group discussions.

- A discussion should be managed so that each member feels a personal responsibility for every other member. Good relationships are essential to efficient working.

- A discussion is used to examine a problem, to seek information or to enquire into a matter.

- In the absence of effective leadership, groups lack direction and individual behaviour which tends to dominate a discussion takes over. Leadership may pass from one to another, changing with group needs.

- A discussion leader should prepare a plan, introduce the subject for discussion, direct and control the group. He should evaluate contributions made and conclude the discussion. A discussion plan enables the discussion to be steered in the desired direction.

- A discussion is opened by briefly outlining its purpose and scope.

- A follow up to the discussion may take the form of a written report or action along the lines of group recommendations.

- Group interaction may be rated using a Bale's type interaction process analysis chart.

- The quality of a discussion is largely the responsibility of its leader.

'Silence, I will not listen to rubbish'

QUESTIONS

1. Outline the main differences between a discussion and a debate.

2. 'Some people are easily influenced by suggestion.'
   (a) Explain the statement.
   (b) Explain how people may be influenced by 'suggestion' during a discussion.
   (c) What is meant by a 'leading question'?
   (d) Specify the conditions which affect a person's suggestibility.

3. 'Leadership is both a function of the social situation and a function of personality, but it is a function of these two in interaction.'
   (C A Gibbs 1947)
   Explain the quotation with reference to the leadership of a discussion group.

4. Prepare a plan and introduction for a discussion on the two main theories of leadership given in Appendix 7.

5. Listen to a discussion taking place during a television programme. Imagine that you are the secretary whose function is to note the main points arising during the discussion. Note the main points and prepare a written report of the proceedings.

6. Observe a small group involved in a discussion. Complete a Bale's interaction process analysis chart showing the behaviour of one of the participants throughout the discussion.

7. There is a tendency for an instructor to see trainee conduct in particular ways and this affects his concepts of individuals. Within your group identify the:
   (a) most popular person;
   (b) most influential person;
   (c) low status members;
   (d) leaders.
   Explain how this kind of knowledge of group dynamics could affect a discussion leader.

8. During a discussion care must always be taken to avoid giving a participant a sense of inferiority. Why is this?

9. What is meant by the statement, 'a discussion is a battle of closed mind with closed mind'?

10. Describe how a discussion leader might restrain an over-talkative group member.

Part 2
Teaching and Learning

5

Understanding the role of perception in the learning process

Perception involves two important processes: the gathering of signals carrying information, and its subsequent decoding in the brain where previous knowledge of such information is stored.

Information is received in the form of stimuli picked up by the five senses: smell, touch, taste, hearing and vision. These senses link the central nervous system with the environment and allow us to react to given stimuli.

The *behaviourist* school of psychologists proposed that animal and human behaviour resulted mainly from the more or less automatic responses of a body to stimuli, playing down the role of the brain as a processor of information. The *Gestalt* school proposed the 'laws of perceptual organisation' including theories of continuity, closure and similarity. Gestaltists suggest that in perception, 'the whole is greater than the sum of its parts' and that 'insight' plays an important part in problem-solving. The brain in some way organises individual stimuli into patterns so that dots, lines or musical notes are combined to form a meaningful whole rather than a set of random entities. They consider that this ability to structure and organise is innate.

At birth, babies are unable to perceive the environment as adults do, although after a while they do learn to perceive and to build up a meaningful picture of the world around them. As time passes, the process of information-gathering and decoding becomes almost automatic and so a knowledge of the environment and learning is formed. The effect of personal experience on the learning process must also be taken into account.

Animals have been used in experiments designed to investigate brain activity. In one experiment a very fine electrode was inserted adjacent to a neural cell in the cortex. The pattern of electrical activity was monitored, amplified and recorded. The record showed bursts of spontaneous activity occurring every few seconds. Such activity continues throughout life, even during sleep, until brain death occurs when no electrical activity can be detected.

When a sense organ detects a stimulus the rate of brain activity increases, and cells in different areas respond, depending upon the nature of the stimulus. It was concluded that the area in which activity was detected was connected with the classification and categorisation of information. In short, the mechanism of perception in animals had been identified, and it is likely that the human perceptual apparatus functions in the same way.

The brain also serves as a storage device. Learning is the process of feeding information into the brain. Information is picked up by receptors located in the sense organs and is interpreted by the perceptual apparatus. The knowledge is then fed into a storage/retrieval system within the brain, where it is stored, possibly as a result of neurological, biochemical or electrical changes in the neural circuitry.

The way in which an event is perceived, therefore, affects the way it is stored as knowledge.

5.1   Perception is an active response to communication

Perception is the interpretation of sensory information received from a person's surroundings through the external senses: touch, hearing, smell, taste and sight.

We are constantly being bombarded with stimuli which reach us from the environment. We become aware of anything directly apprehended by the senses. We perceive it, although not necessarily as it really is.

Stop reading and write down all that you can detect from your surroundings. Perhaps you can hear a clock ticking or smell the coffee brewing, or see a car passing, or feel a warm cup in your hand or taste a Polo Mint. These stimuli are obvious, but there are many other less obvious 'bits' of information reaching you every second, each giving intelligence relating to the nature of the environment.

Much of the information received is either apparently ignored as no action from the receiver is required, or else is responded to in a seemingly unconscious automatic manner. However, particular sensations may be singled out for attention and interpretation. This active interpretation of sensory impressions is known as *perceiving*. Stimuli reach the sense organs and are relayed to the brain, where they are interpreted on the basis of past experience, and the requisite responses made. We perceive by comparing the particular sensation with previous learning and knowledge of identical or similar situations which have been coded and stored in the mind.

Different people perceive a given phenomenon in different ways, and what is perceived depends to some extent upon past experiences, present needs and also upon what we expect and wish to perceive.

In the industrial situation the aim of the instructor is to direct the learner's attention to specific items which he, the instructor, is attempting to communicate. As communication is a two-way process, the learner is required to attend to what the instructor is imparting, to perceive, and hence to learn.

In order for active participation to take place, the learner must find the lesson content interesting and rewarding enough to displace other stimuli competing for his attention. Creating this atmosphere is the main task confronting the instructor.

5.2 Attention defined

Attention is the selective focusing of the mind upon a given phenomenon.

A sudden flash of light, a loud bang or an appearance of the unexpected will all attract our attention. We turn towards the phenomenon and try to make sense of it. If it has disappeared, we maintain our gaze in the direction of its original appearance, or strain our ears trying to detect the origin of the sound. Attention is maintained for a while, and if there is no recurrence of the phenomenon, we soon return to our own private thoughts or to whatever held our attention before the incident occurred.

Attention is a function of our senses, perception and instincts. Our senses detect a change in the environment. We try to relate the change to something we have experienced before and to categorise it in some way according to our previous knowledge of apparently similar events. If we perceive the change to be potentially dangerous, our attention is riveted to the phenomenon and survival behaviour is adopted. Attention can only be maintained if our interest in the event is maintained.

In the instructional situation, audio-visual aids and models initially attract attention. It is the task of the instructor to maintain attention by causing the learner to concentrate on what is being said, by attempting to shut out competing stimuli which interfere with the learning process. If interest is allowed to flag, attention will be lost to more rewarding student activities.

subject-matter. The initial diagram gives an overall picture of the system or process to be discussed, and printed words are kept to a minimum. Each word should count.

Having briefly introduced the subject, a block diagram is displayed. The students' attention will immediately be attracted to the diagram and the general pattern of the whole taken in. Their gaze will shift from one part of the diagram to another until they have a mental picture of the process. Only then will it be possible for the teacher to present verbal information relating to the process effectively. To do so before sufficient time has been allowed to satisfy initial interest in the diagram would be unproductive.

After the relationships between the blocks have been discussed, each block should be studied in depth.

Block diagrams take several forms.

Figure 5.2 shows the movement of fuels from oilfield to filling station.

Figure 5.3 shows important sectors of the mechanical engineering industry. The blocks are not related in any particular way but serve to illustrate the main groups of products. Each sector may then be discussed using another diagram which shows greater detail.

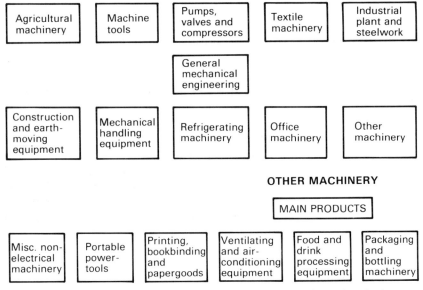

FIG. 5.3   **Block diagram of the mechanical engineering industry**

Note: 'Other Machinery' has been selected for further 'in-depth' study.

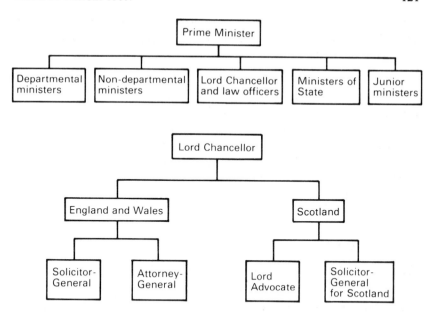

FIG. 5.4   **Block diagram of the Government**

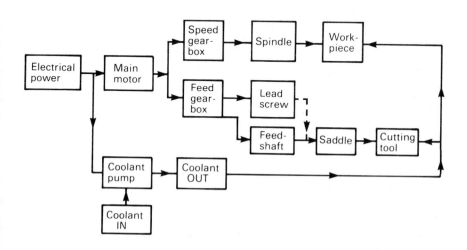

FIG 5.5   **Block diagram of a centre lathe**

Figure 5.4 shows the general form of British government together with one element in more detail.

Figure 5.5 shows a block diagram of a centre lathe. A systems approach showing inputs and outputs has been adopted. Arrows indicate how individual blocks making up the system relate. Using the diagram as an aid helps the instructor transmit an overall picture of the machine to the minds of the trainees. Each block may then be examined in detail using actual machine components wherever possible.

5.6   Perceptual experience defined

Perceiving is the act of attaching meaning to stimuli reaching our senses. The more we attend to a phenomenon, the more we are likely to perceive about it, provided that we have had previous experience of it, or of something related to it. Past experience affects our ability to perceive the nature of a given phenomenon.

Perceptual experience is obtained from exposure to objects or situations. Such experience enables the individual to construct a store of knowledge based upon identifiable objects and to draw upon this store when confronted with the same object or situation at a later date. The process is continuous and the store is being added to daily as learning experiences are encountered. For example, we learn by experience the form, function and attributes of a motor car and also how to react to one when crossing the road. If, while standing in the road, we hear the sound of an engine running or its exhaust noise, we immediately identify the source as a motor vehicle. If we narrowly avoid being run down, we are wary and behave in an appropriate manner when crossing the road on future occasions. If we hear a louder, deeper exhaust noise, we classify the source as a heavy vehicle and, when it appears, find it fairly easy to identify the vehicle as a coach or truck. If, however, the noise of an engine running can be heard but the source cannot be seen, perception is ambiguous. Further information is required before the source can be classified as a motor car, van, truck, coach, bulldozer or stationary engine.

Perceptual experience, then, involves the interpretation of the main features of an object or action based upon information which has previously been categorised and stored in our memory bank.

5.7 The importance of perceptual experience in the learning process.

Any or all of the following may stimulate a learner through his senses: sight, hearing, touch, smell or taste. The awareness of sensory activity will probably cause a response, and the type of response will depend upon how the learner interprets the signal. If the interpretation or perception of the signal could be relied upon, then each person would attach precisely the same meaning to the event. Black or white meanings would be allocated. There would be no errors and no shades of grey. In practice, this is not the case. Discrimination, past experiences and the language available to explain events influences perception.

Discrimination

The ability to differentiate and to discriminate greatly affects perception. *Discrimination* relates to the ability to detect differences between two stimuli. Drawings have been produced by experimenters in order to show that it is possible for a person to perceive a shape either as figure or as a ground. Figure and ground reversal always occur in such drawings. Figures 5.7-5.9 illustrate the effect. If the drawings are studied for a short time,

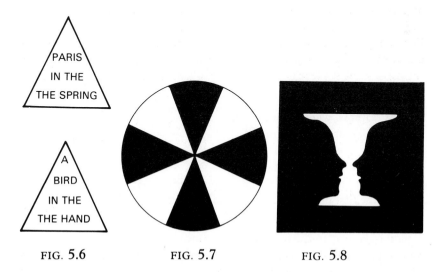

FIG. 5.6   FIG. 5.7   FIG. 5.8

Adapted from *Psychology. The Fundamentals of Human Adjustment*, Norman L Munn, 3rd edition, George C Harrap & Co Ltd.

FIG. 5.9

Adapted from *Introduction to Psychology*, Ernest R Hilgard, Richard C Atkinson and Rita L Atkinson, 5th edition, Harcourt Brace Jovanovich, Inc.

at first, perhaps black stands out as the figure against a white background, and then the next instant, reversal takes place. In no case does the figure merge into the background. Who can say which colour is intended to form the figure?

False perception and optical illusions

Both optical illusions and problems of false perception highlight difficulties encountered in the process of perception. Examples of figures illustrating well known illusions are set out on pages 126-8. Study them before reading on. It would appear that our eyes are not to be trusted!

In his study of the development of sensory organisation, Leeper† used three figures, those of a young attractive woman, an old hag and one which could be perceived either as the young woman or as the old hag. Leeper's subjects were shown a figure of the young woman followed by the ambiguous figure and a high proportion identified the ambiguous figure as that of a young woman. Others were shown a figure of the old hag followed by the ambiguous figure and identified the latter as an old hag. These results suggest that 'recency effects' brought about by prior presentation of one or other of the unambiguous figures, or 'expectation', that is, a readiness to perceive certain aspects of the ambiguous figure (resulting from presentation of the first picture) determines to some extent how things are actually perceived.

A picture similar to the one used by Leeper is shown in figure 5.10. The picture illustrates problems of false perception. At first glance the picture

†Leeper, R 'A study of a neglected portion of the field of learning—the development of sensory organization', *Journal of Genetic Psychology*, 46, pages 41-75.

FIG. 5.10   **Ambiguous figure-ground effects**

Adapted from *Introduction to Psychology*, Ernest R Hilgard, Richard C Atkinson and Rita L Atkinson, 5th edition, Harcourt Brace Jovanovich, Inc.

may appear to be that of an old hag but if gaze is maintained the old hag disappears and is replaced by an attractive young woman. In this case, neither recency effects nor expectation aspects apply, no other pictures having been presented.

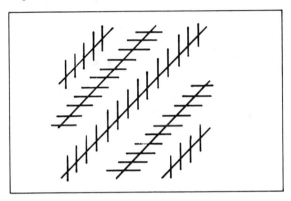

FIG. 5.11   **Zöllner illusion**

In the Zöllner illusion (figure 5.11), the longer lines appear to be converging whereas they are parallel.

In the Hering illusion (figure 5.12), parallel lines superimposed on a system of lines radiating from a central point appear curved.

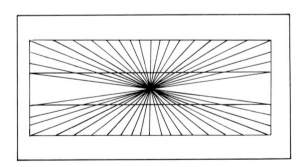

FIG. 5.12   **Hering illusion**

Adapted from *Psychology. The Fundamentals of Human Adjustment,* Norman L Munn, 4th edition, George C Harrap & Co Ltd.

The Müller-Lyer illusions show the effects of adding arrows to lines. The left-hand portion of a straight line which has been divided into two equal lengths by an arrow appears to be longer than the right-hand portion (figure 5.13) as does the lower of two straight parallel lines of equal length (figure 5.14).

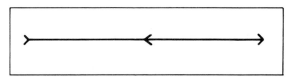

FIG. 5.13 **Müller-Lyer illusion**

Adapted from *Psychology and Everyday Life*, James Breese, Hutchinson Educational 1971.

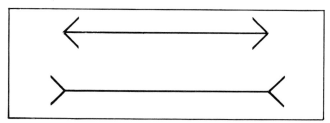

FIG. 5.14 **Müller-Lyer illusion**

Adapted from *Introduction to Psychology*, Ernest R Hilgard, Richard C Atkinson and Rita L Atkinson, 5th edition, Harcourt Brace Jovanovich, Inc.

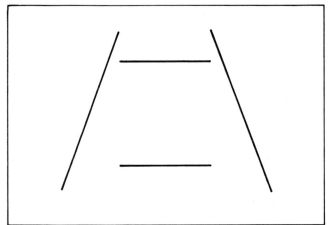

FIG. 5.15 **Ponzo illusion**

Adapted from *Introduction to Psychology*, Ernest R Hilgard, Richard C Atkinson and Rita L Atkinson, 5th edition, Harcourt Brace Jovanovich, Inc.

In the Ponzo illusion (figure 5.15) horizontal lines of equal length are drawn between two converging lines. The upper horizontal line appears longer.

Circles of equal diameter drawn at the centre of each of the clusters shown in figure 5.16 appear to differ in size. The central circle within the ring of smaller circles appears to be larger than the one surrounded by larger circles. The apparent change in size results from placing the central circle in different surroundings.

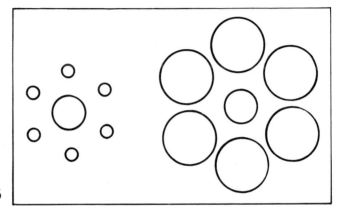

FIG. 5.16

Adapted from *Introduction to Psychology,* Ernest R Hilgard, Richard C Atkinson and Rita L Atkinson. 5th edition, Harcourt Brace Jovanovich, Inc.

Perceptual illusions

A 'sophist' may be described as 'a reasoner willing to avail himself of fallacies that will help his case', while 'sophism' is 'a false argument meant to deceive'.

An illusion results if a person incorrectly formulates an hypothesis relating to visual inputs such as the form of geometrical illusions. If these inputs are misleading then detail of the figure will be incorrectly perceived. In this process the brain could be likened to a sophist and the geometrical illusion to a form of sophism.

Perceptual illusions have been the subject of extensive research but to date no universally accepted theory explaining the phenomenon has been expounded.

Past experiences

Behavioural aspects of perception greatly affect the interpretation of events. Knowledge of results of exposure to a given occurrence is stored in the mind, and when a similar occurrence is experienced, the response made is often biased by what happened during the original event. If, however, there is some small difference which passes unnoticed, the response made may be totally inadequate or incorrect. Attitudes are formed as a result of subjection to an influence, and they lead to a readiness to respond in a predetermined manner, so that resulting behaviour can be a function of either prejudice or opinion.

Language

The quality of perception is greatly affected by the language available to an observer. Appropriate language must be accessible in order for an event to be fully appreciated. If the meaning of an occurrence cannot be explained in words, then the mind cannot efficiently interpret the concept elicited by a given stimulus, given that thought processes involve a kind of inner conversation carried on in the brain.

The role of language in human perception, thinking and teaching is discussed more fully in section 7.1.

Conclusion

From what has been written above, it would appear that if drawings can be perceived in more than one way, and events falsely interpreted in the light of past experience, then it is not unreasonable to suggest that perceptual experience in the learning situation can be plagued by similar processes.

5.8 Motivated experience

Motivation is a term relating to the arousal, control and sustaining of behaviour necessary to satisfy a need or to attain a goal. After a crime has been committed, detectives usually try to establish a motive for the crime. They look for someone who had the opportunity, the means and the motivation to commit the crime.

Fortunately, the majority of people do not resort to crime in order to satisfy needs. Once physiological needs such as hunger, thirst and the like have been satisfied, people tend to concentrate on needs related to self-actualisation, such as self-fulfilment, prestige and esteem.

Intrinsic motivators like challenge, mastery and curiosity frequently lead a person to great efforts in order to attain a goal. The reward for effort comes in the form of inner satisfaction and a feeling of accomplishment after overcoming a problem, acquiring knowledge or mastering some difficult feat of endurance. No obvious reward in a material form results from such effort.

On the other hand, extrinsic motivators involve the satisfaction of needs such as the desire for recognition, praise or financial reward. Gratification can be observed by others and may in some cases be measured in monetary terms.

Motivated experience results from the exposure of learners to tasks which enables them to satisfy particular needs and hence gives rise to feelings of satisfaction when the objective is attained.

Learning takes place from the cradle to the grave. Most people learn something every day, but academic learning is a special case, and such learning can only be accomplished through the concentrated efforts of learners. They must want to learn, be exposed to the appropriate learning environment and be interested in the learning material in order to maintain thier attention.

Motivation, interest and attention are therefore closely interrelated.

Motivated experience results from knowledge gained during encounters relating to the appeasement of needs. People may be confronted with a wide variety of learning situations and yet walk away with little or no change in their state of knowledge. If the situation appears to have no bearing upon their views of the world, or is considered to be irrelevant to their work or future prospects, then they will attend to other matters which they deem to be more profitable.

Important motivators include the desire to qualify so as to improve job prospects, the pleasure experienced in doing a job well, taking a pride in one's work, intellectual achievement and active participation in group activities. Similarly, motivated experience is encouraged by the fear of failure due to falling behind with studies, loss of face with workmates or peer groups, awareness of competition and the prospect of losing one's job.

Motivated experience can be promoted by providing the means by which a learner's needs may be satisfied. The instructor should provide a presentation which directs the learner's interest, and hence attention, to those factors which will prove to be most rewarding. In order to do this, the instructor should outline the purpose of the instruction and its importance to the learner.

Once the learning process has started, interest may be maintained by feeding back progress reports in the form of knowledge of results and by giving praise and reward for correct responses. The presentation should include a variety of teaching media while curiosity may be promoted by using discovery learning techniques where possible. The class should be kept busy, and an element of healthy competition maintained. High-class morale will result from such practices.

5.9 How motivation can be encouraged

The more interested learners become in what the instructor is saying or doing, the more attention they will devote to it and the better they will remember it. If the learner is to remember what is being taught, the material relating to the lesson should be presented in such a way that mental images are easily formed. Once formed, the images may be reproduced at a later date to enhance subsequent extensions to that already learned or to aid recall. The presentation of material should allow the learner to use as many senses as possible rather than to rely on passive learning methods. Where appropriate, the learner should be encouraged to see, hear, feel, taste or smell the objects under discussion and preferably be made to describe them in their own words.

The foregoing assumes that the learner will be highly motivated to learn and that he really wants to learn in order to fulfil a need or desire to acquire knowledge of the subject being presented. However, attitudes already held as a result of former exposure to the subject or instructor and other factors such as feelings, expectations, thoughts and possibly resentment, will affect the learner's perception at a given time. Mental or emotional state will influence interpretation of the learning situation.

Motivation therefore affects our perceptual experiences and the learner's perception of the instructional content will be evidenced by responses and resulting modification of behaviour.

In the instructional situation, the instructor must create a suitable learning environment which incorporates elements designed to attract the learner's attention, and which provides the means by which needs may be fulfilled. The learner should be made aware of the links between the immediate behavioural objectives and the overall aims of the instruction, and also the benefits to be derived in the long run.

Incentives, competition, challenge, ego-involvement and examinations all serve to arouse interest and to stimulate the learner to greater efforts; but probably the most important influence is the standard set by the instructor. The standard should not be too easy to achieve, but should be difficult enough for the learners to attain—if they try.

SUMMARY

● Perception is the interpretation of sensory information received from the environment.

● We perceive by comparing a particular sensation with coded information stored in the brain.

● What is perceived depends to some degree upon past experiences, present needs and what we expect and wish to perceive. Perception is also affected by set.

'Yes,
it's . . .
definitely
a hair brush'

● Attention is the selective focusing of the mind upon a given phenomenon.

- Attention is related to both motivation and complexity of task.

- Sequence of perceiving: background and field, shape, outline, colour, brightness, general classification, identification and naming.

- Sensory overload leads to disruption of attention and breakdown of perception.

- Sensory deprivation leads to boredom and loss of concentration.

'Have I died or am I simply starved of sensory inputs?'

- In order to hold attention the requisite input of sensory information must be provided.

- Excessive detail influences the speed and quality of perception, weakens concentration and leads to confusion. Irrelevant facts overload the trainee's perceptual apparatus.

- Block diagrams eliminate confusing detail and give an overall picture of a process or system.

- Perceptual experience involves the interpretation of the main features of an object or action based upon information which has been previously categorised and stored in our memory bank.

- Discrimination—the ability to differentiate—greatly affects perception.

- Figure and ground and optical illusions are factors which influence perception.

- Motivation is a term relating to the arousal, control and sustaining of behaviour necessary to satisfy a need or goal.

- Intrinsic motivation leads to inner satisfaction. Extrinsic motivation leads to forms of gratification which may be observed by others.

- Motivated experience results from exposure to a task which will enable a particular need to be satisfied.

- Motivated perception can be encouraged by using: incentives, competition, challenge, examinations and situations relating to ego-involvement.

QUESTIONS

1. Define the following:
   (a) perception;
   (b) attention;
   (c) interest;
   (d) motivation.
2. State the effect of the following on a person's perception of an event:
   (a) expectation;
   (b) set;
   (c) past experience.
3. At a given instant many stimuli reach the sense organs. Why is the receiver not equally aware of all of these?
4. List the advantages of using block diagrams during a lecture.
5. How is perceptual experience acquired?
6. What effect does motivated experience have on the learning process?
7. List ways of encouraging motivated perception.
8. What effect does a person's attitude towards a subject and the instructor have on his approach to learning?
9. How could problems of inattention in class be overcome?
10. List factors which influence a person's ability to perceive accurately.

6

Behavioural patterns of adolescence

Adolescence is a phase in the development of a person which lasts from puberty to adulthood. In Britain today, a young person attains adult status at the age of eighteen. He becomes independent and assumes full responsibility for his actions. The several years preceding this momentus occasion are a busy time for the teenager who has to cope with the process of sexual maturation along with psychological, social and physical growth.

Greater freedom from parental control and wider involvement in social pursuits outside the home add to his responsibilities, while media advertisements arouse needs thereby creating a demand for more money. Lack of sufficient cash to fund the changes in lifestyle adds yet more pressure.

During late adolescence an urgent need to acquire the academic qualifications required for a place in higher education or for a decent job together with the transition from school to work bears heavily upon the adolescent.

Academic performance is related to intelligence, and so the rate of intellectual development in adolescents is critical if acceptable standards are to be reached before leaving school.

Piaget (born 1896) began his career as a biologist; he later devoted considerable time to a study of the evolution of children's thinking. He worked in universities in Paris and Geneva and proposed a theory relating to the evolution of intelligence which stresses the significance of maturation and the interaction of a person with his environment. Piaget attempted to describe a sequence of stages through which children gradually acquire knowledge of the world, placing emphasis on the evolution of intelligence over a period of time. He considered that conceptual growth occurs because the child, whilst actively trying to adapt to its environment, organises its actions into *schemata*† through the processes of assimilation and accommodation. A discussion of Piaget's work covering moral and intellectual development is given in Appendix 10.

The language available to an adolescent is another key factor in deciding how well he performs in academic pursuits. Limitations imposed by a restricted verbal code can weigh heavily against him in many educational establishments, which are essentially middle-class institutions.

Finally, social influence processes can greatly affect behavioural patterns and these processes are discussed at some length in section 6.8.

6.1   Physical changes in adolescents

Puberty marks the beginning of sexual awareness and is a maturational and growth period which occurs in the western world earlier now than ever before. It commences at about the age of twelve and usually lasts for about two years, although improved nutrition can hasten this process. During this period, physical changes take place, together with accelerated growth.

Adolescence is a time of psychological, social and maturational growth initiated by puberty. Normal physical development extends through pubescence to the late teens and is a function of both genotype and environment. During adolescence considerable rates of increase in height, weight and brain size are experienced, with girls reaching maturity about two years before boys. Other factors observed include increases in the metabolic rate and blood-pressure, a deepening of the voice in boys, the growth of a beard and increased sweat gland activity.

Adolescents tend to become preoccupied with their bodies. Girls are concerned about the size of their breasts, their height and weight, neither wishing to be too tall nor too fat. Boys are concerned about their height, physique and the size of their muscles—their masculinity. Numerous adolescents experience hypochondriacal preoccupation and the fear of death while many are afflicted by acne, the scourge of teenagers.

Sexual urges and feelings become intense and are accompanied by fantasy and masturbation. Heterosexual relationships become prominent in the

---

†Schemata: 'An active organisation of past actions'. See Bartlett F C *Remembering* (Cambridge University Press, London 1932); also 'Cell Assemblies' in Hebb D O *The Organisation of Behaviour* (John Wiley & Sons, New York 1949).

minds of teenagers, who are naturally attracted to the opposite sex, but to whom sexual freedom is denied by social convention.

Intrinsic aggressive instincts are supported by growth in strength and size, and are evidenced by attacks on extrinsic factors such as parents and teachers, or in acts of vandalism.

Increases in emotional and intellectual capabilities result in the broadening of attitudes and interests, often accompanied by unpredictable change in behaviour and diverse experimentation.

Adolescence is a period when biological, social and psychological development occur simultaneously, bringing conflict and strain, both for the adolescent and for others concerned!

A detailed account of many aspects of adolescent behaviour and development is given in a book entitled *Adolescent Development,* by H W Bernard.†

6.2 The social development of adolescents

The modern adolescent is growing up in a turbulent world. The rapid social change which followed World War II continues at an ever increasing rate. Urbanisation and the growth of cities, together with their attendant infrastructures, has produced a revolution in the fields of communications and technology. Knowledge and the development of high technology required to cope with the demands of a relatively affluent society have caused greater pressures on young people than those experienced in the past. Human aspirations have reached new high levels, fired by the effect of mass media, and modern youth has been caught up in the spiral of increasing industrialisation and consumerism.

Automation eliminates the need for skilled operators although the need for highly skilled technicians remains. Fewer jobs for unskilled and semi-skilled workers are now available as the silicon chip and computer-controlled robots take over. Competition for jobs is now becoming fierce and many school leavers are finding it difficult to obtain employment. To stand any chance of obtaining meaningful employment with prospects, job applicants must obtain good gradings at school and leave with adequate qualifications.

Numeracy and literacy standards become critical. To lack them as a result of underachievement is economic suicide, and for low achievers it means a

†Bernard H W *Adolescent Development* (Intext Educational Publishers, Scranton, Toronto and London 1971).

permanent low level life standard. The need to find a job becomes of paramount importance to a youth, for without a job he lacks status and position in the social world.

Pressures bearing on young people are further increased by the unstable international political situation. Adults appear to give little or no guidance and politicians the world over cannot agree among themselves. Teenagers are aware of the threat of nuclear holocaust, germ warfare and death. Radio and television broadcasts prophecies of doom, eminent scientists cannot decide whether or not the generation of electricity by nuclear power stations is safe, and are unable to agree as to how best to cope with global warming or how to dispose of waste. Poor communications exist between the police and adolescents, especially in the areas of motorcycle spot checks and the searching of teenagers 'on suspicion'. Policemen have earned for themselves the name 'pigs' due to alleged bullying behaviour, a label which the adolescent attaches to them for many years.

Is it any wonder that many young people challenge societal standards, attack conventions and live for the present?

Early socialisation takes place within the family unit. At first, language, culture and moral values are acquired through a process of interaction between the child and members of the immediate family, and later, with a wider circle of friends and acquaintances. Social learning theory suggests that learning takes place as a result of the child imitating those close to him and receiving reinforcement and approval for desired behaviour. Within a nuclear family the parents are directly responsible for dicipline and determine, to some extent, the child's formation of attitudes.

Adolescence is a time when the young person becomes involved in greater activity and social interaction outside the home. Greater freedom from direct parental control and increased mobility bring emancipation and greater personal responsibility. In his search for independence and a new identity, the young adult is drawn into a world in which family links are weakened. The media bombards him with advertisements designed to stimulate demand for certain types of entertainment and products in the huge teenage markets. Money, required to satisfy needs arising from such sources, becomes important, and while wishing to become a free agent, he is not prepared to give up the security and lack of responsibility which goes with continued economic dependence on parents. He lives at home, subsidised by parents, either unable or unwilling to accept full responsibility for his own support.

While living in the family home he comes under pressure from parents to conform to their ideas of social norms. Friction arises as a result of conflicts of opinion. He frequently becomes rebellious and too demanding for parents. Aggressive outbursts are commonplace and defiance of parental authority results. The generation gap becomes apparent. Many people forget the problems of their own transition to adult status, and the adolescent refuses to accept the adult values of the older generation. Parental attitudes towards sex before marriage and adult expectations relating to commitment to work and studies conflict with the way adolescents see things, adding to the difficulties normally experienced in growing up.

Some are unable to make the adjustment to work and cannot find a niche to fill. They become alienated, drop out and seek status in other fields. They sleep around, borrow, scrounge, take drugs, join extremist movements and dress differently in an attempt to beat the establishment. However, the vast majority of adolescents make the transition to adulthood without serious difficulties.

The transition from school to work

The type of school attended, together with the range and level of subjects studied, relates directly to the choice of career available to an individual. Unfortunately, a large majority of pupils have no plan worked out well in advance and little or no idea of their eventual career.

Labour turnover in industry is affected by the school-leaver's choice of employment. Many are attracted to an occupation purely by chance. An advertisement catches their eye, a company has a recruiting stand in a shopping precinct, a friend tells them of a vacancy or the careers master directs them to a few companies.

It is often the case that school-leavers have acquired ideas about what work will be like, and are shocked when they discover that the world of work is completely different to their expectations. The absence of industrial or commercial experience before leaving school was a contributory factor to high labour turnover and poor adjustment to work.

When children are very young they know of only a few occupations, which usually include spaceman, train-driver, policeman, nurse and suchlike. Between the ages of seven and nine they become aware of a wider range of jobs occupied by neighbours, relatives and friend's parents. By the age of twelve, fantasies are discarded and replaced with a first career choice, although these choices do not necessarily accord with academic ability.

At the age of fifteen years, the prospect of leaving school and the need to find a job make the task of career choice more worrying, especially when linked with the transition from adolescence to adult status. Many apprenticeships are geared to a sixteen-year-old entrant, and the decision to remain at school until eighteen adds further anxiety. If pupils stay on until the age of eighteen and fail to pass GCSE, A- or AS-level examinations, they are likely to experience some difficulty in finding a job due to the inflexibility of many training schemes and the difference in wage rates payable which are governed by age.

Teenagers who had failed to make any career decisions found themselves pigeon-holed into jobs, either by their parents or school careers masters, whose main interest appears to be in getting them into *some* kind of job, the actual job being immaterial.

Insufficient guidance was given to pupils. They were often expected to make up their own minds first, and then careers teachers provided information as to how the chosen ambition might be realised. Once in a job, teenagers often complained that the careers staff in schools were unqualified to meet the demands made of them. The staff were considered to be orientated towards the world of the school and out of touch with the real world of work outside the school gates.

Fortunately, over the last ten years, work experience involvement has become more widespread and pupils are now sent from schools to work in factories and offices. There they gain firsthand knowledge of the type of work involved. TVEX and CPVE initiatives linking with local colleges are also helping to bridge the gap between school and industry, in that pupils are able to sample a variety of careers before leaving school.

Many 'day-release' students attending colleges as part of their apprenticeship training are unhappy with their lot. One often hears complaints that one-year 'off the job' training given in training centres for new first-year apprentices keeps them in a disciplined 'unreal' situation for too long. The day-release at college is considered by some students as an extension of school and hence undesirable. Many school-leavers would like a year in which they could sample the world of work, doing a variety of jobs free from related college studies. After this break they would then choose their career, find a job and approach their training with a more enthusiastic and enduring attitude.

Coping with unemployment

An awareness of the very high level of unemployed school leavers prompted the Government to include in its ten-point 'Programme for action'†:

better preparation for working life in initial full-time education;
more opportunities for vocationally relevant courses for those staying on in full-time education;
a £1 billion a year Youth Training Scheme guaranteed from September 1983 a full year's foundation training for all those leaving school at the minimum age without jobs.

The White Paper stressed the importance of the last two years of compulsory education in forming an approach to the world of work and the need for every pupil to be helped to reach full potential for personal development and for the demands which employment will make.

For those school leavers who were unable to obtain employment, the Youth Training Scheme supervised by the then Manpower Services Commission aimed to equip young people to adapt successfully to the demands of employment; to have a fuller appreciation of the world of industry, business and technology in which they would be working; and to develop basic skills which employers would need in the future.

The scheme comprised five main elements:
Induction and assessment—of skills and aptitudes.
Basic skills—numeracy, literacy, communications and practical competence in the use of tools and machines.
Occupationally relevant education and training—both on and off the job.
Guidance and counselling—advice and support throughout the programme.
Record and review of progress—document of progress completed as course proceeds. The standard achieved is recorded in a way recognisable both to trainee and to potential employers.

The scheme produced a valuable pool of partially trained young people who were able to take advantage of the subsequent upturn in employment opportunities while at the same time providing those concerned with a means of gaining self-esteem.

†See: *A New Training Initiative: A Programme for Action,* Government White Paper. Her Majesty's Stationery Office, London, Dec 1981, page 3.

6.3   The intellectual development of adolescents

The growth of intelligence

Up to the age of about ten years, the majority of children are incapable of high-level abstract thought, but with puberty comes a change in intellectual capacity which enables the child to begin to see things in the mind's eye. The child develops the ability to consider various aspects of a given problem and to formulate methods of solution before taking action. Instead of seeing things in purely concrete terms, the young adolescent begins to take an interest in elements beyond the purely physical phenomena encountered in day-to-day life.

The ability to reason, to comprehend and to theorise develops; and this increase in intellectual ability gives rise to a growth in interests, abilities and activities. Intelligence continues to grow throughout adolescence, with females developing verbal intelligence more rapidly than males. However, in the fields of mechanical reasoning and spatial ability, males do much better than females.

Intelligence increases as a result of maturation of the nervous system, exposure to learning situations and interaction with the environment, and peaks during the early twenties. Most people continue to gain in intelligence up to the early thirties although few are equally gifted in the areas of numeracy, literacy, spatial ability and verbal fluency.

Albert Binet was the first to attempt the objective measurement of intelligence, and in 1916 his scales were revised by a team from Stanford University. Scales used to calculate IQ today have been derived from this early work and now incorporate tests designed to assess verbal comprehension, verbal fluency, numerical ability, perceptual speed and logical reasoning.

An account of the results of Piaget's and Kohlberg's investigations of moral development is given in Appendix 10.

6.4   The effect of intellectual development on the learning process.

IQ tests are used to estimate the mental capacity of a person at a given time and relate to present performance over a range of intellectual abilities for which the test has been designed. Coaching and practice affect test results as does the attitude towards the test of the person being tested, while test scores are subject to rise and fall with time.

The intelligence quotient (IQ) is given by the ratio:

$$\frac{\text{Mental age}}{\text{Chronological age}} \times 100$$

and for the average person ranges from about 90 to 110, although college graduates may have IQs of 120 plus.

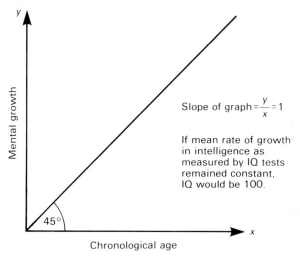

Slope of graph $= \dfrac{y}{x} = 1$

If mean rate of growth in intelligence as measured by IQ tests remained constant, IQ would be 100.

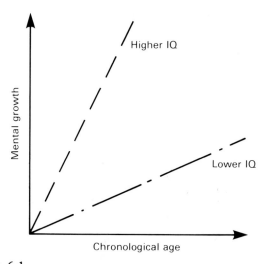

FIG. 6.1

If the mean growth in intelligence as measured by IQ tests remained constant, the graph of mental growth against chronological age would follow a linear law of the form $y = x$, that is, the ratio of mental age to chronological age would always be unity, and the resulting IQ would be 100. In practice, many eleven-year-old boys have IQs of about 85, improving to 110 at the age of sixteen years, reflecting the slower mental growth before puberty and the spurt towards the end of puberty.

Intelligence has been defined as the faculty of understanding. It implies the ability to make satisfactory adjustments to stimuli arising from the environment and the capability to solve problems using abstract language, both verbal and symbolic. In order to learn, a person must be able to perceive and to attach meaning to written and spoken words as well as concrete objects.

Some argue that people are born with innate potential for the development of intelligence, while the acquisition of knowledge results from exposure to contrived learning situations and interaction with the environment. Low academic achievement is considered an indicator of defective intelligence, with mental differences between slow learners and rapid learners increasing over a period of time. Exposure to poorly designed or inappropriate curricular activities relative to the learner's ability also reduces the learning rate. Poor performance judged against academic standards often results in the student 'opting out' and attempting to obtain prestige by creating disturbances, thereby drawing attention to himself.

People develop intellectually at their own rate and should, for prolonged mental growth, be exposed to challenging learning processes for as long a period of life as is possible. This idea is backed up by evidence to the effect that a person who has engaged in further or higher education may well gain a twelve-point IQ advantage over a person of equivalent IQ at the age of sixteen years who has not engaged in intellectual pursuits since leaving school.

Intelligence is maintained by some people throughout life, especially if their IQ is high when younger. In others, with initially lower intelligence, intellectual ability declines progressively from the age of about thirty, while physical loss may also impair intelligence and learning ability. Fortunately, there is a greater maintenance of intelligence with use—if you don't use it, you may lose it!

6.5 Limitations imposed on intellectual development by a restricted verbal code

Language codes

Language is the characteristic feature of communication and is the means by which thought processes are manifested. Languages are sets of rules, and the application of these rules makes possible the formation and understanding of sentences. If the rules are known and the appropriate vocabulary available to the listener, then he will be able to interpret sentences that he has never heard before. Similarly, he will be able to assemble words in a form that will be readily understood by others with access to the same language.

Basil Bernstein refers to two main language codes: the 'elaborate code' and the 'restricted code'.† The elaborate code is the language code of the middle classes and is described as 'universalistic' or 'non-specific', while the restricted code is used by the working classes and is 'particularistic' or 'context bound'. Bernstein emphasises the fact that while restricted-code speakers may use the elaborate code from time to time, such instances will be infrequent during the socialisation of a family. He goes on to say that speech patterns are influenced by one's position in the social structure. As cultural values and life expectancies are linked to social class, the manual worker inevitably finds himself at the low end of the social scale.

The socialisation of children within a family's social group affects their linguistic styles. In consequence, there will be significant differences between the elaborate code of the higher socio-economic groups and the restricted code of the lower classes. The restricted code is characterised by the usage of short, simple and unplanned sentences. This limits the scope of expression. On the other hand the elaborate code enables the middle-class speaker to make his intended meaning clear. The possession of a large number of alternative words makes easy the elaborating of statements.

The difference in language codes greatly affects what is learned and the ability to understand the spoken word. This is particularly evident in schools or other academic arenas where teachers almost invariably use an elaborate code. The teacher's language, while readily understood by the middle classes, is not clearly understood by those who use restricted speech codes. Much of what is said simply washes over the heads of listeners. Consequently, if the language is not understood then the intended concept

†Bernstein B 'Social Class, Language and Socialisation', in Abramson, A S (ed) *Current Trends in Linguistics* (Mouton Press, The Hague 1971).

will not be internalised by the working-class student and many levels of abstraction will be beyond his capacity.

Simple direct speech has its advantages. Many trade unionists and others with working-class backgrounds have achieved important positions in society due to their ability to put forward an argument in a clear manner. In many ways, working-class speakers make more effective narrators, reasoners and debators than middle-class speakers—who tend to qualify each statement and lose the trend of their argument in a mass of irrevelant detail.

A discussion of the main relationships between social class and educational opportunity and attainment is given in Appendix 11.

6.6 The role of instructor expectation on the progress of a trainee

The significance of social context for individual social behaviour and experience

Many people believe that individual human behaviour depends to a large extent upon biological make-up and fixed personality traits which are either present at birth or developed early in life. A person is classified as good or bad, happy or miserable, bright or dull, on the basis of how he presents himself in a given situation. No attempt is made to consider how the same person may behave in a different social context. Superficial impressions are quickly formed and inferences about the characteristics of others drawn on the basis of factors such as dress, speech patterns, colour, facial appearance or posture.

First impressions are important, and the impression formed when meeting someone for the first time will influence behaviour on subsequent meetings. People tend to stereotype others according to beliefs held about others known to them who have in the past exhibited similar characteristics. Traits are attributed on the basis of whatever information is available at a given time, without real justification. We tend to go beyond the facts and read a situation in terms of past experiences of apparently similar behaviour.

Instructor expectations

The instructional situation provides a typical arena in which stereotyping and impression formation can affect the progress and performance of an individual trainee. Experiments have been conducted in which greatly improved performance has been observed in a classroom when randomly selected children were thought by their teachers to have been specially selected, due to their having 'shown great promise'. The influence of social expectations has highlighted the fact that people tend to behave as one would expect them to behave in a given social or work situation. The specially selected children performed better because they believed that greater effort was expected of them. Their teacher's own expectations of the group led him to make greater efforts in order to satisfy these expectations.

The way a person sees himself and the value he places on himself is referred to as the *self-image*. Michael Argyle, in his book, *Social Interaction,*† suggests that each person is constantly being categorised by others and learns to anticipate how he will be categorised, so that he eventually sees himself in these terms. Argyle goes on to say that people are also categorised as being either more, or less, rewarding and prestigeful. This too is anticipated and affects one's self-esteem.

People often adopt the role expected of them. They need to be liked, they need esteem and they need to be valued by others. Individuals who have been deprived of esteem, worth and status often become maladjusted. This fact is worth remembering in the classroom situation as it bears on the trainee's attitude to work, behaviour and achievement.

Categorising, stereotyping and labelling trainees often forms a basis for their adopting the identity expected of them. Instructor expectation and attitude can therefore serve to make or mar the trainee's approach to learning.

6.7   Peer group attitudes

From early adolescence a change in attitudes towards parental authority occurs. Young people experience a need for status and want to become persons in their own right. Pressure to conform to the norms of the adult society in which they live often leads them to seek refuge within peer groups. The peer group or gang, which comprises people of their own age, sex and interests, provides a framework within which a new identity may develop.

The peer group helps the adolescent to break away from close family and home ties and to some extent takes over parental roles. Being a member of the group promotes a sense of belonging, while group rewards take the form of affiliation, friendship, approval, recognition and power.

†Argyle, M *Social Interaction* (Methuen, Atherton 1969) Chapter 9.

Other group members provide support and set expected standards of behaviour. In return, the new member identifies with the peer group leader who normally embodies many of the social characteristics of the group. Conformity to group norms is evidenced by the individual's mode of dress, language and vocabulary used, customs and forms of recreation. Members of the group also tend to own the same sort of vehicle, in the form of scooter, motorbike or car.

If a member of the group behaves in a manner which is unacceptable to the other members, sanctions are applied which may bring the offender back into line. If the sanctions prove to be ineffective, expulsion or rejection by peers results. This rejection can have harmful consequences and will affect the adolescent's ability to cope in a good many areas of day-to-day life.

A student's college group culture embodies many goals, individual roles and codes of conduct. Some teachers appear to be completely unaware of the two basic activities taking place within the classroom. The first, although not necessarily the most important activity as far as the student is concerned, is the learning activity. The second is the interaction of the student with his peers.

Educationalists often assume that all students come to the classroom with an eager and urgent desire to learn, and that all the teacher has to do is harness this energy and direct it to the given learning process. Motivation is the 'in' word; get the students motivated and just pour in the knowledge.

Unfortunately, this concept doesn't always work; 'drive', 'intimidate', 'demand', 'threaten', 'compel' or 'coerce' are words which may be used when speaking of the approach to control and harnessing of student energy favoured by some teachers. Many craft and technician day-release students are attending college only because they have to. It is frequently a condition of the apprenticeship that they shall attend and 'achieve' by passing the requisite examinations. They leave school believing that enforced study is over once and for all and that the world of work means liberation from homework and the need for theoretical knowledge, both of which appear to have no bearing on their practical work.

Then comes the rude awakening. Lectures, homework and academic demands impinge upon free time. Standards are set and educational achievement demanded by training officers and personnel departments. Some students accept the challenge willingly, while many others do so only grudgingly. The latter become 'minimum' men doing the least possible amount of work both in and out of college. The whole 'bit' is an agony to be endured, and the classroom is a place where their own unofficial activities supplant those intended by the teacher. The college day, so far as they are concerned, must be spent as pleasantly as possible according to rules made by themselves rather than by the teacher.

High-flying academic performance may be valued by some, while others view it with utter contempt. The influence of peers and group processes which are operating within the classroom greatly affect the academic approach of an individual and the learning outcome.

In some cases the very fact that low achievers find themselves among a group of higher achievers has the effect of dragging them up by their bootlaces. Nothing succeeds like success and if they are accepted by the group and identify with the leader, they will be encouraged to perform better in an effort to attain a similar standard.

If, however, they are either unable or unwilling to keep abreast of the others, they will probably give in and expend their energies in non-academic directions. Attention will be sought and attempts made to gain power and prestige by adopting some other role. Talking loudly, joking, doodling, moving about the classroom, asking irrelevant questions, frequently visiting the toilets—these and other disruptive forms of behaviour may be engaged in.

As a result, teachers become biased in favour of those who appear to be attending and conforming to their wishes, and resentful to the remainder. Conflict results and leads to belligerency in the classroom. The net result is that little or no learning can take place.

Note: The following publications dealing with social relationships are well worth reading:

Who shall survive? by J L Moreno;

The self-picture as a factor in the classroom, by J W Staines;

British Journal of Educational Psychology 28, 1958, 97-111;

Hightown Grammar: The School as a Social System, by C Lacey;

The Psychology of Interpersonal Behaviour, by M Argyle;

Social Encounters, edited by M Argyle.

6.8 Social influence processes

Social psychology studies the ways in which a person's thinking and behaviour is influenced by others; and social influence processes involve attempts by another person or group to cause an individual to change his opinions or values.

An example is the transient co-operation of American prisoners of war during the Korean War (1950-53). The Chinese used a process known as 'thought reform', a type of brainwashing, to bring about compliance. As a result of the programme, about one-third of the prisoners collaborated temporarily, but at the end of the war only about twenty out of a total of four thousand prisoners chose not to return to the United States.

While rewards or threats of torture can be used to force individuals to comply, social pressures can often achieve the same results. In a series of studies relating to compliance, Asch set out to show that individuals could stand up to social pressures and maintain independence even when others disagreed with them.†

Asch's method required a subject to join a group who were accomplices of the experimenter. The subject was then asked to make a series of perceptual judgements, as were all the others. The group was shown a card on which was drawn three vertical lines of different lengths. Members of the group were asked, in turn, which of the three lines was of equal length to the standard line drawn on another card. The situation was arranged so that the subject always announced his judgement last but one.

Correct choices were easy to make, the lengths of the three lines varying considerably and on many trials everyone gave the correct response. However, on some trials, the accomplices were instructed in advance to give an incorrect answer, the object being to discover whether the individual would conform to the group response or trust his own judgement.

The results of these studies did not support Asch's expectations. Even though the correct answer was obvious, Asch found that in about one-third of the trials an incorrect conforming response was given by the subjects.

Compliance has also been studied by Stanley Milgram.†† One of his studies involved two people: an unsuspecting subject acting as a 'teacher' whose behaviour was being observed by an experimenter; and a 'learner' who was an accomplice of the experimenter.

The apparatus consisted of a variable power supply unit which could be adjusted to give a range of voltage outputs in 15-volt increments from 15

†Asch S E *Social Psychology* (Prentice-Hall, New York 1952).
††Milgram S 'Behavioural Study of Obedience' *Journal of Abnormal and Social Psychology* (1963) volume 67, pages 171-8.

volts up to 450 volts. The power unit with switches labelled from slight shock to severe shock was connected to an 'electric chair'.

Before the learning task commenced, the 'teacher' received a specimen shock to illustrate the punishment to be awarded to the 'learner' for recording an error. Then the teacher, seated in a room with the power unit, was instructed to monitor a learning task carried out by the learner, whom he had observed being strapped into the 'electric chair' in the room next to his.

Each time the learner made an error the teacher was instructed to administer an electric shock by means of the power unit. The shocks were to be increased in severity with every error made.

As the experiment progressed and the voltages increased, the learner started to scream and shout, seemingly in intense pain. (In truth, no shocks were received by the learner although the teacher did not know this.) The screams could be heard by the teacher through the separating wall and this caused him to become concerned and distressed. At 300 volts the learner started kicking the wall after which there was silence. At this point the teacher was told to treat 'no response' to each question asked as a wrong answer and to increase the voltage accordingly. Many of the teachers opted out before reaching the 450-volt (severe shock) mark, but about two-thirds continued the experiment right to the end and administered the severe shock even though the learner was silent (apparently unconscious or dead!). Some teachers asked the experimenter to stop the experiment when the screaming started, but the experimenter insisted that they carry on. Many did so under protest even though they believed that they were causing great suffering by doing so.

This experiment showed that obedience to authority is a powerful influence on a person's behaviour.

Both the Asch and Milgram studies show how differently people behave when placed in situations controlled by others, particularly if those who direct do so from a position of power or authority. Milgram suggests that many people do not know how to disobey authority when placed in a situation such as that described in the experiment above. The extermination camps of the Second World War provide lurid and ghastly examples of the lengths to which human beings will go in order to comply. Perhaps some of the Nazis who operated the extermination devices were themselves victims of a horrible form of coercion which they were either unable or unwilling to resist.

Another social influence process, described by Leon Mann† is labelled 'identification' which 'occurs when an individual adopts the attitudes of a group because his relationship with the group is satisfying and forms part of his self-image'. This indicates that there is a psychological need for a person to be accepted by his immediate group and the wider society in order to have a meaningful existence. If these needs can only be met by adopting certain values and beliefs, many people will end up by making such values and beliefs their own.

In his studies of institutionalisation, Goffman†† describes ways of surviving in mental institutions. Long-term inmates withdraw into themselves, make the institution their home and do not wish to leave it. They become converts to the views staff have of them. Hospitalisation and admission to prison or other types of total institutions are traumatic events that entail fundamental changes in a person's life, and Goffman says that it is a tribute to the power of social forces that social reworking can change the most obstinate diversity of human material.

Internalisation is a social influence process where people *internalise*, that is, inwardly accept information delivered by credible sources which is aimed at attitudinal change.

The mass media exerts a powerful influence on the public at large. Radio and television are very effective means of delivering propaganda, and for the layman, the truth is that which he hears, sees or reads.

Western observers are extremely critical of the way in which major Communist countries disseminate information through mass media sources and by means of educational systems. It is common knowledge that major internal and international crises, tragedies, and activities beyond their national boundaries are played down when it suits them, or else are falsely justified.

The propagandist is expert at delivering the message he seeks to present, and this may not always agree with the truth.

Social influence processes are diverse in both type and scope, and include persuasion, coercion and brainwashing processes, in addition to those already discussed. Persuasion and coercion differ chiefly in terms of the amount and type of pressure exerted. They could be visualised as being at

---

† Mann L *Social Psychology* (John Wiley & Sons Australasia Pty Ltd, 1973) page 127.

†† Goffman E *Asylums* (Penguin Books, Harmondsworth 1968).

either end of a scale ranging from mild inducement or persuasion at one end, to coercion by physical or psychological force or pressure at the other. Coercion is, then, an extreme version of influence processes.

Social influence processes are known by many names, but regardless of the name, their aim is to control the social environment by bringing about a psychological change, whether it be by advertising, brainwashing, political indoctrination or re-education.

Methods of social control include torture or brute physical force, thought reform, interrogation, group pressure and disorientation brought about by lack of sleep, as well as incentives and the provision of an egalitarian and democratic setting, as found in a kibbutz or commune. The effects of social influence processes upon an individual range from gains in self-esteem to the agonies of traumatic experiences.

Institutions are tools of one particular type of social process and take the form of prisons, mental homes and the like. A *total institution* is defined by Goffman as 'a place of residence and work where a large number of like situated individuals, cut-off from the wider society for an appreciable period of time, together lead an enclosed, formally administered round of life'. A total institution therefore affords the possibility of control over its inmates.

The effect on an individual entering a total institution is aptly summed up by Goffman when he writes: 'robbing a person of the props to his identity is indeed to rob him of his identity'. The Chinese used similar ideas in their treatment of prisoners of war. They undermined loyalties and dicipline by prohibiting distinctions in rank, punishing officers and NCOs who attempted to give orders, and encouraging the humiliation of officers. The withholding of mail from home (other than bad news) also served to undermine prisoners' normal social relations.

In the field of behavioural work, concern has been aroused because in any situation where patterns of learned behaviour are sought, if one can control the consequences of a person's behaviour, one can control his actions. The teacher has both the authority and the opportunity to control behaviour and should accept full responsibility for the students' actions while in his charge.

SUMMARY

- Adolescence covers the period from puberty to adulthood and is one stage in the process of maturation.

- Puberty brings with it sexual, psychological and physical changes, together with accelerated growth.

- Early socialisation takes place within the family unit. Adolescence involves greater activity and social activity outside the home. The transition from school to work is a difficult period for the adolescent. Career prospects are greatly influenced by academic performance.

- Most young children are incapable of high-level abstract thought. With puberty comes a change in intellectual capacity. Intelligence increases as a result of maturation of the nervous system, exposure to learning and interaction with the environment. IQ tests have been designed to: assess: verbal comprehension, verbal fluency, numerical ability, perceptual speed and logical reasoning.

- For prolonged mental growth a person should be exposed to challenging learning processes for as long a period in life as is possible.

- Language is an important feature in communication. Bernstein refers to two language codes: restricted and elaborate. The restricted code is characterised by the usage of short, simple and unplanned sentences. Elaborate codes enable the speaker to make his intended meaning explicit by using words which facilitate the elaboration of statements. Teachers should be aware of the limitations imposed on a learner by a restricted verbal code.

- First impressions are important. Beware of stereotyping. Teacher expectations may cause a trainee to make greater efforts. People often adopt the role expected of them. Categorising and labelling trainees leads to their conforming with the identity allocated.

- A peer group contains people of similar age, sex and interests. It provides a framework within which a new identity may develop. The influence of peers and group processes within the classroom greatly affects individual performance.

- Social influence processes may cause a person to change his opinions or values. Individuals may conform to the majority of responses during group processes rather than stand by the evidence of their own senses. Obedience to authority is a strong force in society. Identification occurs when an individual adopts the attitudes of a group. A communicator is more likely to induce attitude change if his credibility is high. Mass media exert a powerful influence on the public. The effects of social influence processes range from gains in self-esteem to the agonies of traumatic experiences.

QUESTIONS

1. Maturation is a natural process of growth. Summarise the important physical changes occurring from puberty to adolescence. Suggest reasons for the difference in rates of development from one person to another.

2. Adolescence is a difficult stage in a person's social development. Give reasons for this.

3. Read Kohlberg's story of 'Heinz's Dilemma' in Appendix 10. What is your opinion of Heinz's behaviour? What would you have done in similar circumstances?

4. Describe the ways in which a person's early social environment may influence his later life chances.

5. Explain the importance of language in enhancing a person's ability to think and reason.

6. 'Intelligence is an inherited faculty of mental ability which is fixed genetically and which may be measured accurately by intelligence tests'. Discuss the statement and the effects of intellectual ability on a person's ability to learn.

7. 'Language codes are influenced by a family's position in the social structure, so that intellectual development and future position within society are controlled by language.' Examine the evidence for and against the statement, using sociology textbooks. See also Appendix 11.

8. In what ways do teacher expectation and the comments made in class affect the progress of learners?

9. Do you think there is a 'youth culture' in Britain? If so, what effect does it have on the progress of a trainee in academic and company-based training?

10. Given that a trainee may have a misguided conception of what others think of him and what he ought to be, how can social influence processes produce a change in his beliefs?

7

Understanding and practising effective lesson preparation

Within industry a training specification is prepared after a job has been studied, its work content listed and skills needed to carry it out identified. The job is broken down into separate tasks and a sequence of operations listed. Key points and areas of difficulty are noted, together with details of standards, machines, safety and inspection requirements. Using a training specification, an efficient training programme may be designed.

With academic learning a person often experiences greater difficulty with perceptive and cognitive learning than with psychomotor activities, and the teacher needs to put a great deal of thought into preparing the lesson plan.

The lesson-planning system shown in figure 7.1 contains the basic elements involved in the production of a lesson plan, while figure 7.22 sets out some aspects for the teacher to consider when producing a plan.

Having produced the plan, and before teaching commences, a number of other factors should be considered, one of the most important being the role of language in the process of learning. Language and learning are mutually dependent. Without adequate knowledge of the language related to a given subject, little or no learning may occur. Teacher talk should be pitched at a level to suit the class and should not (in general) take up too much of the available time. Analyses of classroom interaction have revealed that all too often, teacher talk dominates a lesson. Teachers tend to like the sound of their own voices and this does not necessarily result in learning by the passive listeners (even if they remain attentive to a degree).

The mode of instruction and conditions for learning should also be considered when producing a plan. According to Gagné there are eight classes of learning, ranging from signal-learning to problem-solving (see section 7.6), each class involving a different level of complexity and calling

157

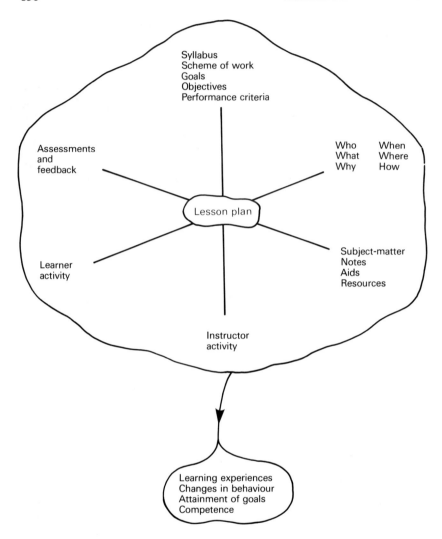

FIG. 7.1   **Lesson-planning system**

for different teaching methods.† The lesson plan should therefore provide
for the appropriate activities and conditions needed to achieve the desired
outcome.

†Gagné R M *The Conditions of Learning* (Holt, Rinehart & Winston, New York
1965) page 58.

Transfer of training should be allowed for when planning the sequence of instruction. When building on previous knowledge the instructor should be aware of the difficulties encountered by students where tasks appear to be similar to those previously learned, but in fact differ slightly. Advantage should also be taken of the positive effects of transfer where existing knowledge or skills may be drawn upon to speed up the learning of similar tasks.

Reviews and recapitulations play an important role in reinforcing knowledge recently acquired, and where learning appears to grind to a halt, a knowledge of the phenomena known as *learning plateaux* may help to explain the temporary lack of progress (see section 7.8).

The plan should incorporate alternative strategies to be employed if class discipline breaks down due to some weakness in presentation or boredom brought about by inactivity.

The quality of presentation and effectiveness of learning depends largely upon a well-thought-out lesson plan well executed.

7.1 The uses of language in teaching

The acquisition of language

Language is essential to human perception, thinking and awareness. It is a universal form of communication adopted by human beings in which a system of symbols or sound patterns conveys readily interpreted standardised meanings to others.

Spoken language is a product of a person's environment and is acquired during prolonged interaction with others who can already converse.

In the beginning, babies make noises in order to signal a need, pleasure or discomfort. The mother interprets the sound and responds by word or action, or both. The baby imitates sounds made by the mother and links these to behaviour; and so learning commences.

Later at school, when responding to questions put by the teacher, children sometimes use incorrect grammar, or words in an incorrect context. The teacher repeats the response correcting the statement and the child registers the correct version, thereby adding to its language store.

English lessons in school account for only a small proportion of a child's waking hours, and so the majority of language acquisition must take place elsewhere. 'Elsewhere' consists of the child's environment and includes family, school and peer-groups. Media such as television, radio, cinema, newspapers and comics greatly influence the vocabulary learned; and the language code adopted by the child is a function of these sources, together with family class, home environment, lifestyle and residential area. Care should therefore be exercised in selecting media to which the child will be exposed.

The pre-school period is an important time for a child in terms of the acquisition of language. Fluency and the range of words known to a child depends, to a large extent, upon the parents' ability to expose the child to correct language forms. A parent should take the trouble to explain the 'whys' and 'wherefores' in answer to a child's questions in order to foster an inquisitive mind. This promotes conversation and further questions. 'Yes/No' answers, or worse still, impatient short snappy replies, discourage the child from asking questions and inhibits its ability to learn.

The student's contribution

Practice is one of the best methods of increasing a person's language store and developing skills in the use of words. Teachers should encourage their students to talk and write as much as is possible in order to get the best out of a given learning experience. This can be achieved by creating a rewarding atmosphere in which students can attempt to put the concept being taught into their own words and are able to discuss the problem as they see it. The teacher can help by carefully choosing the words he uses to introduce the concept, by putting questions and by making the most of the resulting exchanges.

The type of question which elicits a greater amount of student response is of the open-ended type where a number of different answers are often quite acceptable. Reasoning-type questions also call for students to think aloud and to construct from memory a logically organised sequence of ideas; observation questions relate to demonstrations and phenomena which students may observe and which require them to perceive. The type of questions described provide good sources of student activity and are therefore to be preferred to closed questions which have only one acceptable answer, or naming questions which invite a response without requiring the student to demonstrate insight.

In his article 'Language and Learning in the Classroom',† Douglas Barnes outlines some of his findings made during research into classroom

†Barnes D 'Language and Learning in the Classroom', *Journal of Curriculum Studies, 3(1)* (May 1971) pages 36-7.

interaction. He observed eleven-year-old pupils during twelve lessons in various secondary subjects and found that the pupils were, on the whole, passive recipients of instruction, their role being mainly confined to indicating in short answers that they could regurgitate what had previously been taught.

He reported that:

(a) On only eleven occasions did a pupil, by asking a question, or by offering a statement that was not a reply to the teacher, initiate a sequence of interaction.

(b) There were few occasions when pupils could be said to be 'thinking aloud', that is, reorganising learning or solving a problem by verbalising it. Most contributions from pupils were of one word or a little longer.

(c) On only two occasions was there exploration of the meaning of a word, though definitions were asked for and given.

(d) Only in one lesson (physics) did pupils frequently mention out-of-school experience in order to relate it to new ideas being learnt.

Barnes's research also embraced an examination of teachers' demands on pupils. His study of teachers' questions revealed that:

(a) In many lessons a majority of the teachers' questions asked for factual replies.

(b) Teachers hardly ever asked questions to get information which they did not possess: they used questions mainly to test recollection of what had been taught previously.

(c) In some lessons pupils were asked to read aloud: this often implied that they were to go over a sequence of thought given by the teacher. Teachers hardly ever followed a brief reply by requesting the pupil to expand it or make it more explicit. Teachers not infrequently interrupted pupils who did try to answer at length.

(d) Questions which asked pupils to refer to first hand experience outside school were almost absent.

Clearly, the shortcomings in teachers' presentations of curricular knowledge shown up in Barnes's research must be overcome if students are to benefit by more active participation in learning. The same sort of thinking should be applied to the training of industrial staff, so that trainees may be more

FIG. 7.2　**Flanders' interaction analysis categories**

TEACHER TALK	Response	1. *Accepts Feeling.* Accepts and clarifies an attitude or the feeling tone of a pupil in a nonthreatening manner. Feelings may be positive or negative. Predicting and recalling feelings are included. 2. *Praises or encourages.* Praises or encourages pupil action or behaviour. Jokes that release tension, but not at the expense of another individual: nodding head, or saying 'Um, hm?' or 'go on' are included. 3. *Accepts for uses ideas of pupils.* Clarifying, building, or developing ideas suggested by a pupil. Teacher extensions of pupil ideas are included but as the teacher brings more of his own ideas into play, shift to category five.
	Initiation	4. *Asks questions,* Asking a question about content or procedure, based on teacher ideas, with the intent that a pupil will answer. 5. *Lecturing.* Giving facts or opinions about content or procedures; expressing *his own* ideas, giving *his own* explanation, or citing an authority other than a pupil. 6. *Giving Directions.* Directions, commands, or orders to which a pupil is expected to comply. 7. *Criticizing or justifying authority.* Statements intended to change pupil behaviour from nonacceptable to acceptable pattern; bawling someone out; stating why the teacher is doing what he is doing; extreme self-reference.
PUPIL TALK	Response	8. *Pupil-talk–response.* Talk by pupils in response to teacher. Teacher initiates the contact or solicits pupil statement or structures the situation. Freedom to express own ideas is limited.
	Initiation	9. *Pupil-talk–initiation.* Talk by pupils which they initiate. Expressing own ideas; initiating a new topic; freedom to develop opinions and a line of thought, like asking thoughtful questions; going beyond the existing structure.
SILENCE		10. *Silence of confusion.* Pauses, short periods of silence and periods of confusion in which communication cannot be understood by the observer.

Flanders, *Analysing Teaching Behaviour*, © 1970, Addison-Wesley Publishing Company, Inc, chapter 3, page 34, table 2-1. 'Flanders' Interaction Analysis Categories (FIAC).' Reprinted with permission.

highly motivated in their approach to the acquisition of skills, together with relevant knowledge.

Analysing periods of oral work

Ned Flanders developed a social interaction model by which classroom interaction could be recorded and analysed. He classified the statements and behaviour of students and teachers into ten categories (see figure 7.2).

An observer sits in a class and at the end of each three-second period categorises and records the communication behaviour of that period. Alternatively, a tape recording may be made of the lesson and categorised later. The results are then analysed and the percentage of time given over to each type of behaviour calculated.

TABLE OF RESULTS										
Category	1	2	3	4	5	6	7	8	9	10
Total										
%										

A high proportion of categories 5, 6 and 7 would indicate that the teacher had been very direct, whereas a high proportion of categories 8 and 9 would indicate an indirect style with high student activity.

In his unit, 'Intervening in the Learning process',† David Moseley writes: 'Despite all that we hear about child-centred education, the ordinary teacher loves the sound of his own voice', and gives a table of typical results following an analysis of classroom discourse.

Teacher asks questions	10%
Other teacher talk	50%
Pupils ask questions	5%
Other pupil talk	20%
Silence or confusion	15%

FIG. 7.3

†Moseley D 'Intervening in the Learning Process' (Open University) OU Course E281 Unit 16, page 14.

He then goes on to say that the table shows that in a class of forty, on average, each pupil talks for less than 1 per cent of the time available while the teacher may be talking for 60 per cent of the lesson (see figure 7.3).

TASK

1. Tape record one of your own instructional periods or lessons and carry out an analysis.

2. Given that a class consists of thirty pupils and that a lesson lasts two hours, calculate the time occupied by each category shown in figure 7.3.

    Calculate also the average amount of time each student spends talking.

    For the solution see page 371.

Language used by teachers

The teacher must always be conscious of the language he is using. There is often a gulf between teacher and student because, in general, teachers tend to use an elaborate code of language which is not readily understood by all. Technical terms also produce barriers and hinder learning if used thoughtlessly and without adquate explanation. Students will imitate the teacher and learn to use technical terms without really knowing their meaning, and so the teacher must ensure that he is handing over the meaning as well as the words.

Teachers need a far more sophisticated insight into the implications of the language they use, and they should recognise the linguistic and conceptual difficulties experienced by students. A 'register of language' should be built up to suit the teaching environment and the verbal exposition pitched at a level to suit the students. A picture or chalkboard sketch is worth a thousand words, and it is better that the concept be understood from the picture backed up and reinforced by words than to rely on words alone.

Examples of teacher talk

Case hardening of mild steel

Carburising in solid media described.

FORMAL LANGUAGE

This process is based upon the principle that carbon will dissolve interstitially in solid iron, provided that the iron is in face-centred cubic lattice form which obtains above the upper critical temperature for the steel under consideration.

The mild steel components are packed in carburising media together with energisers such as sodium carbonate and barium carbonate. During the heating process, carbon diffuses into the surface of the steel, thereby increasing the carbon content up to the limit of solid solubility.

INFORMAL LANGUAGE

The hardness of a steel depends upon the amount of carbon present in it and how we heat-treat it. Mild steel doesn't contain much carbon. Therefore, if we try to harden it, we don't get much luck.

Sometimes we need a shaft which is tough and able to withstand shock loadings but which, at the same time, possesses a hard wear-resistant surface. Mild steel is relatively tough but as it doesn't harden very well we have to increase the carbon content of the outer skin. Then, when we heat-treat it correctly it will provide a hard wear-resistant surface and still possess a tough core.

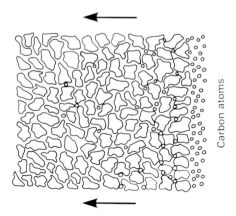

Carburising-diagrammatic representation of steel absorbing carbon atoms

We start by carrying out a process called carburising, during which carbon soaks into the surface of the steel, thereby increasing its carbon content.

The shaft is packed into a steel box surrounded by carbon-rich material, such as charcoal, and a chemical energiser, such as soda ash. Chemical firms supply these materials ready for use. A lid is placed on the box and sealed

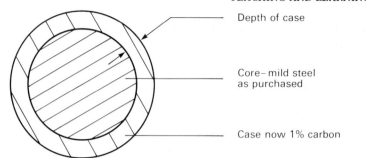

Depth of case

Core – mild steel
as purchased

Case now 1% carbon

A carburised shaft

with fire clay. If we leave the box like this nothing will happen to the steel shaft. But, if the box is heated to about 900–950°C known as the upper critical temperature range for mild steel, the shaft undergoes a change in structure.

The iron atoms which make up the shaft rearrange themselves and allow small carbon atoms from the charcoal to creep into spaces between themselves. These small spaces are called interstices.

The surface of the mild steel shaft absorbs carbon just like a sponge soaks up water. The energiser speeds up the process; that's why it's included. The box remains in the furnace for about six hours, and during this time carbon penetrates to a depth of about 1 mm all over the shaft.

The furnace is switched off and the box cools down to room temperature. The carbon remains in the steel; it cannot escape. The shaft now has a case containing about 1 per cent carbon and the core remains the same as it was originally, with about 0.15 per cent carbon. If the shaft is later subjected to the correct heat treatment process it will have a tough core and hard case—but that's another story.

Which of the two examples do you consider to be more suitable for a craft apprentice or inexperienced trainee?

7.2 The imbalance of superiority between instructor and trainee

There is frequently a psychological imbalance between the instructor and trainee, especially in the more formal classroom situation. This is particularly so in the case of mature trainees who have not been exposed to 'book-learning' for many years. The classroom itself is likely to bring back memories of schooldays and schoolmasters. Memories of cold, detached figures commanding obedience from their podiums by virtue of the authority vested in them as teachers, subservience to the teacher's whims being an accepted role for the pupil.

In further education and in industrial situations, a different type of imbalance is perceived by the trainee. The instructor possesses superior skills and ability. He is the master of his craft or subject, and as the source of information or fountain of knowledge, he directs the activities of the trainee, who engages in set tasks while the instructor supervises. The instructor is a source of social reinforcement and holds the power to reward or punish the trainee according to his performance. If the trainee does well he may be praised; if he performs badly he runs the risk of being criticised, which results in a loss of self-esteem.

Power is based on the instructor's expertise and position. The instructor should be aware of this imbalance in power and should take steps to reduce the accompanying emotional tension by providing a secure atmosphere in which learning may take place.

Steps should be taken by the instructor to redress the imbalance as early as possible. A warm, friendly attitude should be adopted, backed by an enthusiastic approach towards the task of instructing. Trainees should be encouraged to speak freely and if similarities between the instructor and trainee are perceived, these similarities tend to increase, resulting in enhanced self-esteem for the trainee.

The instructor should avoid sarcasm and should at all times be respectful to the trainees. He should display patience, tact and diplomacy and be willing to help trainees through difficulties.

Integrity and high personal standards should go a long way towards overcoming the inevitable initial imbalance.

7.3 Designing a training plan

The need for training can arise from a variety of sources. The more common areas where training or retraining can be most effective include situations in which there is evidence of production inefficiency and poor worker relations. A selection of these might include:

excessive tool breakage;
high machinery down-time;
excessive cycle times;
poor quality;

high scrap-rates;
unsafe working practises;
high accident rates;
poor motivation;
grievances;
absenteeism;
high labour turnover;
poor communications.

Having identified the need, the next step is to think about preparing a course of training designed to improve matters.

A planning questionnaire is a useful aid to preliminary thinking. Its function is to give a broad outline of some of the important factors relating generally to course design, and to give greater insight to the problem.

After completing the questionnaire, a clearer picture of the training needs and overall requirements of the proposed course should emerge, and a training programme may then be designed.

The programme should follow well-proven and established teaching practice. The outcome of the course should be that learning shall have taken place; that is, a relatively permanent change in behaviour will have occurred as a result of the practice and experience encountered during the course of instruction.

Preparing a course

PLANNING QUESTIONNAIRE

1. What are course objectives?
   What is training required for?
   Is the purpose to:
   teach manual skills?
   impart information and increase knowledge?
   improve attitudes?

2. What is nature of group?
   Will it be:
   co-operative or obstructive?
   hostile?
   suspicious?

3. Which instructional method would be best:
   lecture?

lesson?
demonstration and practice?
case study?
role-play exercise?
discussion?
syndicate?
programmed learning?
learning package?
film and discussion?

4. Who will give the instruction:
management?
training officer?
instructor?
specialist guest lecturer?

5. What aids will be required?

6. Where will the instruction take place?

7. How long will it last?

8. How will terminal objectives be measured?

9. Who will conduct follow-up?

10. How much will it cost?

TRAINING PROGRAMME FORMAT

A typical training programme format is given in figure 7.4. Each step follows a logical sequence. The starting point is the writing of objectives stating in behavioural terms what the trainee is expected to be able to do as an outcome of training. Then, an overall plan of instruction should be laid out, following the form of the examples shown in figures 7.5, 7.6 and 7.7. Detailed lesson plans should then be produced (see section 7.9). The remaining steps follow conventional teaching practice.

7.4 The structure of a lesson

A lesson consists of three main stages: an introduction, a developmental stage and a conclusion. Some teachers like to start a lesson with a short written quiz based upon the previous week's work, or, in the case of mathematics, some quick easy mental arithmetic questions. This approach involves the whole group and gets their heads down. The main point is to get every member of the class working as quickly as possible. Delays in getting

```
┌─────────────────────────────┐
│ Write aims and objectives in│
│ behavioural terms           │
└─────────────────────────────┘


┌─────────────────────────────┐
│ Devise plan of instruction  │
└─────────────────────────────┘


┌─────────────────────────────┐
│ Select instructional material│
│ required to satisfy aims    │
└─────────────────────────────┘


┌─────────────────────────────┐
│ Organise in short logical   │
│ steps                       │
└─────────────────────────────┘


┌─────────────────────────────┐
│ Grade in order of difficulty│
└─────────────────────────────┘


┌─────────────────────────────┐
│ Introduce material at appropriate│
│ level of difficulty         │
└─────────────────────────────┘


┌─────────────────────────────┐
│ Allow student to learn at own│
│ pace                        │
└─────────────────────────────┘


┌─────────────────────────────┐
│ Involve student by active   │
│ participation               │
└─────────────────────────────┘


┌─────────────────────────────┐
│ Evaluate progress           │
└─────────────────────────────┘


┌─────────────────────────────┐
│ Feed back knowledge of results│
└─────────────────────────────┘


┌─────────────────────────────┐
│ Master each section before  │
│ going on to next            │
└─────────────────────────────┘


┌─────────────────────────────┐
│ Evaluate programme and modify│
│ as necessary                │
└─────────────────────────────┘
```

FIG. 7.4   **Training programme format**

FIG. 7.5 **Training specification**

Job:	To operate a 'Thermpack' heat-sealing machine in the Surgical Disposable Products Department
Title:	Heat Sealer Operator (Hyperdermic Needle Packaging)

Stage	Action	Instructor	Time Allocated (hours)
	Induction		
1	The company and its range of products. Markets and quality standards.	Line manager	½
2	Tour of works.	Section supervisor	1
3	Company rules. Conditions of service and fringe benefits.	Personnel officer	1
4	Health and Safety at Work Act and accident prevention, fire, safety and hygiene.	Safety officer	1
	Basic training		
5	Demonstration of heat sealer.	Process worker	¼
6	Adjusting temperature control.	Training supervisor	¼
7	Setting air cylinder operating pressure.		¼
8	Loading unsealed hyperdermic needle packs to machine.	,,	½
9	Locating plastic sealing strip.	,,	¼
10	Operating heat-sealing platen.	,,	¼
11	Cropping surplus plastic material.	,,	¼
12	Ejecting heat-sealed packs.	,,	¼
13	Checking condition of seal.	,,	½
14	Reporting of defects and breakdowns.	,,	¼
15	Maintaining clean working conditions.	,,	½
16	Practise to reach experienced worker standards.	,,	16
17	Appraisal of performance.	Line supervisor	½
	TOTAL PROGRAMME TIME	. . . .	23½

FIG. 7.6   **Plan of instruction: practical teaching course for instructors**

Session	Lecture Topic	Group Activities	Student Preparation
1	Introduction to course Components of a lesson Specifying learning objectives	Discussion—further examples of stating objectives Tutor talk on verbal exposition Set assignment	Short talk
2	Lesson-planning and preparation	Discussion on lesson-planning Short talks by students	Lesson plan
3	Interrelationships in the classroom	Presentation of lesson plans by students	
4	Informal methods including questions and answers and discussion	Discussion on use of original methods Presentation of lesson plans by students	Discussion
5	Display, demonstration and the learning of concepts	Examples by tutor of skills analysis and concept-teaching Discussions led by students	Demonstra-tion
6	Classwork, practical and project activities	Presentation of demonstrations by students Brief by tutor on micro-teaching	Micro-teaching
7	Evaluation of work	Microteaching	
8	Final review of course	Questions and answer session Students' comment on course design and presentation	

FIG. 7.7   **Educational technology—an introductory course for instructors**

Programme

The lecture programme will consist of a survey of teaching aids and will concentrate on giving the instructor a knowledge of the existing range of media. It is hoped that the students will acquire the practical skills of using these aids and preparing material. There is available a range of handout material dealing with technical data and methods of preparation and use of those items of equipment covered in this survey.

Period	
1	*Introduction*—introduction to the course: aims; programme; resources available for instructors' use; an approach to the use of teaching aids.
2	*Display*—a survey of non-projected aids for classroom use: the chalkboard, newsprint pad, felt and magnet boards; charts, diagrams, classroom displays.
3	*Reprographics*—methods of producing class handouts: spirit and ink stencil duplication; small offset; copying techniques—heat, transfer, dyeline, xerox; economic considerations.
4	*The overhead projector*—the projector: its uses; siting; methods of use; as a writing surface; as a projector; masking and overlay techniques; simple movement; experiments.
5	*Still photography*—applications of photography to classroom use; equipment; economics; strip and slide projectors, screens; back projection.
6	*Cine photography*—film projectors: standard and super 8 mm, 16 mm; sound equipment; economics; loop-film projectors.
7	*Recorded sound*—the use of sound recordings in the classroom: equipment; record and tape techniques; methods of recording from broadcast and live performances; use of tape/slide synchronisation technique.
8	*Educational radio and television*—national programmes; local stations; CCTV; use of video-recorders; television as a classroom aid.

things moving encourage social conversation and once this has started it is not always easy to focus attention on the subject to be discussed. The results of the quiz can be checked quickly by the group after exchanging papers, and areas of difficulty can then be revised.

Lesson aims and objectives should be given in the introduction proper, together with reasons for their inclusion plus some form of incentive. If the 'reasons for' and 'incentives' can be related to the group's world, there is likely to be a greater commitment to work hard during the lesson.

The developmental stage is used to introduce basic principles and to build up knowledge progressively. Students are led from the known to the unknown and from the easy to the difficult in small steps. The group should be actively involved in 'doing' for much of the time. The teacher organises activity in the form of teaching/practising, note-taking, discussing, working through handouts and answering questions. The developmental stage should occupy most of the lesson.

The conclusion enables the teacher to consolidate the new work, to check the effectiveness of the lesson and to 'look forward' by briefly outlining the subject for the next session. Sometimes an objective-type test is set which covers the lesson's subject-matter, in order to evaluate effectiveness. Homework may then be set.

7.5   Desirable features to include in the lesson

The lesson should be structured so as to provide a variety of activity for both teacher and student. The use of audio-visual aids adds lustre to the lesson, but they should not be used purely as gimmicks. Each aid introduced should serve a specific purpose and should back up what the teacher is trying to get over rather than replace him. The more senses employed by the learner during instruction the better, and for this reason, a wide range of aids should be employed.

The teacher should set goals aimed at making learning intrinsically rewarding to the student and the lesson should include a means of providing feedback and knowledge of results to all concerned.

An important feature of the lesson is the practice stage. Consideration should be given to the question of whether or not massed practice should be used. Massed practice is more suitable for less able students or where work being studied is simple, especially when applied to job instruction. Distributed practice is more suitable when the material to be learned is complex and where a considerable amount has to be absorbed. However, once learned it is retained longer than by using the massed practice technique.

Perhaps one of the more important features of a lesson is the 'question and answer' method of developing a subject. This method is particularly useful in the teaching of manufacturing technology, where the students can contribute by relating their work experience to the discussion.

Question and answer techniques

Starting the lesson

The use of a short question and answer session at the beginning of each period of instruction can assist the instructor in several ways. Questions can be used to arouse the trainees' interest and curiosity, while at the same time allowing the instructor to determine the existing level of knowledge of the subject. No matter how complex the subject for discussion may be, a good number of responses will relate in some way to the subject. The trainees' replies may need to be modified in some respects and this can be done by correcting or enlarging the statement and repeating the new version to the group. Trainees should never be ridiculed or told that their answers are totally incorrect, or they will clam up completely. They will not wish to be embarrassed by the instructor in the event of their uttering an incorrect response. They will remember that there is safety in silence and the instructor will have lost them.

During the lesson

If questions are allowed to flow naturally as the lesson develops, the result will be greater participation by class members. The thing to bear in mind at all times is that, in general, trainees learn most when they are actively contributing to the instruction.

Many of the questions asked by trainees are directly related to statements made by the instructor, or to theory and calculations written on the chalkboard. Wherever possible, the question should be broken down into a series of mini-questions and thrown back to the group, so that the trainees formulate their own answers to the problem. If, after cueing, this ploy fails, the question will have to be answered directly by the instructor.

Questions may be asked by trainees because they are confused. An observant instructor should never allow matters to reach this stage. The expressions on the faces of individuals will signal bewilderment, and an able instructor will take steps to restore the balance before complete confusion exists. He can do this by repeating his subject-matter more slowly or by putting it another way with a series of check questions interposed at suitable break points.

Key questions should be thought out by the instructor when planning the instruction and these should be included in the lesson plan long before the lesson commences. Planned questioning serves to stimulate, encourage and consolidate learning as instruction proceeds and creates self-confidence in the trainees, especially if they are rewarded with praise for correct responses.

Concluding the lesson

A prepared list of questions relating to the subject-matter taught may be put to the group towards the end of the lesson. This technique enables the instructor to evaluate his instruction and the trainees' learning. It also serves to reinforce key points and stimulate the brighter students, while encouraging slower learners to show that they know too.

Questioning techniques

Use unambiguous language which is easily understood.

Use questions which cover the subject step by step.

Put questions to the whole group—name person to respond.

Choose respondent at random, while at the same time making sure that the person chosen is capable of correctly answering the particular question.

Repeat answers slowly.

Give praise for correct responses.

Encourage slow learners by cueing until correct response is elicited.

Avoid irrelevant or trick questions.

Questions with Yes/No answers have a 50/50 chance of being answered correctly by guessing and should be avoided.

The use of incomplete statements by an instructor as a form of questioning requires little effort on the part of the trainee. Be on your guard against this practice. As an instructor you will be tempted to put words into the mouth of a trainee who is unable to answer. When the question has been answered you are 'off the hook' and many instructors will go to great lengths to achieve this.

FIG. 7.8   **Summary of questioning techniques**

Any weakness apparent may be rectified there and then, and the lesson plan modified to overcome the difficulties shown up.

7.6 Methods whereby a student learns

Learning as a process of maturation

As we grow older we learn by experience. We are exposed to a wide variety of events in our social environment and learn something during each encounter. We learn by interacting with people, places and things. Without this interaction we should know little more than on the day we were born.

Some things are learned accidentally. We touch a hot object, get burned, and learn that hot objects should not be touched with bare hands. Later, perhaps in the workshop, we may have to handle hot objects in the course of our work. We remember our earlier unpleasant experience and take precautions. We extend our knowledge to include the wearing of protective equipment when handling hot objects.

The tempo of learning can be accelerated by arranging contrived situations in which the learner is exposed to stimuli which would not normally be experienced during the process of maturation. The relatively permanent change in behaviour resulting from such exposure is known as *learning*, and some of the main processes employed are discussed below.

Learning process

A formal learning process comprises a teacher, a learner, a set of behavioural objectives, elements of instruction and interaction between the teacher and learner, responses and reinforcement, and a means of testing and evaluating the outcome. The teacher is responsible for providing a set of conditions under which learning may occur, while the learner must display a willingness to participate actively in the process.

In his book *The Conditions of Learning*,† Robert Gagné classifies eight varieties of learning, each calling for a different set of learning conditions and higher level of mental ability than that preceding it. The classes are:

Signal learning	Multiple discrimination
Stimulus—response learning	Concept learning
Chaining	Principle learning
Verbal associate learning	Problem solving

†Gagné R M *The Conditions of Learning* (Holt, Rinehart & Winston, New York 1965) page 58.

Gagné suggests that each class of learning should be mastered before tackling higher levels. This would entail competence in seven classes before attempting problem-solving at the highest level.

Signal learning

Signal learning involves the learner in responding to a signal. It is a form of classical conditioning—a technique relating to the conditioning of behaviour. Ivan Pavlov (1849-1936), a Russian physiologist and psychologist, discovered it during investigations of salivation in dogs.

A dog was placed in a harness. A bell was rung (stimulus), but the dog did not react (no response). Later the bell was rung again, but this time, food was presented a split second after the sound. The dog salivated (responded). This stage was repeated several times and each time the sound of the bell produced a salivary response in anticipation of the arrival of food. Pavlov called the sound of the bell a 'conditioned stimulus' and the behaviour resulting, i.e. the salivation, a 'conditioned response'. The dog had learned to associate the sound of the bell with the impending arrival of food, and the two events had become a 'learned association'. Pavlov's work was far more involved than this; but, nonetheless, we can conclude from this result that human behaviour can be influenced by subjecting a learner to a process whereby certain conditioned stimuli result in conditioned responses.

Examples of signal learning include the reaction of a pedestrian to the sound of a car horn or the appearance of the family dog when it hears the sound of a biscuit-tin lid being removed.

The instructor can make use of the theory of learned association in both theoretical and practical training. The following practical example illustrates the theory.

When setting up tools in a single spindle chucking automatic such as the Warner & Swasey 3 AC, it is necessary to switch the 'machine control' to 'hand control'. The setting operation uses a very slow turret feed rate, and the point at which the forward feed ends cannot be easily detected by observation. However, a red 'end hand feed' signal lights up on the control panel when the turret reaches its full forward position.

The trainee will need to stop chuck rotation and check workpiece lengths when the turret is fully forward. He watches and waits until the turret feed motion stops, observes the red signal light (conditioned stimulus) and stops chuck rotation (response). Having once associated the red signal light with end of turret feed, he subsequently responds by stopping chuck rotation

FIG. 7.9
(Photograph by courtesy of Warner & Swasey Turning Machines Ltd, Halifax, England)

immediately upon observing the red light. He no longer attempts to observe the turret slowly feeding forward to the end of its stroke.

Stimulus–response learning

'Trial and error learning', 'operant learning', 'instrumental learning', 'instrumental conditioning' and 'need reduction' are all names used to describe stimulus–response learning. The stimulus–organism–response model of learning attempts to explain how a learner comes to behave as he does when presented with a stimulus situation. The general argument is that a stimulus is more likely to elicit a response if similar responses have, in the past, been beneficial to the learner and have been rewarded or reinforced. Examples of reinforcement are approval, praise, encouraging words and gestures, and material rewards.

Trial and error learning

This type of learning results from trying out one form of response after another until the correct response is discovered. The correct response is often rewarded in some way.

E L Thorndike (1874-1949) an American experimental psychologist, believed that human behaviour could be studied and analysed in terms of stimulus (change in environment) and response (behaviour resulting from attempts to adapt to the change). He based this belief on research carried out on animal behaviour.

Thorndike observed the behaviour of animals during a series of experiments and as a result drafted his 'law of effect' which suggests that behaviour which is followed by reinforcement will tend to be repeated, while behaviour which is not reinforced or which results in discomfort will be less likely to occur.

In one of Thorndike's experiments, a hungry cat was placed in a cage incorporating a release mechanism which could be operated by the trapped animal. Outside the cage, food was placed which the cat could observe. At first the cat prowled around the cage scratching and trying to escape. It tried many kinds of random behaviour in an effort to reach the food. After a while the cat operated the release mechanism by chance, escaped and consumed the food. On subsequent trials the cat's activity became less random and was concentrated in the area near the release mechanism. Eventually the cat was able to release itself almost immediately after being placed in the cage. It had learned the location of the release mechanism and how to secure its freedom.

Human beings placed in similar situations often resort to the same sort of behaviour when presented with a problem. Coach-drivers and taxi-drivers are often given classroom instruction in finding their way about large cities. By studying maps they attempt to learn key routes from one location to another using a maze-type format. They make a series of straight-on, left and right turn decisions, until the correct sequence is obtained.

The maze learning activity given below from the Open University Course E 281 is used to illustrate trial and error learning. Read the instructions.

Activity

TRIAL AND ERROR LEARNING

For this activity you will require a sheet of cardboard with a hole in it, and a maze which has a starting point A and a finishing point B (see figure 7.10).

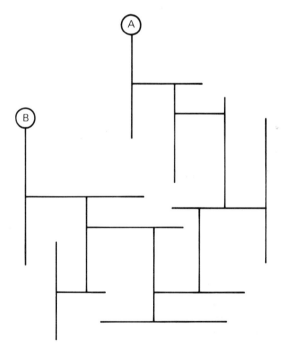

FIG. 7.10 **From Unit 6, Open University Course E 281, reprinted with permission.**

(Adapted from a suggestion by Stones, 1966.)

1. Place the cardboard over the maze so you can see the starting point of the maze A through the hole.

2. Try to get from one end of the maze to the other, making sure that no part of the maze is visible except through the hole. Count the number of errors you make. Every turning that leads into a blind alley counts as an error.

3. Repeat the procedure in 2 until you can get from one end of the maze to the other without making an error on *two* successive trials. Count the number of errors you make on each trial.

4. Fill in the number of errors you make on each trial in the table:

Trial	Errors
1	
2	
3	
4	
5	
6	
7	
8	
9	
10	
11	
12	
13	
14	

5. Draw two axes at right angles. Let the horizontal axis represent the number of trials and the vertical axis the number of errors. Draw a graph showing how the number of errors varies with the number of trials.

6. Your own 'Learning Curve' should look like the graph opposite:

Learning curve

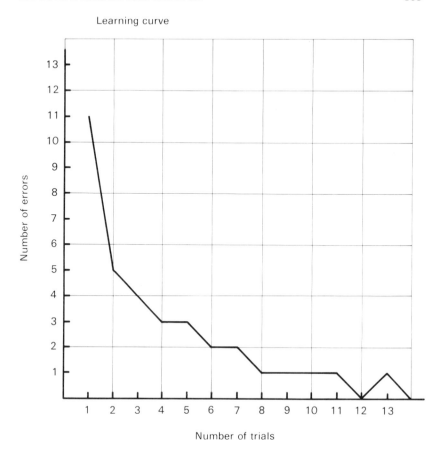

Number of trials

7. Make notes on how you learned the maze.

Make up a cardboard sheet with a hole in the centre. The cardboard must be large enough to cover all parts of the maze at all times. Now carry out the activity.

Instrumental conditioning

This is a form of stimulus–response learning in which an active response in the form of desired behaviour is rewarded. The response is instrumental in producing the reinforcement, hence the name 'instrumental conditioning'. If the required response does not occur, then there is no reinforcement.

B F Skinner (born 1904), an American psychologist, introduced the idea of operant conditioning, a form of instrumental conditioning. The subject of an experiment operates on the environment in order to produce a desired effect. To illustrate the principle, Skinner used a box later known as the 'Skinner Box' into which a hungry rat was placed. The box was fitted with a bar and a food tray. By pressing the bar, a pellet of food was delivered to the food tray. Pressing the bar was instrumental in providing the reinforcer. Motivation for the rat's behaviour was provided by means of its hunger drive, and reinforcement for its bar-pressing activity was in the form of the pellet. Like Thorndike's cat, the rat's behaviour was at first purely random. The food appeared only as a result of the rat pressing the bar during the course of its investigation of the box. At first, the rat was rewarded only on each occasion that the bar was pressed. The rat soon associated the bar-pressing with the appearance of food in the tray and it continued to press the bar and eat the food until its hunger drive was satisfied.

Skinner later investigated reinforcement schedules relating either to the period of time or number of non-reinforced responses between successive reinforcements. This resulted in Skinner concluding that behaviour could be 'shaped' by reinforcement. He listed four categories of reinforcement:

(a) fixed time interval;

(b) variable time interval;

(c) fixed ratio (number of unreinforced responses per reinforced response);

(d) variable ratio (first response after variable number of unreinforced responses is reinforced).

Experimenters have shown that schedules (b), (c) and (d) tend to produce higher levels of response than (a).

The practising teacher can make use of Skinner's results to elicit and reinforce learners' responses, and reinforcement techniques are widely used in programmed learning instruction and teaching machines.

Gestalt or insight learning

Gestalt theory stems from speculation about learning by a number of psychologists, including Koffka, Köhler and Wertheimer. Gestalt psychology is a psychological theory which stresses the importance of pattern, organisation and seeing things as 'wholes' rather than as collections of individual elements. Gestaltists believe that: the whole is greater than the sum of its individual parts.

For some, the sounds of individual notes are meaningless, but when combined produce music which may be recognised and enjoyed. A highly tuned and 'blue-printed' racing engine, when reassembled and tested, has many properties not apparent to the observer when laid out as components before assembly. The whole highly organised structure becomes much more meaningful than does knowledge of its elements.

Wolfgang Köhler (1887-1967),† a German-born psychologist, considered that there was much more to learning than purely stimulus–response behaviour. In order to justify his beliefs, he carried out experiments designed to investigate how animals solved problems.

In one experiment Köhler placed a banana outside a cage containing a chimpanzee. Two sticks were available to the chimpanzee, neither of which alone was long enough to reach the banana. The chimpanzee tried unsuccessfully to reach the banana with its hands and feet. It then tried using one of the sticks and was once again unsuccessful. After pausing, presumably to cogitate, the chimpanzee suddenly joined the two sticks together and, using the resulting single long stick, was able to reach the banana. It then proceeded to rake the banana towards the cage.

Köhler concluded that the solution came suddenly when the chimpanzee had surveyed the whole problem after its unsuccessful attempts. In a flash of 'insight', the chimpanzee had 'seen' the connection between the two sticks and the banana after perceiving the relationships essential to the solution.

In another experiment yielding the same sort of conclusions, a banana was dangled from the top of a cage beyond the reach of a chimpanzee. A number of boxes were placed inside the cage. The chimpanzee tried to reach the banana by standing on top of one box after another but was unsuccessful. No single box was high enough. The animal tried in vain to reach the banana. Then, after a while, it stacked one box on top of another. It leapt on top and was able to reach the banana. Again, the solution was attributed to insight.

In problem-solving, insight is the name given to the process involving the perception of relationships leading to a solution. The learner surveys each element of a problem and calls up previous knowledge and rules from his memory store. Perceptual organisation takes place as he tries to formulate a pattern of activity which will solve the problem or arranges the links connecting various elements into the correct sequence. All aspects of the problem are surveyed; then, in a flash of insight, the solution suddenly becomes apparent and the requisite responses are made. The problem is solved and the method of solution may be repeated or applied to other

†Köhler W *The Mentality of Apes* (Harcourt, Brace & World, New York 1927).

problems with similar parameters. The problem has been solved by insight brought about by a complete understanding of all relationships appertaining to it.

Teachers can help students to gain insight by using examples and diagrams which illustrate rules and by using the 'Socratic' method of questioning, where the student's replies help him to identify his errors and discover the correct answer for himself.

Chaining

Response chains and *learning sets* are learning structures in which elemental steps are mastered and linked together to form a procedure. Having once acquired the knowledge, a learner will be able to carry out routine sequences almost automatically.

The procedure normally adopted in an instructional situation covering the motor responses involved in, say, inspection operations or setting up machine tools, is as follows: the teacher demonstrates each step in the correct sequence; the learner memorises the sequence, performs individual links and then connects each one to the next. He repeats the chain in the correct order with the instructor cueing and reinforcing as required until an error-free demonstration can be repeated many times.

Having acquired the chain, a learner should be able to apply it to new operations of a similar nature. Poems, quotations, definitions, physical laws and procedures for solving mathematical problems are other examples of chaining.

The table in figure 7.11 summarises the stages involved in learning response chains:

Participator	Procedure	Remarks
Teacher	Establishes form and content of chain	Discriminates
Teacher	Demonstrates each link	Explains
Trainee	Learns each link of chain separately	Verbal prompts
Trainee	Repeats sequence in quick succession	Avoids forgetting
Trainee	Repeats chain several times	Reinforces
Trainee	Masters chain	Satisfaction
Teacher	Rewards trainee for correct chaining	Immediately

FIG. 7.11

Verbal association

One example of *verbal association* is *naming*. In order to be able to name an object, such as a cone or cube, the observer must see the object, recognise its shape and know its name. If these three conditions are met, the observer will be able to say, 'This is a cone', or, 'This is a cube'. We can see from this that naming is an elementary form of learning met in everyday life.

When unusual objects are experienced or when new concepts are introduced during a lecture the names sometimes give a clue as to their nature. Take the word *pyrometer*. The word breaks down into two parts: *pyro* and *meter*. *Pyro* relates to fire or heat and *meter* to measuring. A pyrometer is a temperature-measuring device. The learner associates *pyro* with an existing mental image, say, a heat-resistant Pyrex dish or perhaps a pyre, a pile of wood for burning a dead body! Similarly, *meter* may be associated with a parking meter or speedometer, both used for measuring. The examples drawn from experience act as coding connections and help to give meaning to the new word.

Definitions are frequently made up of several concepts; a statement such as, 'a vector quantity involves both magnitude and direction', can be translated as 'how big' and 'course or line'. A mental image of a vector diagram helps to connect the words in a meaningful way (see figure 7.12).

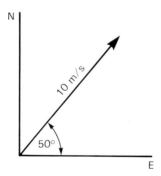

FIG. 7.12

Poems, quotations, physical laws and procedures for solving mathematical problems are other examples of verbal chaining. The form of a commonly used phrase is often memorised, so that many people will be able to say almost without thinking: 'at this moment in time', 'unaccustomed as I am to public speaking', 'I regret that I shall be unable to attend the meeting', etc.

Many partially formed verbal chains are stored in the brain ready for recall when the opportunity presents itself, so that new chains are more readily learned if the coding cues are strong enough.

Multiple discrimination

Discrimination is the act of discriminating or discerning that which constitutes a difference between two or more objects. It involves making judgements or observing characteristics. In psychological terms it relates to the detection of differences between stimuli in the perceptual field.

Multiple discrimination learning requires the learner to be able to distinguish objects or words from a very wide variety of items, many of which bear similarities and thus lead to problems of interference. The learner must also be able to identify likenesses and differences in objects and to construct chains of words in correct and unambiguous sequences.

In a practical situation the trainee must be able to discriminate between physical characteristics of objects or processes. The table below sets out some common applications:

Factor	*Knowledge of concept of*
Light/heavy	Relative density
Bright/dim	Luminous intensity
Rough/smooth	Surface finish assessment
Hard/soft	Hardness testing
Wet/dry	Humidity
Hot/cold	Temperature
Colour	Optical spectrum

Concept learning

Groups of objects with common features are known as *classes*, while general ideas about classes are known as *concepts*.

A concept can be defined as the 'properties, essential qualities or relationships common to a class of objects. Concepts may relate to concrete things in the real world or to abstract ideas such as beauty, fairness, equality, honesty or justice'.

If we consider the word *house*, a mental image of several of the following may form: large house, small house, mansion, council house, farmhouse, lodge or villa. The word *house* probably brings to mind several different types of building, so that when we are thinking about houses we are thinking about a *class* of buildings.

If we are presented with a set of photographs which includes many different types of houses together with a variety of other objects, we shall be able to sort the houses into a class and reject the remaining photographs. This is because the houses incorporate common features such as walls, windows, doors and roofs.

Concepts are formed as a result of experiences within the physical environment as well as through verbal communication related to events. In addition to the physical attributes of a house, such as bricks and mortar, ideas about the functions of a family within the house are also built into the concept. Having once acquired the concept *house*, we are able to discuss houses or read about them using mental images drawn from our imagination and hence learn without actually seeing the real thing.

In the classroom, when a word is written on the chalkboard or spoken by the teacher, a response of some kind will be forthcoming. This is because the words represent real things in the minds of the students. The response may be in the form of physical behaviour at the mention of a word because the word has signal significance. On the other hand, students may recall abstract ideas suggested by the word because the word has semantic significance—going beyond the recognised simple meaning of the word to form a general concept from consideration of particular instances.

In general, when teaching concepts, the teacher should move from the concrete to the abstract, from the known and familiar to the unknown, and should, wherever possible; relate examples or analogies to the students' lives.

Principle-learning

A *principle* is a fundamental truth on which others may be founded and is made up of a chain of concepts. A chain of concepts such as 'molecules', 'energy' and 'heat' may be combined to form a relationship like: 'molecules gain energy when heated'. In the same way, more complicated principles such as: 'action and reaction are equal and opposite', 'the force on objects in circular motion is directed towards the centre', and, 'pure metals increase in resistance when their temperature is increased', are made up of a number of concepts linked together in a specific sequence. The important point about chaining of concepts is that for the principle to be correctly stated, the appropriate verbal chain must be assembled in the correct sequence.

Principles learned from verbal chaining may or may not be meaningful. If principles are learned by rote, that is, by repeating or performing without regard to meaning, there will be a strong probability that the trainee will be able to solve only certain examples. Slight changes in the order of wording problems, or problems requiring 'in-depth' knowledge of the application of principles will result in the learner giving in. To be successful in problem-solving, the learner will need to be able to recall the verbal chains in correct sequence, to understand individual concepts and to be aware of the relationship between them.

Perhaps a better approach to principle-learning is that put forward by Gagné, who suggests that a thorough knowledge of the lower orders of learning should be mastered before attempting principle learning and problem-solving.† This requires that words denoting general ideas and concepts formed when different objects are seen to possess common features should be forged into well-learned chains making up the principles. Having once acquired a number of principles relevant to a given problem, the learner can combine them in order to solve it.

The teacher can help by relating his teaching of principles to situations which the learner will meet in his day-to-day life, and by using appropriate teaching aids. For his part, the learner can speed up problem-solving by verbalising his repertoire of principles while working on the problem. Such practices tend to produce more accurate solutions, reducing the number of errors made along the way.

Problem-solving

A *problem* is a matter in which it is difficult to decide the best course of action. An academic problem usually arises as a question propounded for solution or as a proposition in which some outcome or end-product is required. Such problems involve the application of one or more principles.

Problem-solving is the most complicated form of learning behaviour. It leads to the formation of new principles of a higher order. The learner is required to consider the problem and to organise knowledge of several principles at one time in order to reach a successful solution.

†Gagné R M *The Conditions of Learning* (Holt Rinehart & Winston, New York 1965) pages 60, 153.

If the learner is able to express his thoughts in words and to propound fundamental principles bearing on the problem, he will be well on the road to solving the problem. This type of activity is met daily within industry. A problem arises and two people get together to discuss a solution. We often hear conversations similar to the one following:

'We had a case like this once before. Do you remember? We used a larger element in the heater to increase the fluidity of the plastic, then we were able to reduce the moulding pressure. If we do the same with this job we should be able to get over the problem—provided we reduce the cycle time.'

'Yes, but if you do that, will the cavity fill completely? Another thing, will the plastic cool down sufficiently before it's ejected?'

'I've just thought of another problem. Distortion. Some of the work distorted on the shorter cycle.'

The discussion of the problem will probably lead to a decision based upon a mixture of past experiences and principles relating to the moulding process. The example illustrates Gagné's proposition that once a problem has been solved, something has been learned and added to the learner's capabilities.

Trial and error learning can waste a lot of time and the learner runs the risk of learning redundant and incorrect responses in his efforts to reach a solution. Problem-solving which is guided by a teacher is much more productive. It involves the combination of learned principles to achieve some end, and once this end has been achieved, the principles involved may be transferred to many other situations. Learning achieved by problem-solving is retained for a long time and is seldom forgotten.

In formal academic situations the teacher should analyse the problem and ensure that the learner has all essential concepts and principles involved in the problem before being introduced to it. While problem-solving is taking place, the teacher should be on hand to guide the learner through the maze towards a solution. Students should be able to see the overall pattern and should make use of any positive transfer of learning available (see section 7.7).

Figure 7.13 summarises the stages involved in problem-solving.

Learning skills

Some tasks are performed frequently. They often form basic components of other more complicated tasks, so it is necessary to perform them well,

FIG. 7.13   **Problem-solving**

Participator	Procedure	Remarks
Teacher	Prepares and describes problem	
Trainee	Analyses problem and identifies its nature	Exhibits state of readiness
Teacher	Outlines possible approaches or lines of thought	Does not reveal solution
Trainee	Keeps all relevant principles in mind and applies them to the problem at one time	Contiguity
Teacher	Cues and directs trainees' efforts when required	Keeps trainees on right track
Trainee	Discovers solution	Activity is reinforced
Trainee	Forms new higher-order principle from existing principles	Has learned something new
	Remembers solution and is able to apply principles to other similar but novel problems	Is less likely to forget principles

accurately and with as little effort as possible. These basic operations are called *skills* and include walking, manipulating arms and legs, writing, reading and typing. If these skills are not well learned, they consume a great deal of time and energy, and higher ordered activities of which they form part are less efficiently performed.

Skills demand a lot of practice and eventually their performance becomes more or less automatic. Many skills relate to motor or physical activity only; but there are many parallels in what are almost exclusively mental activities.

Fundamentals of sensorimotor skills

Filing metal with a hand file is an example of a sensorimotor skill in which muscular movement is prominent but is controlled by sensory stimuli. Filing a block of metal is not purely a mechanical operation but also includes brain activity which may occur without our paying conscious attention to it.

A manual skill involves a decision-making process in which a choice of muscular response is made to suit the pattern of incoming sensory signals (see figure 7.14).

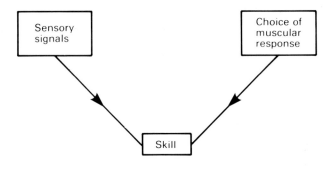

FIG. 7.14

A skilled performance involves rather more than carrying out a pattern of skilled movements. The craftsman must discriminate between competing stimuli and select only those appropriate to the task on hand (see figure 7.15).

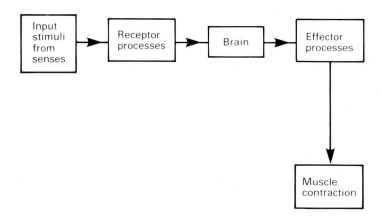

FIG. 7.15

When considering the skills involved in a filing operation, the following should be borne in mind: senses such as sight and touch; pressure (kinaesthetic sensitivity); hand and body movements.

In order for a person to pick up the file from the bench, the following must occur:

(a) The eyes must observe the location of the file.

(b) Information is transmitted to the brain.

(c) Brain initiates hand movement.

(d) Hand grasps file handle and exerts suitable pressure.

This information is represented diagramatically in figure 7.16.

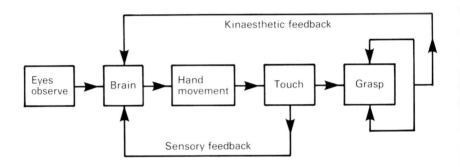

FIG. 7.16

Once the filing operation commences, a good many more input signals relating to the filing are received by the brain and kinaesthetic senses really come into play. A stronger grip is required on the file handle. Downward and forward force is required to actually cut the metal. The file must be stopped momentarily at each end of the cutting stroke to enable a change in direction to take place. The plane of filing must be constantly monitored to ensure squareness and flatness of the surface produced. The cutting force must be adjusted so as to obtain the desired surface texture and to ensure that the component is within specified dimensional tolerances. Inefficient cutting action must be detected and remedial action thought out, and so on.

7.7 Transfer of training

The effect of learning one task on the learning of another and the extent to which past learning can be applied to new situations affects the transfer of training.

Positive transfer occurs when previous training or experience assists in the acquisition of knowledge or ability involved in another task. *Negative transfer* occurs when previous learning interferes with and hinders the learning of another task. *Neutral transfer* applies to a situation where previous knowledge neither aids nor hinders a learning process, and obviously applies to a task which is completely different from anything a trainee has experienced before.

Maximum positive transfer occurs when the new task is extremely similar to previously learned tasks. Negative transfer occurs when the new task is different, but bears some similarity to what has previously been learned. In such instances the stimuli may appear to be the same, but require different responses to those assumed (see figure 7.17).

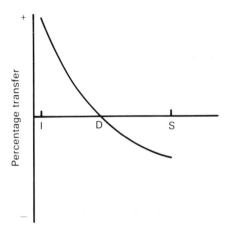

I – Tasks *X* identical to task *Y*
S – Confusing similarity between tasks *X* and *Y*
D – Tasks *X* and *Y* completely dissimilar

FIG. 7.17 **Graph showing % transfer of training between tasks *X* and *Y***

Two general theories apply to the transfer of training: the *identical elements theory* and the *transfer through principles theory*. The first theory holds that if tasks *X* and *Y* contain identical elements, positive transfer will occur and the rate of learning will increase, giving faster times to experienced worker standard (EWS). The second theory holds that fundamental principles, once learned, can be applied to a variety of problems based upon general objectives and concepts of certain classes, resulting in positive transfer.

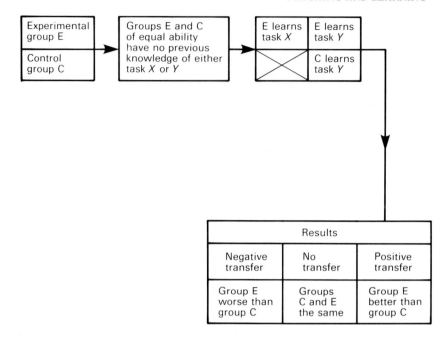

FIG. 7.18   **Evaluating transfer of training**

A diagram showing the form of an experiment used to evaluate transfer of training is given in figure 7.18.

The aim of the experiment is to compare the performance of each group in learning task *Y*. Neither group should have any previous knowledge of task *X*. The experimental group first learns task *X* and then learns task *Y*. The control group does not attempt task *X*, but attempts task *Y*. After completing the learning sessions, each group's performance on task *Y* is evaluated and compared. If the experimental group performs better than the control group, positive transfer of knowledge from task *X* to task *Y* is assumed. If the experimental group performs worse than the control group, negative transfer is assumed. If both groups perform the same, no transfer is assumed.

In industry, when a person is retraining and is faced with performing a new job, his previous experience will probably affect his performance. As in academic learning there will be elements of both interference and positive transfer and these factors should be allowed for when designing the training programme.

7.8 Learning curves

A learning curve may be drawn by plotting performance against a time base (see figures 7.19 and 7.20).

Data

Day	1	2	3	4	5	6	7	8	9	10
Performance %	15	27	40	43	47	50	50	65	80	100

TASK

1. Over which period was:
   (a) highest rate of increase in performance attained?
   (b) Lowest rate of increase in performance obtained?

2. Describe what was happening to the trainee between day 6 and day 7.

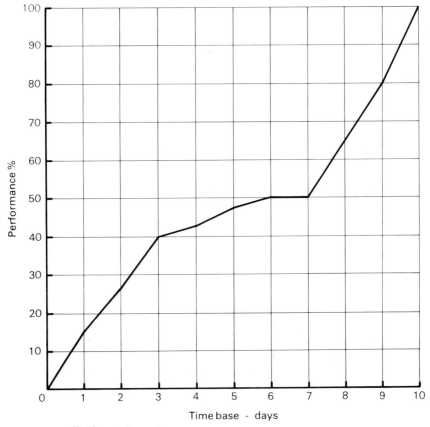

Time base - days

FIG. 7.19 **A learning curve**

1100	Type longer words—alas, dad, salads, flasks, falls. Eyes on BB.	VE	Touch-typing	CB
1105	Type simple sentences—ask a lad; a lass has a flask.	VE	Touch-typing	CB
1110	Paper release lever. Routine for putting work in folders, covering machines.	VE and Dem.	Take work from machines	Dem. mach-ines
	Summary	VE	Cover machines	
	Class dismissed			

FIG. 7.26 **Lesson plan assessment sheet**

Lesson plan assessment

Rating scale: Score: _____

Excellent   5
Very good   4
Good   3
Fair   2
Poor   1

Element	*Rating*	*Remarks*
Stating of learning objectives		
Logical development in suitable steps		
Variety of methods and activities		
Use of resources		
Adequacy of student involvement		
Checks of learning		

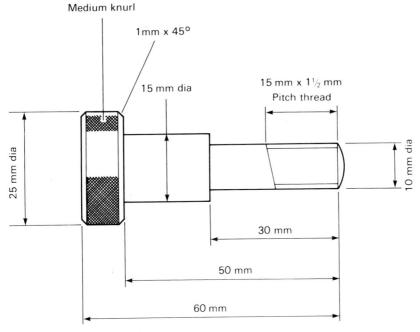

Material: 25 mm dia BDMS

FIG. 7.27   **Knurled screw**

Figs. 7.27-30 adapted from *Production Technology for Technicians Book 1* by H H Marshall with kind permission of Pitman Books Ltd, London.

dealing with capstan and turret lathes. The text provides a very good explanation of many aspects relating to the production of the knurled screw shown in figure 7.27.

An operation sheet, tooling layout and table of standard times taken from the text have been reproduced in figures 7.28, 7.29 and 7.30 respectively.

TASK

1. With the aid of the figures given, prepare detailed lesson plans covering the following learning objectives *relating to the manufacture of the 'knurled screw' using a capstan lathe.*

   Objectives
   The expected learning outcome is that the student will be able to:
   (a) prepare an operation sheet showing the correct sequence of operations;

Operation Number	Operation	Tool and Tool Material	Position on Machine	Cutting Speed m/min.	Spindle Speed rev/min.	Feed Rate mm/rev	Time min.
1	Feed to bar stop	Bar stop	Turret	—	—	—	0.06
2	Turn 15 mm dia.× 50 mm long	Roller box. H.S.S.	Turret	40	500	0.4	0.25
3	Turn 10 mm dia.× 30 mm long	Roller box. H.S.S.	Turret	40	840	0.4	0.09
4	Form the end	Roller ending box. H.S.S.	Turret	—	840	—	0.15
5	Cut screw thread	Die head. H.S.S.	Turret	8	150	1.0	0.07
6	Knurl	Knurling tool	Turret	8	100	Hand	0.10
7	Chamfer head	Form tool. H.S.S.	Cross-slide Front tool box	40	500	Hand	0.15
8	Part off	Part off tool. H.S.S.	Cross-slide Rear tool box	40	500	0.2	0.13

Productive time	1.00
Non productive time	0.62
Total machining time	1.62
Add 15% contingencies	0.25
Total cycle time	1.87

FIG. 7.28 **Operation sheet**

(b) draw a tooling layout;
(c) calculate the correct spindle RPM for each operation;
(d) calculate the total:
   (i) time required for each operation;
   (ii) productive time per component;
   (iii) non-productive time per component;
   (iv) time allowed for contingencies;
   (v) cycle time.

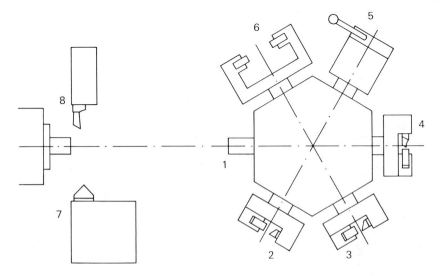

FIG. 7.29 **Tool layout**

| | Time | |
Operation	min	sec
Change Speed	0.05	3
Change Feed	0.05	3
Index Tool Post	0.06	3.5
Engage Feed	0.02	1.5
Feed to Bar Stop	0.06	3.5
Chuck in 3 Jaw Chuck	0.75	45

FIG. 7.30   **Lesson plan D**

Standard Plan—Lesson One	Assumes no previous knowledge
Greet client:	
Put at ease	
Drivers licence and eyesight checks	
Establish prior learning and experience	
Agree objectives	
Allow for questions and clarification	
Explain:	
Cockpit drill:	
Door	
Seat	
Steering	
Seat belt	
Mirrors (all)	
Blindspots	
Fuel level	
Foot controls:	**Instructional terms:**
Accelerator (Gas pedal)	Set gas. More gas. Less gas. Off gas.
Footbrake	Cover brake. Gently brake. Firmly
	brake. Off brake. Gently brake to stop.
Clutch	Cover clutch. Clutch down. Slowly
	clutch up. Feet still.
Hand controls:	
Handbrake	Apply handbrake
	Release handbrake
	Prepare handbrake
Gear lever	Hand on gear lever palm towards
	me/you
	Select (1, 2, 3 or 4) (5) (Reverse)
Steering wheel first	Steer left or right (Use aid)
	Position of hands (Ten-to-two)
Switch gear:	
Indicators	
Lights	
Horn	
Wiper/washer front and rear	
Heater	
Visual controls:	
Speedo	
Fuel gauge	
Water temperature	
Warning lamps	
Ignition lights	
Practice:	
Starting procedure	
Insert key	
Check handbrake is applied	
Check gear lever is in neutral	
Remove steering lock	
Switch-on ignition	
Check warning lamps	
Set gas	
Start engine	
Release keys ⎱ When engine	
Off gas ⎰ starts	
Switching-off	
Moving off:	*Emphasis on:*
Flat	Safety
Uphill —handbrake start	Mirror—look behind mirror
Uphill —clutch control	Signal if necessary
start	Safety
Downhill—1st Gear	Control and co-ordination of hand and
Downhill—2nd Gear	foot controls
From behind a parked car	(Later)

(cont.)

Steering	Straight line
Stopping:	
Uphill	
Flat	Safe and convenient position
Downhill	
Review progress	Complete Driving Report
	Record of Driving Lessons or
	Progress Checklist Profile
Look forward	
Lesson ends	

Based on an outline plan provided by John Coleman ADI, IAM RAC Registered Professional Driving Instructor, Blandford, Dorset.

Note: It will be seen that this plan differs from the other examples in that timings and details of aids have been omitted. This is because each lesson is individually negotiated with the learner. Content, time spent on each element will depend on rate of progress. What is important is that the Driving Instructor has analysed each element in terms of knowledge and skills involved and carefully prepared a logical sequence of learner activity.

Properly organised instructors will have in their cars diagrams, flash cards, sketch pads, dummy steering wheel and other aids to back explanations and to make things clearer for the learners.

Assessment and feedback will be ongoing throughout with an evaluation before ending the lesson.

7.10   Discipline

'Training or mode of life in accordance with rules'. 'Order maintained by control'. 'Subjection to control'.

The word *disciplinarian* describes a person who enforces strict discipline. At school he is the cane-wielder, in the Brigade of Guards he is the drill-sergeant. When we hear the word discipline we immediately think of domination, severity, obedience, subjugation, restraint and punishment.

As an instructor we must avoid being labelled as a strict disciplinarian if it is at all possible. It is better to be referred to as a 'just', 'unbiased', 'fair', 'impartial' or 'firm but fair' instructor. Most instructors could, if they wished, keep the group 'screwed down'. The whole lecture could pass without a murmur being heard from the group, but it is doubtful as to whether any learning will have taken place.

Discipline in the lecture situation is a two-way process, a state of discipline depending upon mutual recognition of relative responsibilities.

In his abdication speech on 11 December 1936, King Edward VIII said: 'But you must believe me when I tell you that I have found it impossible to carry the heavy burden of responsibility and to discharge my duties as King as I would wish to do, without the help and support of the woman I love.' In the classroom it is impossible for the instructor to discharge his duties effectively without the support of the trainees and vice versa. A knowledge of relative responsibilities is therefore necessary to enable discipline to be maintained and for useful learning to take place.

Rules

INSTRUCTOR'S RESPONSIBILITIES

To plan the period of instruction.

To provide adequate material.

To prepare detailed instruction.

To tell the trainee what is expected of him.

To fit material to individual's level of experience.

To deliver information in a manner easily assimilated.

TRAINEE'S RESPONSIBILITIES

To work to instructions of the instructor.

To respond to reasonable requests.

To remain silent while another is speaking.

To listen while another is speaking.

To remain seated unless requested to move.

Infringement of the rules

Unfortunately, not all trainees are highly motivated all of the time and there will be a tendency for disruptive behaviour to occur when there is a conflict between the group task and individual desires. It is the manner in which the instructor deals with the situation that reveals his attitude to the group and his ability as 'policeman'. There are no hard and fast rules for dealing with breakdowns in communication in the classroom. Perhaps a good start would be to consider the following quotations and evaluate your own performance with these in mind:

'Personally I'm always ready to learn, although I do not always like being taught.' *Sir Winston S Churchill*

'This person was a deluge of words and a drizzle of thought.' *P. DeVries*

People are inquisitive by nature. Challenge and mastery are great motivators. Thousands of people attempt crossword puzzles, explore caves and watch TV quiz programmes. Learning is taking place from the cradle to the grave; however, different people prefer different methods of learning and so the method of instruction being used may not suit every individual. A perceptive instructor will identify those trainees who appear to be flagging, he will notice the glazed eyes, the fidgeting, the chin-on-chest attitude, the doodling, the murmur of conversation and the laughter when his back is turned. These are danger signals indicating that the time has arrived for contingency plans to be put into action.

If we accept that there is no such thing as an uninteresting subject, then we must assume that our presentation is lacking in some respect. By trying a different approach, introducing an activity or audio-visual aid to give impact, interest may be revived. If all else fails, and as a last resort, dictate some notes; this seldom fails to restore order.

Verbosity and a seemingly endless stream of words promote passivity and boredom on the part of the trainee. This state of affairs leaves plenty of scope for undesirable behaviour to replace attentiveness. Even the most willing listener can only take so much, and after about fifteen minutes' exposure would succumb and either fall asleep or seek other forms of activity. Learning is an active process. We learn by doing. So bait the hook to suit the fish and keep them biting. Keep the lesson going and avoid gaps of inactivity.

Verbosity promotes boredom and undesirable behaviour replaces attentiveness

Dealing with the infringement

If the infringer does not respond to a modified approach to lecture presentation and refuses to join in the group activity, then action must be taken. The majority of the group will expect this. Sometimes group reaction to the disturbance will be sufficient to curb the infringer's efforts to disrupt and to draw attention to himself. Lack of reinforcement and rejection by his peer group are powerful demotivators for actions which do not conform to accepted group goals. However, care must be taken that the instructor does not unwittingly reinforce the infringer's behaviour by outright public admonishment; this might be just what he is hoping for. If he finds that he is irritating you, he will try it again or else one of his friends will.

Each infringement of rules is an individual affair and the instructor must avoid penalising the whole group for the actions of a single person. Avoid the temptation to base the method of control on the behaviour of minorities. Do not make threats. You may be challenged and may not have the authority to carry out your threat. It is better to provide reasonable opportunities for the infringer to save face. In any case, if you win by force, you lose. Irish? Not really. If you embarrass the trainee you will most probably have lost him for the duration of the course, and as the aim is to increase his store of knowledge you need him on your side. So, avoid confrontation in public unless you wish to make use of group pressure.

Alienation from the group and the attending isolation is the last thing most individuals want and rejection is, for most, unbearable. Praise and reward are better than blame and punishment and remember that even a small amount of success can give a sense of achievement, so use a positive rather than a negative approach. Aim for an increase in activity, co-operation, creativity and interest rather than authoritarianism, compulsion and passivity, and never make sarcastic remarks.

Try reason first. Try to be just and try to be unbiased.

If the infringer fails to respond then you will have no alternative but to apply sanctions in accordance with the agreed rules.

Well, perhaps nobody wanted to come—perhaps they'd all like to go—but they're not going. Because they're going to behave—and that's what we all have to learn in life—we have to learn to behave!

Ruth Draper—*The Children's Party*

Case Studies

THE BREAKDOWN OF DISCIPLINE

You are the course tutor. Read the case studies and decide what action you would take in order to overcome the problems.

1. Nicholas Blake is sixteen years of age and commenced a Technician Apprenticeship in August. All apprentices employed by the company spend their first forty-eight weeks undergoing 'off the job' training at an industrial training centre remote from the company premises.

   Nicholas obtained good GCSE results in Maths, Physics, English, Technical Drawing and Metalwork before leaving school. He has been enrolled in Level II of the A5 BTEC Mechanical and Production Engineering Programme at a nearby college, where attendance for one day and one evening each week is compulsory. At first, Nicholas adapts to the college work, but towards the end of the Autumn term starts skipping evening classes, arrives late in the morning, has frequent dental appointments and fails to submit assignments. His continuous assessment marks are generally quite high except in the case of Manufacturing Technology where he has failed his first assessment test. During a Manufacturing Technology lesson, one of his friends with GCSE grade A qualifications asks him why he has been 'skiving'. Nicholas tells him that he is bored stiff with college work; that he has covered much of the work before at school; that he cannot see the relevance of college work to his practical training and that he has no confidence in the Technology teacher's ability to get the subject-matter across.

   During the same lesson the Technology teacher asks Nicholas several questions aimed at drawing him into the discussion. Nicholas deliberately offers feeble or irrelevant answers. The teacher responds by answering his own questions and explains matters in great detail in an attempt to make Nicholas understand. The rest of the class start talking and become restless, safe from the eye of the teacher. The lesson becomes a shambles and Nicholas now feels that he has the measure of the teacher.

   Having quietened down the class by dictating a few notes, the teacher directs another question to Nicholas.

   Nicholas blurts out, 'Don't keep asking us questions. It's obvious that we don't know the answers. You're the expert. You tell us!'

   The class explodes with laughter and the teacher rushes out to see the course tutor.

2. Steve Brown is a big fellow aged seventeen and although towering above his classmates he is good-natured and certainly not a bully. He left school at the age of sixteen with GCSE grade A in English and grade C in Maths, Metalwork and Physics. He obtained employment as a craft apprentice with a large engineering company.

Wherever possible the company encourages its craft apprentices to follow Technician further education courses and Steve is now enrolled in the second year of an A5 Mechanical and Production Engineering course at college. Having managed to scrape through the first year of the course with bare pass grades after several retests, Steve now finds the second year very heavy going. This is not surprising, since he is no great academic.

From his very first day at the college, Steve has found himself in trouble. During an initial safety lecture for the entire first-year intake his chair collapsed with an almighty crash, drawing unwanted attention to himself. The lecturer in charge reported him for horse-play. Week after week something just had to happen which landed him in trouble. It was largely his own fault for he had set himself up as the class clown. Now, whether he likes it or not, his mates look to him for leadership in disruptive tactics in the classroom. Any attempt to co-operate with the teacher is seen as an act of weakness by Steve and his cronies, so that anyone wishing to learn is ridiculed and soon discovers that there is safety in silence.

At the company Steve is well liked by the men in his section and he throws himself into his work with great gusto. He tends to rush things so that although his output is high, the quality is low and accuracy doubtful.

His long-suffering teachers have tried to make allowances for his unco-operative behaviour in class. The company has been advised on several occasions of his misdemeanours and he has had several warnings both from the teachers and his training officer.

The crunch comes when Steve returns late to class after lunch reeking of beer. The teacher remarks on his lateness and points out the fact that College rules state that no student will be admitted to class after consuming alcoholic beverages. Steve responds by telling the teacher to 'get stuffed'.

The teacher refers the matter to you for action.

SUMMARY

- Language is essential to human perception, thinking and awareness. Fluency is related to the range of words known.

- Teachers should encourage their students to write and talk.

- Many teacher's questions call for factual replies only or test recall of what has been taught.

- Ned Flanders developed a system of recording classroom interaction.

- Teachers tend to like the sound of their own voices.

- Teachers should be conscious of the language they are using.

- Technical terms should be defined in simple familiar language where possible.

- There is frequently a psychological imbalance between instructor and trainee. Power is based upon the instructor's expertise and position. The instructor should avoid sarcasm. He should display patience, tact, diplomacy and integrity.

- A training plan may be designed around a questionnaire.

- A lesson consists of three stages: introduction, developmental stage and conclusion. Lesson aims, objectives and incentives should be presented during the introduction. The development stage is used to introduce basic principles and to build up knowledge progressively. The conclusion enables a teacher to recapitulate and consolidate.

- Lesson structure should include a variety of activities including question and answer sessions.

- Learning occurs during the process of maturation.

- Robert Gagné classified eight varieties of learning: signal learning; stimulus–response learning; chaining; verbal associate learning; multiple discrimination; concept learning; principle learning; problem-solving.

- E L Thorndike observed stimulus–response behaviour in animals. Behaviour followed by reinforcement is likely to be repeated.

- B F Skinner introduced the idea of operant conditioning, a form of instrumental conditioning. He observed the behaviour of hungry rats using an apparatus later known as the 'Skinner Box'.

- Gestalt psychology (Koffka, Köhler and Wertheimer) stresses the importance of pattern and organisation: 'The whole is greater than the sum of its individual parts.'
  In problem solving, 'insight' is the name given to the process involving perception of relationships leading to a solution.

'Waiting for the penny to drop'

- Tasks performed frequently form basic components of other more complicated operations. Skills well learned save a great deal of time and energy. Practice leads to more or less automatic performance.

- Positive transfer of training assists the learning of a new task. Negative transfer hinders learning.

- A learning curve is obtained by plotting performance against a time base. A plateau is a period of no improvement preceded and followed by improvement.

- Lesson-planning is important.

- Discipline depends upon mutual recognition of relative responsibilities. Verbosity promotes boredom and inactivity—undesirable behaviour replaces attentiveness. Never penalise the whole group for an individual's indiscretion. Avoid confrontation in public. Try reason first.

QUESTIONS

1. Many teachers tend to be middle-class due to their family background or academic achievements. If this is true, they will probably use an 'elaborate language code' during lessons. How will this influence the effectiveness of their teaching?

2. Using the example of teacher talk entitled 'Case hardening of mild steel":
   (a) prepare a set of 'closed' or 'naming' questions based on the text;
   (b) rewrite the questions in an 'open-ended' form designed to elicit greater student response.

3. Observe a lesson and record the communication behaviour using a Flander's Interaction Analysis report form. Analyse the results and decide whether the teacher has used a 'direct' or an 'indirect' style.

4. Many students believe that while in the classroom there is safety in silence. How can a teacher modify this belief?

5. You are requested to produce a training plan for your company. The area concerned is *safety* applied to a particular machine or process of your choice. Answer the questionnaire (see section 7.3) and draw up a training plan.

6. Prepare a list of questions to be used for a 'question and answer' session during instruction on the safety training course in Question 5 above.

7. Give an example of each of the following classes of learning:
   (a) Signal learning
   (b) Stimulus–response learning
   (c) Chaining
   (d) Verbal association learning
   (e) Multiple discrimination
   (f) Concept learning
   (g) Principle learning
   (h) Problem-solving

8. Describe a practical situation in which positive transfer of training may occur.

9. Design a lesson plan to cover any BTEC unit objective.

10. Using a Lesson Plan Assessment sheet, rate a lesson plan produced by one of your group. After rating, discuss the plan with the originator.

8

Understanding and using teaching methods

Management is the process or activity of carrying out a number of diverse activities in such a way that certain defined objectives are achieved.

A manager is responsible for creating conditions under which the desired objectives may be achieved by the combined efforts of a group of people. In an educational situation the teacher is responsible for the management of instruction and for the development of resources so that students may learn most effectively.

Henri Fayol (1841–1925) was the head of a large French mining and engineering company and was appointed when the company was near to bankruptcy. He saved the company and became a pioneer of modern organisational management by developing the first approach to functional organisation. For him, functional organisation required that work and task be structured and organised 'into bundles of skill' where everyone understands his own task. He proposed five essential elements of management: planning, organising, co-ordinating, controlling and commanding. These elements apply equally to the role of teacher as a manager of both learning resources and learning situation.

In his book *Management of the Total Enterprise*, † Robert Katz outlines three types of management skills: technical skills relating to what is to be done; human skills concerned with how it is done; and conceptual skills concerned with why it is done. These three skills may be related to the learning process.

Technical skills concern the preparation of course work based upon a set of learning objectives and an assessment specification for evaluating terminal

†Katz R L *Management of the Total Enterprise* (Prentice-Hall, Englewood Cliffs, NJ 1970).

behaviour, Human skills are concerned with the methods of presentation and resources to be used; while conceptual skills are concerned with needs, expectations, motivation and validation.

The teacher is charged with overall responsibility for ensuring that the three elements are met. When given a set of behavioural objectives he must provide an environment in which the objectives may be best achieved, and select the teaching method best suited to the subject-matter and type of learning involved. As in industry, constraints such as time available, student ability, resources and space must be considered so that the method chosen meets the conditions existing.

Different methods of instruction call for different arrangements of teaching media, and while there is no hard and fast rule, Bloom's three main categories of learning—cognitive, affective and psychomotor—could be used as a basis for deciding the mode of instruction. Cognitive domain learning may be taught using any method of teaching, although conventional lessons and programmed instruction are to be preferred. Affective domain goals are probably best achieved using discussion, case study or role-play methods where responding, valuing and organising behaviour may be given free rein. Psychomotor learning is best acquired by active physical participation so that either demonstration followed by practice, experiment or project work may be employed. Some common teaching methods are descibed below.

8.1 Teaching methods described

Job instruction training

With the advent of World War II came a rapid increase in demand for armaments and many other war materials. Factories were drained of manpower in order to swell the armed forces and these men had to be replaced. Large numbers of workers were recruited to cope with the vastly increased demands made on British industry. Female labour was introduced on a large scale and men were directed to factory work from non-essential industries. These workers needed to be trained, and trained quickly. To meet this need, job instruction techniques were developed which are still widely used today.

The traditional method of job instructional training involves the seven main stages set out in figure 8.2. The whole job is demonstrated and explained by an instructor while the trainee observes. The trainee then tries to emulate the instructor and endeavours to reach experienced worker standards. En route, learning plateaux (see section 7.8) are normally encountered which hold up this progress. After a while the trainee overcomes his difficulties and reaches the required standard.

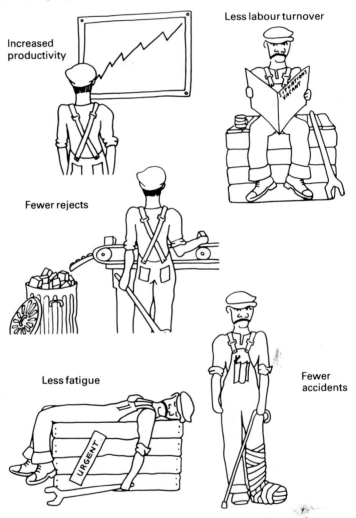

FIG. 8.1   **The results of analytical job instruction**

Artist: Brian Snape
Reproduced by kind permission of R Bailey BSc, PhD, Principal, Bournemouth and Poole College of Further Education.

FIG. 8.2   **Comparison of job instruction methods**

JOB INSTRUCTION	
Analytical method	*Traditional method*
Analyse job	Demonstrate whole job
Carry out skills analysis	Demonstrate whole job with explanation
Demonstrate and explain whole	Demonstrate whole job slowly
Demonstrate each skill element	Trainee practises whole job while instructor supervises and corrects
Trainee practises each skill element until proficient	Trainee builds up stamina
Move to next skill element	Transfer trainee to production situation
Combine skills into whole job	Follow-up
Trainee builds up stamina	
Transfer trainee to production situation	
Follow-up	

The analytical method is based upon a skills analysis for the job concerned. The job is studied and broken down into skills elements which are demonstrated separately. The trainee practises and masters each element after which he is required to combine the individual skills into a complete job. Time to reach experienced worker standard by this method is usually shorter than by the traditional method. Learning plateaux are reduced or eliminated with consequent savings in training time, while the trainee benefits by experiencing less frustration.

A closer look at the analytical method

Before preparing a job instruction plan the job itself should be analysed and the following questions asked:

What is done?	Where is it done?
Why is it done?	How is it done?
When is it done?	Who does it?

FIG. 8.3　**Tutor and National Bus Company supervisors discussing a skills analysis**

Having established answers to these questions and agreed the method, a skills analysis is carried out.

The skills analysis

A *skill* is the ability, either innate or acquired by practice, which enables a person to perform a job expertly.

A skills analysis is carried out in order to separate job factors into their component parts, so that a training plan can be devised and used to train workers to perform the necessary operations effectively.

Each factor is analysed under three headings:

> Function
> Knowledge required
> Skills involved

Function 1 of the example shown in the table of job factors in figure 8.4 involves the operator in adjusting a temperature control. In order to do this

FIG. 8.4 **Table of job factors**

JOB FACTORS Job: Heat-sealing (Thermopack machine)		
Function	*Knowledge*	*Skills*
1. Adjust temperature control	Scale-reading incre-ments Temperature-setting Means of adjusting	Aligning control knob with scale markings
2. Set air cylinder operating pressure	Pressure gauge readings Pressure settings Means of adjusting	Adjusting air regulator valve
3. Load unsealed hyperdermic needle packs to machine: (a) checks unsealed packs (b) picks up loading device; (c) opens jaws of loading device; (d) lifts out load; (e) transfers load to sealer; (f) clamps load in machine; (g) returns loading device.	Recognises incomplete packs Number of packs per load Loading device to be full Location required Locking control operation	Grips in left hand Operates trigger using correct pressure Force required to raise load Locating packs in holders Actuates locking control Left hand to table and release
4. Locate sealing strip: (a) picks up sealing strip; (b) locates strip in machine.	One strip only required between locating dowels	Separating strip from stock Smooths strip flat
5. Operate heat-sealing platen; operates air cylinder control.	Location of control	Presses control button
Complete table for all operations shown in training specification (see figure 7.4)		

correctly the operator must know the specified temperature at which the machine is required to operate. He must also know how the temperature may be adjusted and how to interpret scale markings. The skills element involves the co-ordination of hand and eye movements so that the control knob may be aligned with the desired scale marking (see section 7.6.). Each function is classified in the same way.

Therbligs

Frank Bunker Gilbreth, an American engineer, studied the basic elements of body movement used by workers when carrying out a variety of operations and produced a list of *therbligs* (an anagram of 'Gilbreth') to represent these movements (see figure 8.5). Each therblig represented a movement or reason for the absence of movement and is represented on a chart by a specific colour, symbol or letter.

A 'therblig chart' showing a sequence of individual therbligs can be produced from either of the following:
(a) carrying out a detailed examination of the 'job analysis';
(b) filming the sequence of operations executed and then performing a 'film analysis' in which a frame-by-frame examination of the film reveals each movement;
(c) producing a 'man-type flow process chart' which records the worker's movements.

Each therblig should then be analysed in order to identify the skills involved in terms of:
(a) what is done;
(b) how it is done;
(c) left hand movements;
(d) right hand movements;
(e) body movements;
(f) vision;
(g) touch;
(h) kinaesthetic sense;
(i) other senses.

Results of the analysis highlight:
(a) particular difficulties;
(b) suitable break-points in instruction;
(c) needs for special apparatus (simulators);
(d) level of manual dexterity desired;
(e) degree of concentration involved.

FIG. 8.5 **List of therbligs BS 3138:1969**

Reproduced by permission of BSI, 2 Park Street, London W1A 2BS from whom complete copies of the document can be obtained.

Symbol	Name	Colour
⊂⊃	Search	Black
⊂◻⊃	Find	Grey
⟶	Select	Light grey
∩	Grasp	Red
⌂	Hold	Gold ochre
⌣	Transport load	Green
9	Position	Blue
#	Assemble	Violet
U	Use	Purple
#	Disassemble	Light violet
0	Inspect	Burnt ochre
8	Pre-position	Pale blue
⌒	Release load	Carmine red
⌣	Transport empty	Olive Green
℅	Rest for over-coming fatigue	Orange
⌢	Unavoidable delay	Yellow
⌴	Avoidable delay	Lemon yellow
℗	Plan	Brown

The advantage of carrying out a skills analysis is that the following are identified:

(a) sequence of operations;
(b) key elements of task;
(c) hand skills involved;
(d) other sensorimotor skills involved;
(e) necessary co-ordination of movement;
(f) kinaesthetic senses involved;
(g) need for learning aids;
(h) need for special exercises and practice;
(i) estimate of cognitive aspects of task;
(j) estimate of training time.

Demonstration, explanation and practice

Having identified the knowledge required and skills involved using a job-factor or therblig analysis, the instructor can set about planning the instruction in detail. Ways and means are then developed whereby the trainee may practise the individual skills elements making up the whole job.

The instructor gives several demonstrations of the complete operation, with explanation, to give the trainee a clear picture of what he should be able to do at the end of the training session. A single skills element is then demonstrated while the trainee watches. The trainee then practises each element until all skills elements have been mastered. The trainee then combines individual skills elements into a complete cycle of operations. Practice follows until the trainee reaches experienced worker standard.

Case study

EMPLOYEE TRAINING

Stan Roberts, a fifty-year-old plating department operative, looked glum. After working on the nickel-plating line for over ten years, he had just been told that a new automated continuous operation plating plant was to be installed, and that his job would go, along with the jobs of five of his workmates. His supervisor had explained that in order to improve productivity the new plant would be directly linked to the machine tool line which produced the components to be plated. This innovation would dispense with the need for loaders, thereby putting him out of work.

The supervisor had, however, outlined two other employment possibilities within the company. The first of these related to a new position as a line-inspector whose job would be to ensure that rigid quality standards were maintained. Statistical sampling techniques were to be introduced and applied to the new automated process. The inspector would implement these techniques. The second related to a vacancy for a power guillotine operator. This job entailed the cutting of metal sheets to a given size using a hand-operated machine.

Stan went home that night and thought things over. He didn't like the way in which the supervisor had dropped the bombshell. The supervisor had announced the news in a completely off-hand manner with no apparent concern for his feelings, and had made no effort to allay the fears that any man of his age might justifiably experience. Stan knew that he was not an ambitious type and quickly decided that he did not want the responsibility that went with the inspector's job, even if he was offered it. Besides that he had no head for figures and disliked any form of paperwork. He considered that he was too old to bother with book-learning and made up his mind to opt for the job of guillotine operator, even though he knew the job was noisy and required considerably more physical effort than he was used to. He convinced himself that any sort of job with the company would be better than taking redundancy pay and running the risk of a long spell off work. In his younger days he would have taken a chance, but now he had lost much of his former confidence. He wanted to remain where he felt safe, among his workmates in a familiar environment.

The next day Stan spoke to his supervisor and announced his willingness to train as a guillotine operator.

A month later the new plant had been installed and Stan was taken by his supervisor to the press shop where the guillotines were located and introduced to George Hunt, the foreman.

'Morning George. This is Stan Roberts, the bloke I spoke to you about. We've finished with him now, so I'll leave him with you. I've notified Personnel. I'll have to get back to the plating shop. Soon as me back's turned things go haywire. Can't leave some of them morons for more than a few minutes.'

George nodded understandingly, then turned to Stan and said, 'Right, let's make a start. I'll show you the guillotine you'll be using.'

The two walked into the press shop where Stan soon became aware of the thumping of presses and the clatter of metal. Looking around he noticed that only about one-half of the operators were wearing ear muffs, and wondered how the other half could stand the racket.

After stopping once to give a weedy-looking man a rollicking for pouring coffee from his flask, George stopped at an unattended guillotine.

*'He told me
any fool
could do this job'*

'This one will be yours,' he said. 'I'll show you how to operate it. It's dead easy. Any fool could do this job so you won't need to worry.'

Stan winced.

'Right. This is the isolator. Push the lever down to switch on the power. Press the green button; that starts the motor. Pick up a sheet like this, slide it under the guard and push it up against the stop. The setter adjusts the stop for you. Push this knob to the right to clamp the sheet. Then press these two buttons—one with each hand and the machine automatically crops the metal. When the blank has been cropped, unclamp by pushing the knob to the left. The sheet is released and the guard rises. See?'

'Yes,' replied Stan.

'Okay, I'll show you again. Push the metal forward to the stop. Clamp the sheet like this. Press the two buttons. Unclamp, and away you go again. Right! Now you do one while I watch.'

Stan pushed the sheet forward. Clamped the sheet. Pressed the two buttons and guillotined off his first blank. He then repeated the operations without fault several times with George watching.

George seemed to be satisfied and said, 'Right, You've got it. Told you there's nothing to it. Keep going. The machine's got a counter on it. You've got to make sure you do your number, so don't hang about. I'll pop back later if I get a minute'.

Stan was left alone and didn't see any more of the foreman that morning.

By lunchtime the following had happened:

(a) The inspector had discovered that:
  (i) a large number of blanks had been guillotined with edges not parallel;
  (ii) several blanks were cut too narrow;
  (iii) offcuts were mixed with correctly sized blanks;
  (iv) thicker gauge blanks had been cut in error to the same dimensions as the original blanks.

(b) A narrow offcut had jammed between the blades of the guillotine causing the drive belts to slip and wear rapidly. The drive motor had become over-loaded and the fuses had blown.

(c) Stan had gashed his hand on a sharp edge and also had a bad headache.

(d) Stan was ready to give in. He'd had enough for one morning.

DISCUSSION

1. If you, as the Plating Shop Foreman's immediate superior, had over-heard his conversation with George Hunt, what action would you have taken?

2. How should the incident in which George caught the weedy-looking man pouring coffee have been handled?

3. Why did Stan wince?

4. What was wrong with the way George gave his demonstration?

5. How could the unfortunate happenings of Stan's first morning in the press shop have been avoided?

6. What would be the likely result of failing to wear ear muffs in the press shop environment?

7. What steps should be taken to improve Stan's attitude to his new job?

8. Assuming that the Plating Shop Foreman had been advised well in advance of the management's plan to install the new plating equipment, consider how you would have broken the news to the men affected.

9. Discuss the effects of occupational change upon older workers.

10. Outline some of the problems encountered when the need for retraining older staff arises.

Programmed instruction and teaching machines

Each trainee uses a training machine while a teacher is at hand to offer guidance and help whenever required.

Using linear programmes, the subject-matter is presented in discrete steps known as *frames*, each of which poses a problem or gives one unit of information. Each frame requires a response, usually asking the trainee to answer a question or complete a statement based upon the information given.

In branching programmes the frame contains much more information than that of the linear programme and is usually followed by a multiple choice type question. The trainee selects an answer from the options provided and presses a key which signals his choice to the machine. The machine communicates the correctness or otherwise of his choice to the trainee, and if correct, moves to a new frame which often indicates why the answer is correct and presents new information. If incorrect, the trainee is directed to that part of the programme which is designed to remedy the error.

Having entered the programme at a level commensurate with his existing knowledge of the subject, maximum participation from the trainee is ensured because he works alone at his own pace and receives adequate reward and reinforcement for correct answers. The programme presents a challenge, and the immediate feedback of results helps to maintain motivation so that the trainee is encouraged to give all his attention to the programme.

The advantage of the programmed learning method is that the subject-matter is carefully presented in small interrelated steps and is graded in difficulty so that the trainee should make few mistakes. The method ensures a high probability of successful learning.

Flexible and open learning

Flexible learning opportunities are offered in the form of open-learning schemes involving college based, work-based or home-based study using specially designed or adapted resources and supported by tutors. Open-learning enables people to fill gaps in their education and training, to attain qualifications post school, to update their work-based skills and to meet identified training needs.

Instructor skills needed to support open-learning include: an awareness of what flexible learning is all about; competence in tutoring and counselling; writing and adapting open-learning materials and other work directly relating to open-learning such as monitoring and evaluating resources and methods.

The Open College described by Lord Young as 'the college of the air', is an initiative designed to enhance the competency of people already in work and those not available for work. It is a relatively new national approach to education and training which places emphasis on learning rather than teaching.

The College follows other leaders in the field of open-learning such as: The Open University, The National Extension College and Open Tech. It is intended to attract people back into education and training and to provide interesting and easy to study high quality, cost effective training. The College uses open-learning techniques supported by broadcasting and local centres where guidance and facilities are made available, so as to provide learning where, when and how it is needed. Successful performance in Open College courses provides credits which may lead to the award of National Vocational Qualifications.

The lecture

The lecture is an economical means of transmitting factual information to a large audience, although there is no guarantee that effective learning will result. The method is autocratic in form and allows little or no room for active audience participation, while at the same time, providing little feedback to the speaker as to the effectiveness of his presentation.

The method is popular in universities and the like where the aim is to provide a framework of ideas and theories which can be developed and considered in detail subsequently, either by private study, or in seminar groups supervised by a tutor. The lecture cannot cope with a wide diversity of ability and in itself provides no opportunity for the audience to clarify misunderstandings although a limited question and answer session usually follows.

A famous educationalist once declared that a university lecture is a means whereby the contents of the speaker's notes are taken down into the students' notes without passing through the minds of either. If the lecture is read from notes by an uninspiring speaker, the audience will soon fall asleep. It is difficult for a person to concentrate for very long, due to lack of active participation, and some experiments have suggested that twenty minutes is the best one can hope for.

Lectures at the Science Museum in Kensington are usually well attended and are very successful. The reasons for their success stem largely from the fact that the lectures are well prepared, rehearsed and supported by audio-visual material. The lecturers exhibit enthusiasm and imagination and are able to set the scene for meaningful and intrinsically motivating learning experiences. A complete contrast to the lectures described above.

In general, lectures do not result in a noticeable change in attitudes held, while retention of information disseminated is also poor. Tests on recall applied immediately after lectures have shown that students may retain less than 40% of content , falling to 20% one week later. Those results show how ineffective the lecture is as a means of teaching, especially in the case of below-average students.

Instructing by demonstration

A demonstration is a practical display or exhibition of a process and serves to show or point out clearly the fundamental principles or actions involved. Teaching by demonstration is a useful tool available to the instructor and plays an important part in the teaching of skills. The recommended sequence for planning and delivering a demonstration is given in figure 8.6.

Practice session

A practice session should follow immediately in order to reinforce procedures. If the actual equipment is delicate or expensive, a cheaper simulator should be substituted for the real thing.

Trainees learn best by doing. There is no substitute for practice in the acquisition of a skill. During the practice session, the instructor should give individual attention and should correct errors and omissions quickly. Bad habits and unsafe working procedures are difficult to erase once established.

After confidence has been built up, factors such as accuracy, style, rhythm. speed and quality can be concentrated on; while ensuring that any target set is within each trainee's mental and physical capacity.

Watch for signs of boredom. Once a trainee has mastered a technique there is no further challenge. Move him on to another stage, but do not confuse boredom with fatigue. Do not flog a flagging horse. Think of some way of reviving the trainee.

Reward with praise wherever possible. Praise acts as a reinforcer. Never blame a trainee. No good can come of this. Aim to stimulate, not to distress. No one deliberately sets out to make mistakes. Be positive. Look at your instructional method and try a new way.

Project work

Trainee behaviour in the learning situation has been grouped by Bloom into three domains or areas: cognitive, affective and psychomotor (see section

FIG. 8.6   **Instructing by demonstration**

Sequence	Remarks
Preparation Plan demonstration	Include key factors Logical sequence
Obtain apparatus Rehearse demonstration	Do not leave anything to chance Perfect sequence and delivery
Delivery Lay out apparatus	Each element in correct order
Establish rapport	Create suitable atmosphere for learning
State aims	What you intend the trainees to achieve by the end of the session
Show end-product	Establishes in trainee's mind the need to participate
Demonstrate silently at normal speed	Repeat several times. Allows trainee to focus attention on process. Arouses curiosity
Demonstrate at slow speed	Describe hand or body movements and senses involved
Ask trainees to explain process	Trainees think for themselves and are actively involved
Discuss safety aspects	Forewarns and creates awareness of inherent dangers
Ask for volunteer to attempt demonstration	Encourages competition. Other trainees asked to spot mistakes
Each trainee attempts demonstration	Remainder watch and comment. Instructor corrects faults

2.3). The use of project work provides a means by which the instructor can develop abilities in each of these fields.

A project may be set either as an individual task or as a small group undertaking. The project may be designed as a learning process in which group members are faced with new concepts and unfamiliar activities, or on the other hand, as a device for the integrating of several previously mastered individual skills. Whichever method is selected will involve the trainee in activity relating to one or more of Bloom's domains.

The cognitive domain will embrace such thought processes as identifying key factors inherent in the problem, seeking information relevant to mastery of the problem and using the information to solve it. This domain also includes the ability to plan and to implement a scheme of work designed to complete the task and the ability to communicate the contents to other group members.

The affective domain provides for the development of latent aptitudes or traits such as perseverance, leadership and creativity; and the ability to provide teamwork spirit or individual efforts.

The psychomotor domain includes drawing-office design work and practical skills involved in the manufacture and assembly of project details.

If a group project is set, account must be taken of each trainee's social skills as shown by the way he gets along with other group members. As an instructor, once again, you must know your men and try to arrange group membership so that the group will be cohesive.

Modern research has shown that when appointing a group leader it should be borne in mind that successful leaders are usually more intelligent than the other group members and are often extroverted, assertive and self-confident. They tend to have a high rate of participation in group discussion, to integrate group activity and to be task-orientated. In the event of a snag or problem, they suggest remedial action and attempt to secure group co-operation and consensus.

Allocation of work to each group member is the responsibility of the group leader. He will have to decide whether each member will be made responsible for a particular stage of the work or whether he will be involved in all aspects of the project. Before decisions can be made, the leader will have to consider whether to allocate a task on the basis that a member is good at a particular type of work or because he needs practice in a given area. Time available to completion and the probability of achieving objectives set at the right quality level must, of course, be an important factor when making these decisions.

Algorithms

An algorithm is a set of instructions designed for solving problems in a finite number of steps. It should be laid out in such a way that the reader knows exactly what is to be done in order to solve the problem as quickly as possible.

Algorithms usually have only one entrance or starting point although they may have several exits or finishing points corresponding to the possible solutions or outcome of the problem.

Each step of the algorithm should be unambiguously laid out and should be easy to interpret. It should leave the reader in no doubt as to what to do next, so that if instructions are correctly followed, a successful solution is guaranteed.

The algorithm shown in figure 8.7 illustrates the general principle of 'go', 'no-go' gauging used in an engineering inspection situation. It forms part of a training element, prepared by the Engineering Industry Training Board, designed to assist instructors and trainees in the development of satisfactory levels of skill in operator training.

The algorithm has only one starting point, in this case, the box containing the command: 'Try the "go" end of the gauge to the workpiece'. Then follows a set of YES–NO decisions when a question is asked either leading to further commands or to a logical conclusion. The algorithm has three possible exits or conclusions, one of which indicates that the gauged component is acceptable, the other two rejecting it as unacceptable.

Algorithms are excellent aids to problem-solving and are ideal teaching devices in a practical situation although they can be used for the solution of mathematical problems.

A typical application for an algorithm is in the diagnosing of faults in motor cars and electrical devices reducing the role of the instructor to a minimum while trainee activity is maximised.

Developing the skill of using the gauges

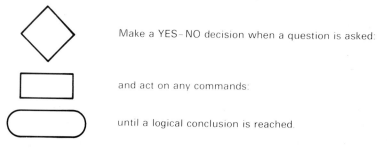

Make a YES–NO decision when a question is asked:

and act on any commands:

until a logical conclusion is reached.

(Fig. 8.7 continued overleaf)

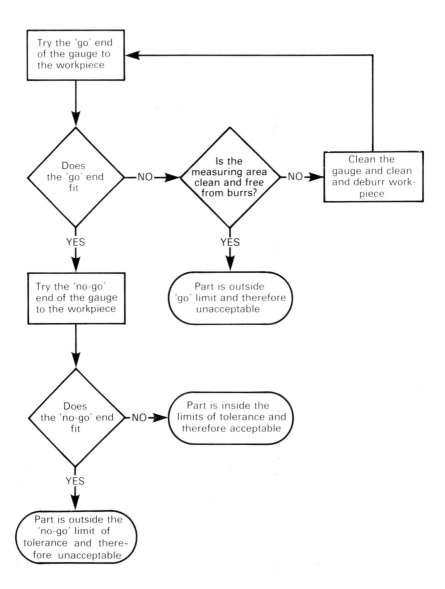

FIG. 8.7   **General principles of 'go', 'no-go' gauging**

(© Engineering Industrial Training Board, Watford, Herts. 1973. Reproduced from 'Training Element C2' EITB, page 10)

In his article 'Innovation and Education',† John McCafferty, Director of Studies, Unilever Management Training Centre, introduced the algorithm shown in figure 8.8 in order to draw the attention of the reader to:
(a) the issue of whether an innovation problem exists in his or her company;
(b) investigate some initial stages of the problem-solving process.

In other words, he was not only trying to stimulate the reader's interest, but also using the technique as a method of problem identification, together with some suggestions as to what the initial stages of the analysis should be.

The simplicity of an algorithm can encourage individuals to make the first steps in problem analysis, and in McCafferty's personal view is useful in tackling problems (e.g. diagnosis of faults in motor cars). He suggests that algorithms can be used successfully in pre-negotiation meeting plans where industrial relations issues are being discussed.

The design of algorithms has the advantage that it disciplines a person to think in a realistically structured way towards a whole range of problems.

Finally, it helps others to focus on appropriate options open to them.

Fault diagnosis

An informative paper entitled 'Fault Diagnosis', written by Mr G Chamberlain, Senior Training Advisor to the Food, Drink and Tobacco Industry Training Board, is given in Appendix 8. The paper, which deals with diagnostic skills and the use of algorithms, was published in the *Plant Engineer*, volume 24, No. 2, March 1980, and has been reproduced by kind permission of the author and the Institution of Plant Engineers.

Participative learning

Participative learning methods involve the trainee in actively participating in the task rather than passively soaking-up information as in the conventional 'chalk and talk' lesson. The trainee is encouraged to make a verbal commitment to the learning process so that material, tutor and group are linked by a near continuous dialogue. Success depends on the attitude, style, personality, awareness and sensitivity of the tutor, together with his knowledge of and skill in using teaching methods which promote trainee involvement.

†McCafferty J *'Innovation and Education' Education & Training* Vol 22, No. 9, October 1980.

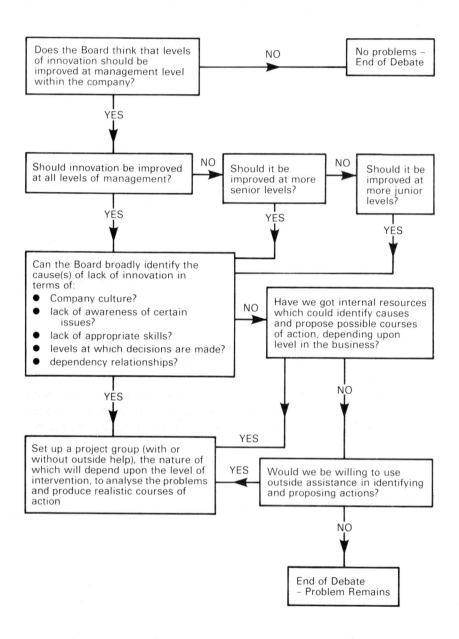

FIG. 8.8

Under the general heading of Participative Learning can be grouped the following teaching techniques:

Case Studies   Simulation Exercises
Role-play   Instrumental Team Learning
Discussions   Problem Solving

Each of these methods is now being used by major training establishments and Peter Finney, Technical Training Instructor, Southern Gas, has described participative teaching in the following way:

'In any teaching or training situation there are four major factors continually interacting: the tutor, the trainee, the material and the learning environment. The environment forms a framework within which affective domain goals such as rapport between student and tutor, student motivation and good relations between group members may be realised. Other factors such as the nature of the topic and the time of day may also work for or against the successful attainment of group aims.

Participative learning methods have been used within the Gas Industry in a variety of training situations ranging from conventional lessons to instrumental team learning. The "conventional lesson" can become participative if the tutor makes a conscious effort to involve students during the main body of the lesson. The tutor in this situation should always be working towards obtaining verbal commitment from the students. At the other end of the spectrum is "Instrumental Team Learning" where the tutor acts purely as an administrator. Throughout the entire range of participative learning methods the interaction of elements, that is: tutor, trainees, material and learning environment, will vary in intensity and in the way that they dominate the teaching situation.'

Case studies

Case studies are based on real life situations or problems which are frozen and presented in one of the following forms:

Written   Film
Spoken (taped)   Role-play
Closed-circuit Television

Case studies create subject awareness and interest and by actively participating people can learn from others. As peer groups are frequently involved there are less inhibitions within the group and participation by all members helps to fill out an experience giving an understanding of behaviour. The method can also be used to pass on skills, knowledge and attitudes.

In general, complex cases should be avoided in order to eliminate overloading the students' capacities although suitably difficult cases may be written for use by management trainees or even degree students.

Role-play

Role-play is a dynamic version of the case study and is often based on counselling or human relations problems. Role-play itself gives many of the advantages of the case study method but is limited to very simple situations where only one or two learning objectives are involved.

Students either take the part of characters themselves or watch actors or tutors play out the situations. Where students are to be involved care should be exercised in selection. A student can easily be embarrassed and mentally shattered if made to look silly. Perhaps the most suitable type to participate would be an outgoing person sometimes described as a 'social extrovert'.

Discussions and simulation exercises

Discussion is a useful tool of the trainer and takes three distinct forms:

Pre-planned
Partially planned
Spontaneous

In the pre-planned discussion, conclusions are known and opening statements are formulated together with important factors arranged in correct sequence. With partially planned discussions, opening statements and conclusions may be known but the rest of the discussion must be planned as the theme is developed. It goes without saying that spontaneous discussions can result in greater freedom and bigger rewards in that the tutor can grasp certain statements made and expound them to any level he chooses. However, care must be exercised by the tutor to ensure that he is fully conversant with the subject matter otherwise chaos will ensue. All three discussion types may be either guided or non-guided depending on the control required by the situation or by the tutor.

Simulation exercises are very similar to discussion although they usually relate to practical work.

Instrumental team learning

This is a series of learning techniques comprising the following elements:

Team effectiveness design

Team member teaching design
Performance judging design

Team effectiveness design

With this technique, students are divided into teams of about five persons. Each individual reads a manuscript and then attempts to answer an associated question paper. They then rejoin respective teams. A time limit is set by the tutor and using the completed papers the team discusses answers and formulates a reasoned answer to each question. During the discussion no reference may be made to the original manuscript. When the team has answered all questions both individual work and team-work are scored against a key provided by the tutor. The scores measure both individual and team performances.

If team interaction has been effective, the team score will normally be higher than any individual score. The key provides the correct answer together with the rationale behind the answer, so that the student is able to reinforce the learning objectives without re-statement by the tutor.

The last stage in the Team Effectiveness Design technique is the teamwork critique. A period of time is provided for team members to criticise their individual performances within the team and to analyse team effectiveness. The critique may take the form of a guided discussion with the tutor in the chair or the team may wish to undertake the analysis themselves.

Summary of technique

Stage 1   Students read manuscript and answer questionnaires
Stage 2   Students join teams and decide on answers to each question
Stage 3   Scoring of individual and team answers
Stage 4   Team-work critique

Team member teaching design

The basis of this instrument is that the student will learn a section of work and then teach other group members. As the teaching is performed by a peer group member nobody will feel out-of-place and 'in-depth' discussion of subject matter will occur. The whole procedure is controlled by students.

Group size controls the number of segments that will comprise the subject matter. One subject segment is allocated to each student for individual

Team effectiveness design

Advantages

Student responsible for learning (motivates)
Immediate feedback of results and achievements
Re-usable subject matter
Direction of learning can be controlled
Teams compete against a standard
Experiences of individual team members are beneficial to group
Teams could influence a disinterested member
Administrator needs to be a subject expert
Students learn to reject inappropriate material
Material can be set up at short notice
Large number of suitable subjects

Disadvantages

Construction of instruments is difficult, time-consuming and
   requires specialist knowledge
No use for acquiring skills, or for subjective material
Trainees must be literate and capable of participating in
   group interaction
Failure to complete pre-work reduces group effectiveness
Unco-operative attitude within teams inhibits learning (domin-
   ating, 'switching-off')
Material may require frequent updating which could be difficult
Could be used inappropriately because it is easy to administer
Requires accommodation for syndicate work
Needs careful time management

Uses

Useful for – 'levelling' (testing previous knowledge)
             – rules and regulations
             – legislation
             – product knowledge
             – business topics
             – facts and comprehension
             – codes of practice

(Source: Peter J M Finney)

preparation and at this stage students are told that their understanding of not only the individual material but also that presented by other team members will be tested.

After the team assembles, one student starts by teaching other members his segment. He does this without referring to original material. The rest of the team ask questions and take notes to aid learning.

Each student in turn presents a segment and after all segments have been delivered a test covering the whole subject matter is applied individually, followed by scoring.

At this point four different comparisons are possible:
total score by each individual;
average individual score for each team;
score each student made in his teaching segment;
a within-team comparison of how well each team member taught his segment of information.

The last step is the team-work critique in which the team gathers to discuss their performance. Within this framework it can be seen that the four different comparisons can be used to great effect in clarifying learning objectives.

Summary of technique

Stage 1 Individual preparation
Stage 2 Team-work
Stage 3 Testing and scoring
Stage 4 Team-work critique

Performance judging design

This instrument allows students to learn the criteria that apply to performing a particular skill. It requires the student to be able to produce a workpiece as evidence of his skill level. The workpiece can be compared with those produced by others and evaluated by the students themselves using their own criteria.

A two-page report on a given subject set by the tutor is an example of individual preparation where the students working alone produce some item of work. Teamwork now follows and the object of this is to develop relevant criteria for judging the particular work objective. This may be done in a number of ways. The team may be given 'expert' criteria and asked to discuss them to ensure full understanding or they may be asked to develop

Team member teaching design

Advantages

Promotes in-depth study of one "chunk"
Competitive element motivates team members
– individual effort essential
– requires commitment
Time element
– large amount of learning in short time
Easy to administer
Can aid confidence and social skills
Students control learning process (acts as 'subject matter expert')
Re-usable

Disadvantages

Depends on students identifying key points (no control of direction)
– reading skills of student crucial
– needs close monitoring
– student presentation skills crucial
Requires concentration and preparation
– time-consuming
Students concentrate on own 'chunk'
Causes stress
– undermines confidence
Subject must be capable of suitable segmentation
Need for full access to all information
Individual ability may not match subject suitability
Absence or poor preparation can jeopardise team results

Uses

Segmented topics of complex nature (extensive application):
  supervisory/management level
  codes of practice
  instructional skills
  technical subjects
  legislation
  products

(Source: Peter J M Finney)

Performance judging design

Advantages

Responsibilty placed on student for learning
Criteria can be set by students
General uplifting of standards
Students learn to exercise critical judgement
Students more receptive to 'in-team' criticism
Reinforces learning by rapid feed-back
Can be used for subjects which can be measured by an original
set of standards

Disadvantages

Uneven mix of students in team can lead to uneven rate of
learning
Possible rejection by colleagues
Criteria that is acceptable to group may not be so to individual
Relies on learning administrator being a subject matter expert
Criteria limited to students' level of knowledge—'blind leading
the blind'
Could induce negative teaching
No guarantee of correct feedback for students effort
Disruptive member can have a 'domino' effect on team or group
Complicated to administer
Limited application

Uses

Learning of any skill which has an effective criteria

Selected skill areas i.e.
– learning a new skill
– to improve and perfect existing skills
– selling techniques
– servicing a boiler
– installation of appliances

(Source: Peter J M Finney)

their own set of criteria together with rationale. In order that each team arrives at a similar set of criteria, one member of each team meets with representatives of other teams and thrash out a common set of criteria.

Judging performance comes next. Individual material is collected by the tutor and coded so that authorship is unknown to others. The material is then passed out to different teams. One group-member reads the report and the other members criticise it against their developed criteria. This procedure is repeated until all reports have been dealt with. A written critique is attached to each report and the reports returned to the tutor who then passes them on to their respective authors, as he alone knows the identification code. At this stage each author reads his report and its critique to the team. This enables the team to offer help, advice and suggestions to individual team members. Each student is then given another assignment which is different yet similar in nature to the first and is now able to put into practice his improved skill and knowledge in the particular subject area. As before, work is coded and distributed for critique. This cycle can be repeated until students reach any pre-determined level of ability.

Summary of technique

Stage 1   Individual preparation
Stage 2   Team-work
Stage 3   Performance judging
Stage 4   Critique
Stage 5   Second assignment
Stage 6   Repeat procedures

Problem-solving—task-centred

The main advantages of group problem-solving exercises are that they involve mutual participation, criticism and correction behaviour by group members. Members tend to express themselves more freely and take advantage of the fact that the group is leaderless and free of control by the instructor.

A group task such as the Anchor Food puzzle (see figure 8.9) is set, and the group is asked to form the five pieces of cardboard into a perfect square. Although the example given is an elementary problem, the method can be applied to more difficult examples, and such problems as determining the shortest route to be taken by a delivery van calling at several widely dispersed destinations, shoploading and the like, can be attempted.

FIG. 8.9   **5-piece puzzle**

(Reproduced by kind permission of Anchor Foods Ltd, Swindon).

The aim of the exercise is to study the behaviour pattern of a group when presented with a problem. A non-participating observer records his impressions of the process on a report form and when the problem has been solved, feeds back his observations to the group. Observers may be changed after each exercise and it has been found that the observer learns more about group behaviour by looking at the process than by actual participation in the problem-solving.

There are several types of report form available depending upon the particular aspect of behaviour being studied. One relates to recording the number of times each member of the group speaks; another records the type of statement made by each person. These statements are usually classified as being related either to the task itself or to group cohesion. Other factors which may be recorded include interpersonal communication skills, communication patterns, major roles and leadership styles.

A comprehensive study of group behaviour during a problem-solving session or discussion can be made by completing a 'Bale's interaction process analysis chart' (see figure 4.1). An observer scores each occurrence of the twelve categories of interactions on the chart and, when completed, it gives an overall picture of the behaviour witnessed during the group discussion. As it is near impossible for a single person to score the whole group, only one person at a time should be reported on unless several observers are employed. The chart should be discussed by the group on completion of the problem.

PROBLEMS TO SOLVE

1. THE TARTAGLIA

Three missionaries and three cannibals are on the north side of a river. Transport them across to the south side by means of a boat which holds only two at one time. All the missionaries and only one cannibal can row. Never, under any circumstances or at any time, may the missionaries be outnumbered by the cannibals.

2. THE SUN—MINDBENDER

Arrange eight counters on a draughts board so that no two are in the same line—across, down or diagonally.

3. DAILY MIRROR—MIRRORGRAMS

Rearrange the letters below to make the name of a Shakespearean play:
SORRY I'VE FEW WORDS IN THEM

Rearrange the letters below to make the name of a sportsman:
A CANOE IS BEST

8.2   Microcomputing

The following article by P. Yeandle† outlines the ways in which microcomputers can change modern teaching methods:

'Within education there is a great scope for using the microcomputer to improve our students' learning capacity since the new technology affords new approaches.

†Paul Yeandle, *Micro*, No. 2 (Bournemouth & Poole College of Further Education, March 1982).

Between 1973 and 1977, the National Development Programme investigated CAL (Computer Assisted Learning) over a variety of subject areas but emphasised the need to "institutionalise". By that they were implying the need to build-in computer use into the framework of the learning process rather than use computers as a novelty once the work had been covered by traditional methods.

In particular, this was taken up by the Schools' Council in conjunction with Chelsea College. Now there are packages available in a number of subject areas including Biology, Chemistry, Economics, Geography and Physics. With the set of programs come teaching notes as well as student work and investigation sheets. The computer is used not only as a teaching aid but also as an experimental tool.

Computer Assisted Teaching (CAT) is essentially the use of the computer as a demonstration device similar to the way the teacher uses other visual aids, but with more sophistication.

We need not make too much of the distinction between CAT and CAL. Both approaches are designed to improve student learning and both to be fully effective must be incorporated within teaching strategies, and not used merely as a supplement to existing method.

Some programs available could be used either in or out of class without the teacher necessarily being present whilst others are designed to demonstrate more effectively than traditional methods, to the whole class.

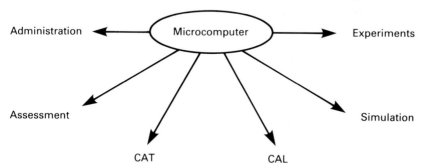

There are many ways in which a microcomputer can assist in improving the learning achievement of a student and assist the teacher. Some of these benefits are considered below.

1. SIMULATION

With a screen capable of displaying intricate dynamic diagrams and pictures, the microcomputer can simulate an experiment (as defined in its widest sense) or the workings of a mathematical model which no other device has adquately done before. Although there is no complete substitute for the 'real thing', some experiments are difficult, indeed impossible to carry out. The computer can overcome many of these difficulties by simulation.

Danger—Where dangerous substances, e.g. radioactive materials, are in use, any experiment is limited to weak and ineffective sources. Use the computer to display dynamically, more elaborate experiments and supply results for the students to analyse.

Cost—Test an economic model of a firm or country, even to the extremes of bankruptcy.

Scale—Investigate the universe on one hand or atomic particles on the other.

Difficulty—The computer can demonstrate effects experienced under water, in the tropics or in arctic conditions while seated in the classrooms.

Time—Using a computer, simulate in an hour, a year's trading in a business game. Equally we can, repeat the rather tedious Millikan experiment 50 times or harmonise a tune in four parts in several different ways under different restrictions.

Thus the student can perform the traditional lab experiments and then take this a step further with the use of the microcomputer.

2. EXPERIMENTS

The laborious chores of having to perform many repetitive calculations can cloud the real point of an experiment. How much more convenient for the student to work out just one calculation, check it using the computer program which then processes all other calculations. The programme could even guide the student through the various steps of each calculation.

Early microcomputers were not easy to use as controllers of other equipment but more recent versions including PETs are more flexible. Programmed control of an experiment provides a new approach to demonstration in the laboratory.

3. CAL AND CAT

Parts of many courses are more readily suited to the student working at his own pace rather than at a class average speed which encourages the brighter students to ease up and the less bright to give up. In an ideal world the student would receive individual attention.

This is partly possible with the microcomputer provided the student receives the necessary human interaction at appropriate times.

CAL programs need to be of the very highest quality. They must be "user friendly" at all times, interactive in asking for a student to respond in simple terms to questions after covering new material and sophisticated enough to anticipate a wide variety of replies whether right or wrong.

CAT programs require the teacher to build the use of microcomputers into his teaching scheme. After an introduction to a topic would follow experiments or investigations where appropriate and then the use of the microcomputer to extend and reinforce points already made. Conclusion and assessment would follow.

The follow-up is necessary because for some students, particularly in the early days, the fascination of using the computer can detract from the object of the exercise.

CAL and CAT programs available in a central resource such as the computer centre or library can provide for revision in a topic, self assessment, catching up on missed work and a useful method of remedial teaching.

4. ASSESSMENT

The use of multiple-choice questions has been queried as to their validity but as a form of instant assessment, is very convenient once a bank of suitable questions have been formed.

How easy it would be to use the microcomputer to perform this task especially when one program could select randomly from different question sets and provide an assessment at the end.

The ability to assess subjectively would be more difficult.

5. ADMINISTRATIVE TASKS

Probably the teacher's greatest burden is the administrative work associated with structured courses. Where several staff are concerned with a specific area of work it would be a great asset to have a computer perform many of the tedious tasks automatically.

It only requires the staff to pool their efforts in defining and initiating a computer solution and thereafter record keeping can become a minor problem.

BTEC is a prime area of attack.

Some departments of a college have a need for record keeping such as product details or information sources. These can be kept on microcomputer files but consider the task you are undertaking before embarking along these lines. A manual system may still be more efficient and less time consuming.

CONCLUSION

The opportunity is here for the teacher to enhance his teaching ability.

However, before using a computer, the teacher should consider carefully whether the use will provide a better method than that given by traditional methods. If one merely replaces the other without increased effectiveness, the gimmick of using a computer will rapidly wear off and the teacher will regret the excess work he has created for himself.'

8.3   Microtraining

The aim of microtraining is to help inexperienced instructors and teachers acquire and develop basic training skills. Microtraining incorporates such _lements as lesson-planning, verbal exposition (lecturing or addressing the group), questioning and discussing. It encourages the participants to be self-critical. The technique promotes the learning of social skills involved in controlling and motivating groups, and heightens perception. It also serves to validate new approaches to the teaching of a subject.

The trainee teacher prepares a short lesson or the opening of a lesson and delivers it to a small group. The lesson, usually devoted to a particular skill, lasts up to fifteen minutes. The whole group is video-taped while the lesson is in progress. After the lesson, the tape is played back to the group. The group discusses the presentation and suggests improvements. The trainee teacher then repeats the lesson with another group incorporating the improvements agreed.

8.4   Preparing and presenting a short instruction

Microtraining enables the instructor to plan and deliver a short piece of instruction before launching into longer sessions. The instructor is able to receive early feedback on his performance and valuable guidance from experienced tutors. Each session of micro-training should deal with only one aspect of teaching such as introducing a topic, explaining a single aspect, organising a short question and answer session, giving directions, using aids or gaining the attention of the other trainees.

Microtraining may be rated using one of the following rating schedules.

A programme of teaching skills entitled *Microteaching* by George Brown is published by Methuen and Company Ltd of London.

FIG. 8.10   **Rating a lecture**

Allocate marks to each section using the following rating scale:

Poor	*Fair*	*Good*	*Very Good*	*Excellent*
1	2	3	4	5

1. **Presentation**
   1.1   Was the introduction satisfactory?
   1.2   Were the key points presented in logical sequence?
   1.3   Were the explanation and development clear?
   1.4   Conclusion: key points restated, content summarised, action recommended. Plug line?

2. **Information**
   2.1   Was the content related to subject of talk?
   2.2   Was the terminology clearly understood?
   2.3   Was the information easily assimilated?
   2.4   Were the facts and figures supported by evidence?

3. **Interest**
   3.1   Did the speaker hold your attention?
   3.2   Did the speaker relate facts to audience's experience?
   3.3   Were the appropriate visual aids used?
   3.4   Was there an opportunity to ask questions?
         If so, how were they answered?

4. **Delivery**
   4.1   Was the speaker relaxed?
   4.2   Was his manner warm and friendly?
   4.3   Did the speaker's eyes roam over the whole group?
   4.4   Did the speaker have any irritating mannerisms?

5. **Speech and language**
   5.1   Was verbal exposition clear?
   5.2   Was the appropriate language code used?
   5.3   Were the important points stressed or emphasised?
   5.4   Were the concepts introduced explained in simple language?

Rating % = Total mark×4

FIG. 8.11

Factor	Poor						Excellent
	1	2	3	4	5	6	7
Clarity of objectives							
Appropriateness of objectives							
Organisation of lesson							
Selection of content							
Selection of materials							
Beginning of lesson							
Clarity of presentation							
Pacing of lesson							
Group participation and attention							
Ending of lesson							

Adapted from: 'Stanford Teacher Competence Appraisal Guide'.

SUMMARY

- Job instruction training techniques were developed during World War II.

- The traditional method of job instructional training involves seven stages.

- The analytical method is based upon a skills analysis for the job concerned.

- A skills analysis is carried out in order to separate job factors into their component parts.

- Frank Bunker Gilbreth produced a list of 'therbligs' (see BS 3138:1969). Therbligs represent movements.

- In programmed instruction, subject-matter is presented in small interrelated steps, each graded in difficulty. The method ensures a high probability of successful learning.

- The lecture is autocratic in form and allows little or no active audience participation. A lecture can reach a large audience.

- A demonstration is a practical display or exhibition of a process. It is used to show fundamental principles or actions.

- Project work enables cognitive, affective and psychomotor skills to be developed. The method allows for the integration of several previously mastered individual skills.

- Algorithms are excellent aids to problem-solving.

- Fault-finding requires a log of faults and their associated symptoms to be compiled. The appropriate action to be taken to remedy the fault can then be added, and the information gathered can then be displayed.

- Group problem-solving involves mutual participation, criticism and correction behaviour by group members.

- The behaviour pattern of a group engaged in problem-solving may be studied and recorded on a Bale's interaction process analysis chart.

QUESTIONS

1. What should a teacher do:
   (a) to prevent his class becoming too noisy?
   (b) if the class becomes noisy?

2. Defining specific objectives before instruction is given prohibits invalid learning experiences even though exploration of these could well increase the overall store of knowledge obtained by the trainee. Should this exploration be allowed?

3. Is there one best sequence of instruction for all trainees as laid down in many linear programmed learning packages? If not, should the scheme be flexible, in order to take account of the many different approaches to learning and to allow trainees to use their own initiative?

4. What steps should be taken when planning a lecture in order to maintain the audience's attention? When would you use a lecture in preference to other methods?

5. Write a realistic case study relating to problems arising as a result of the need to retrain one or more workers. The text should include material which enables the group to examine, analyse and diagnose the

problems. The case study should then be discussed by small syndicates who later report to the whole group.

6. Prepare and give a demonstration involving the use of an apparatus. Explain how you would incorporate a demonstration in the teaching of a psychomotor skill.

7. A lampholder fitted with a 240 volt 100 watt lamp is connected by insulated cable to a 13 amp fused plug. The lamp does not light up when switched on at the wall socket to which it is connectd. Design an algorithm to solve the problem.

8. Initially, the role of a tutor in microtraining is to help the trainee instructor to improve his teaching. How should the tutor set about this task?

9. Rate a microtraining session using each of the rating sheets given in section 8.3.

10. 'Trainees learn something from hearing instructors talk, more from talking themselves, most of all from what they actually do.' Explain this statement.

Part 3

Audio-visual Aids

9

The purpose and use of aids

Stand in front of a group holding a picture of something they have neither seen nor heard of. Try to describe the picture in words without displaying it. Ask the group to name the 'something'. There is a high probability that you will receive a wide variety of suggestions.

It is difficult to convey new ideas and unfamiliar information by words alone. We hear words but often have little or no understanding of the ideas and concepts behind them. For words to have meaning they must be related either to personal experiences or to known 'concrete' objects.

We meet with aids in everyday life. Travelling in an Underground carriage we look up at diagrams showing lines and stations. In the car we observe road signs giving warnings and directions. At railway stations or in airport lounges we observe visual displays showing departures or we listen to announcements. These types of aid form 'one-way' communications and like a good many educational aids such as films, television and radio, give the observer little chance of stopping the presentation to ask questions or to clarify difficulties he may be experiencing. 'Two-way' communication is ruled out with any form of mass media.

To be successful in the classroom, aids must supplement the teacher's work and should be flexible in their application. The learning resources centre may well be jammed full of the latest multi-media teaching aids, but this will be of little use to a teacher who lacks the know-how that they require or who does not have the time to set them up in the instructional situation. Before using any aid the teacher must be fully conversant with its operation and application. He must also rehearse his presentation before confronting the class.

Aids serve to open up more channels for the communication of information and create a variety of sensory impressions. When using aids the teacher does not have to rely solely upon his talking and the students listening for the transmission of knowledge. Aids enhance the process of perception and retention and consequently improve the efficiency of learning.

Boredom is an enemy that the teacher is constantly fighting. It is extremely difficult to maintain attention for periods of longer than about fifteen minutes without involving the student in active participation. Aids serve to brighten up a presentation and help to maintain attention, while in many cases they substitute for the real thing, which may be unavailable or too large to bring into the classroom.

While the experiences of handling the actual object, participating in a process or observing a factory in operation involve the use of all senses and provide the best aid to learning, well-thought-out aids can act as effective substitutes.

The value of aids

A good aid helps to overcome the limitations of word-only communication. It should appeal to as many senses as possible at one time (see figure 9.1). Some of the advantages of using aids are listed below, while advantages and disadvantages are compared in figure 9.3.

Aids:
form a focal point and attract attention;
arouse interest;
invoke co-operation;
challenge within the limits of a learner's ability;
supplement description and help to explain words;
give an accurate impression of the concept;
illustrate relationships;
promote retention and memory;
stimulate imagination;
consolidate what has been learned;
save teaching time.

The overall function of an aid is to supplement the teacher's exposition and to help him overcome the limits of verbal communication. The aid should provide a shared experience which cannot be conveyed vividly and realistically purely by word of mouth.

Generally, the use of aids goes some way to providing a stimulating classroom environment, promoting a desire to learn and enlivening teaching.

Use the right aid, at the right time, in the right place, in the right manner.

FIG. 9.1   **Summary of senses used relative to aid employed**

Aid	Senses used		
	Eyes	Ears	All
Actual equipment			★
Chalkboard	★		
Blanket board	★		
Books	★		
CCTV & video	★	★	
Drops and charts	★		
Epidiascope	★		
Films	★	★	
Film strip	★		
Magnetic board	★		
Models			★
Overhead projector	★		
Radio broadcasts		★	
Slide/tape programmes	★	★	
Tape recordings		★	
TV broadcasts	★	★	

9.1 The function of an audio-visual message

Boredom results from lack of involvement. Audio-visual aids relieve boredom and mental fatigue by providing a focal point for attention. Movement against a background of sound brings the subject-matter to life and involves the use of two senses. In general, the more senses involved in a learning situation, the better the learning outcome and ability to recall. If we rely only upon what we hear we shall not achieve much, as only about twenty-five per cent will be remembered after forty-eight hours has elapsed. If, however, visual presentations are backed up by sound, followed by discussion and some kind of practice, we shall be able to recall a good deal more.

In about 1907 an advertisement for Sloan's Backache and Kidney Oils used the caption, 'Every picture tells a story.' The picture was designed to sell the product. Similarly, the words 'kills pain' on liniment packaging were very effective, and a business report of the time indicated that 'the concern is recorded as one of the largest of its kind and goods are sold extensively throughout the country' (USA). In both cases the visual imagery conveyed the manufacturer's message with some impact.

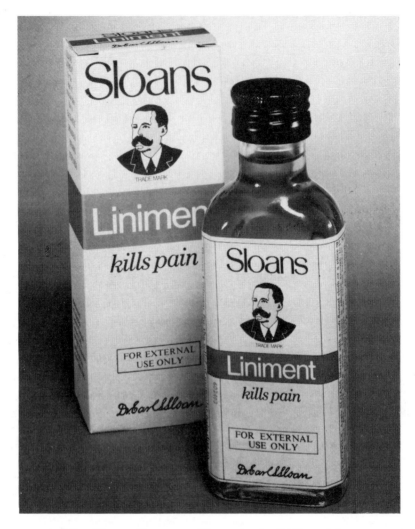

FIG. 9.2   **Sloans linament. Note words, 'kills pain'.**

(Reproduced by kind permission of Warner-Lambert (UK) Ltd, from a photograph
supplied by Christine Warwick, Product Publicity Manager)

The purpose of audio-visual aids is to introduce stimuli materials in a way
which increases the impact of information being passed to the listener. The
aid serves to transmit, amplify and distribute the message in a manner which
is more effective than straight-forward lecturing or reading.

Today, a great deal of effort is being devoted to curriculum development and to devising ways and means of improving the presentation of information. The role of audio-visual aids as a supplement to chalkboard, textbook and teacher's talk is growing in importance, and ready-made aids are freely available.

There is a tendency for some to adopt the role of innovator and to use aids simply because they are on the shelf. Before using an aid, the following basic question should be asked: 'Does the learning objective call for a visual aid, and if so, does the available aid meet the objective?' In any event, use of the aid should be validated and its impact evaluated.

9.2 Identifying the behavioural objective which might apply to the use of given aids

The function of an audio-visual message is to provoke some form of response in those who are exposed to it. The particular response resulting from exposure to the aid should conform to the behaviour expected as an outcome of the set learning objective. As previously discussed in section 7.9, the lesson plan should have been written and aids prepared in advance, so that teaching materials and sequences are arranged to give the best possible framework in which effective learning may take place.

The aid should therefore be chosen for its function and for its predicted effect on the audience. Slow-motion film may be employed to demonstrate movement of machine parts, workshop operations, sporting activities or the chip being torn away from parent metal during a cutting operation. Slides or transparencies are very effective for a multiplicity of activities. X-ray films of welded joints may be projected. Music or languages can be recorded and played back on tape. Engine construction can be shown by cut-away models or sectionalised engines, while 'mobiles' can be manufactured from card and projected by OHP.

Any or all of the aids may be used to attract and maintain attention, to illustrate relationships, to explain the meaning of words or concepts, to invite challenge or to consolidate what the instructor has said.

9.3 Aids available

Pictorial aids

Visual aids should be large enough to be seen by everyone present and should display the minimum amount of detail required to be effective.

FIG. 9.3   **Advantages and disadvantages of audio-visual aids**

Advantages
Larger groups may be involved.

Cost per person is relatively low for large groups.

Demonstration time is reduced.

Chalkboard work is reduced.

Form and content of lesson is varied.

Information is more readily disseminated.

Replay can be immediate.

Management of resource material is straightforward.

Facilitate perception, transfer of training, reinforcement and retention.
Aids are cheaper than field trips.

Eliminate safety hazards relating to actual equipment.

Avoid need for actual equipment.

Enable instructor to preview and rehearse lesson in advance.

Are better prepared and presented than much classroom teaching.

Disadvantages
Initial cost may be high.

Some programmes prohibit interaction between trainee and instructor.

Speed of introduction of facts may be too fast for easy assimilation.

Too much detail confuses the trainee.

May be used to entertain rather than purely as an instructional aid.

PHOTOGRAPHS

The main value of using photographs lies in the fact that they are a true record of something and will be accepted as such by the viewers. Photographs should be presented individually for perusal in order to avoid the tendency for viewers to divert attention to others. Many photographs carry too many details, which tend to mask the essentials, and wherever possible, complementary diagrams should be provided. Photographs of 'before' and 'after' situations and those taken at frequent stages during a project or experiment are valuable aids to recall.

PICTURES

Black and white pictures are often reproduced on handouts and summary sheets. The photocopier can be used to reproduce pictures on OHP transparencies and significant parts highlighted with colour before projection (see figures 9.4, 9.5 and 9.6). Important details may be enlarged and reproduced inside a balloon (see figure 9.4).

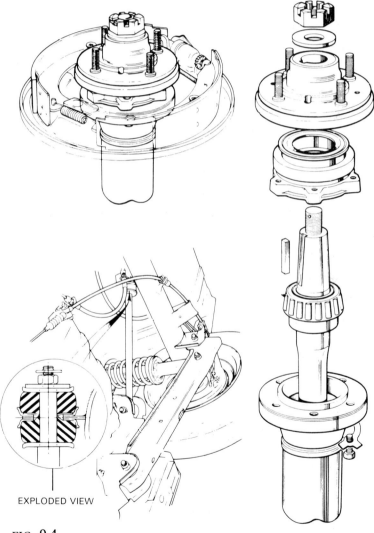

EXPLODED VIEW

FIG. 9.4

(Source: *Dolomite Sprint Repair Operation Manual.* British Leyland Cars Ltd)

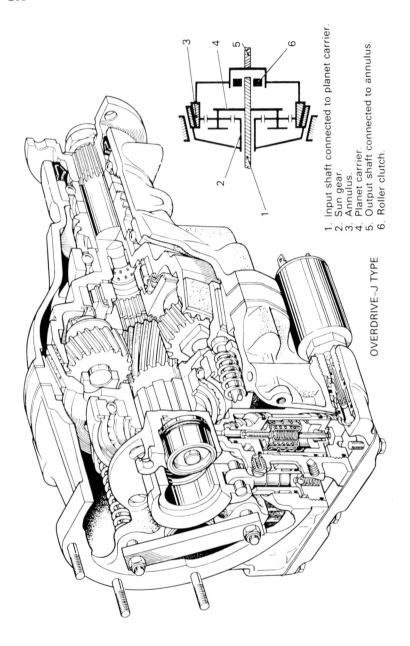

1. Input shaft connected to planet carrier.
2. Sun gear.
3. Annulus.
4. Planet carrier.
5. Output shaft connected to annulus.
6. Roller clutch.

OVERDRIVE–J TYPE

FIG. 9.5
(Source: *Dolomite Sprint Repair Operation Manual.* British Leyland Cars Ltd)

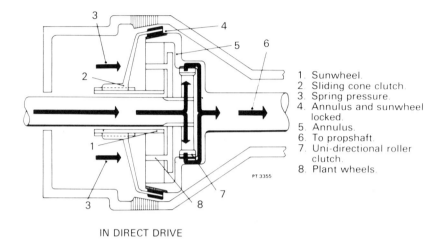

1. Sunwheel.
2. Sliding cone clutch.
3. Spring pressure.
4. Annulus and sunwheel locked.
5. Annulus.
6. To propshaft.
7. Uni-directional roller clutch.
8. Plant wheels.

IN DIRECT DRIVE

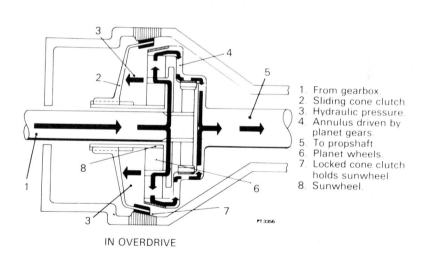

1. From gearbox.
2. Sliding cone clutch.
3. Hydraulic pressure.
4. Annulus driven by planet gears.
5. To propshaft.
6. Planet wheels.
7. Locked cone clutch holds sunwheel.
8. Sunwheel.

IN OVERDRIVE

FIG. 9.6
(Source: *Dolomite Sprint Repair Operation Manual*. British Leyland Cars Ltd)

Descriptive pictures contain facts and information and are intended to give meaning to unfamiliar words. Action pictures contain people doing things or machines working and are used to encourage thought and enquiry. Emotive pictures appeal to the emotions and are used where people are required to discuss their feelings about the subject of the picture.

DIAGRAMS

Line diagrams illustrate essentials without clouding the presentation with excessive detail. Block diagrams may be used to represent mechanisms or processes schematically rather than the actual object (see pages 119-21). Line diagrams are frequently used to illustrate principles.

TABLES AND CHARTS

Tables and charts give information and are used to represent ideas, statistics and trends. Each aid should have a clear title picked out in bold type and all data should be enclosed in a box.

GRAPHS

Graphs are used to illustrate experimental data, mathematical and trigono-metrical functions, statistical information and trends. When graphs of multiple functions are required, different types of lines or different colours should be used to represent each function. Graphs serve to support words and to create interest. Trends may be identified, statistics interpreted and functions related using graphical aids.

CARTOONS

Political cartoons are provocative and form an ideal backcloth against which current affairs may be discussed. Cartoons are symbolic and require a background of knowledge for interpretation; they are excellent aids to the teaching of supervisory management subjects.

CHARTS

Bar charts, histograms, pie charts, flow and organisational charts are commonly used to represent proportions or relationships. The visual impact of charts brings figures to life and tends to be more meaningful than a list of numbers or percentages. Suppose that in a certain factory the number of staff employed on various jobs is given in table opposite.

The information can be represented by either of the diagrams shown in figures 9.7, 9.8, 9.9 and 9.10.

Type of personnel	No. employed	Percentage
Machinists	140	35
Fitters	120	30
Clerical staff	80	20
Labourers	40	10
Draughtsmen	20	5
Total	400	100

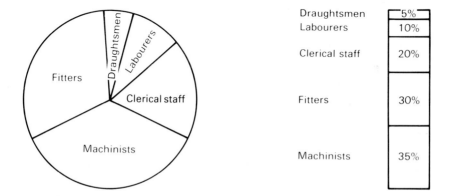

FIG. 9.7 **The pie chart** FIG. 9.8 **100% bar chart**

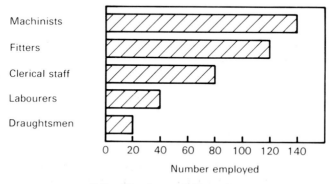

FIG. 9.9 **Horizontal bar chart**

(Source figs. 9.7–9.10 BTEC First-Mathematics for Technicians by A Greer and G W Taylor. Stanley Thornes (Publishers) Ltd, Cheltenham)

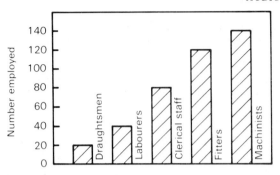

FIG. 9.10   **Vertical Bar Chart**

FLIP CHARTS

Large sheets of newsprint or cartridge paper are assembled in a pad and hung from an easel. Lesson content or key information is written on the sheets, either before the lesson or as the lesson proceeds. When each sheet has served its purpose it may be flipped over the top of the easel revealing the next blank sheet or prepared set of notes. Faint pencil lines may be used to outline diagrams, tables and notes, which are thickened in using felt pens or crayons as the lesson develops.

WALL CHARTS

These are large charts often supplied free by industrial concerns. Many wall charts contain too much information to be readily assimilated in one go. Wording and other detail is relatively small and therefore unsatisfactory for displaying as an aid during the lesson. The content often summarises a specific topic and the chart is best used as a reinforcer. The chart should be displayed in a workroom, laboratory or well-lit passage where it can be seen, but where it will not distract and interfere with the teaching of other subject-matter.

Boards

CHALKBOARDS

Chalkboard work should be kept legible and coloured chalks used for easy differentiation. The upper part of the board should be used wherever possible, and when writing on the board, talk to the group—not the board. Prepare the outline of complex drawings in advance. Faint lines should be drawn in pencil or chalk which may be seen by the instructor, but not by the students. Build up diagrams or mathematical solutions step by step, in logical sequence. Technical words, key words and definitions should be highlighted using coloured chalks. Summaries should be developed as the lesson progresses, and may later be used to recap and reinforce lesson content. Rub off non-essential notes, worked examples and unwanted material as soon as the students have finished taking it down.

FLANNELBOARD

A board which is covered with felt or beize. Aids to be displayed are fixed to the board by attaching coarse sandpaper to the back of each cardboard figure. The board is used to display a series of events, sets of items, hairstyles, development of fashions, key headings which form a summary, and so on. Sections through engine assemblies may be built up using different coloured material.

WHITEBOARD

A smooth white plastic finish is applied to the board. Water-based felt tip pens are used to write on the board and the writing may be erased using a damp cloth. Spirit-based pens may be used where permanent lines or layout is required. Banda fluid often removes writing produced by spirit-based pens. The board may also be used as a projection screen for overhead projectors.

MAGNETIC BOARDS

A steel sheet often painted white, green or black, to which magnets will be attracted. Cardboard cut-outs or other aids have small magnets stuck to the reverse side. The magnet must be strong enough to support the weight of the aid. Several thicknesses of card may be applied to the board when building up mechanisms, but the card used for such applications should be thinner than normal, as the magnetic attraction becomes weakened and there is a risk of the cards falling off during the demonstration. Aids are easily moved about the board and can be added or removed at will.

An example of the use of such aids is where alignment testing is to be demonstrated in the classroom before going to the workshop for practicals (see figures 9.11-9.14). Using cardboard cut-outs of a hollow spindle, centres, mandrels, dial test indicators, a machine table, reflectors, collimator and directional arrows, a large number of tests can be demonstrated on the magnetic board. Figures 9.18-24 illustrate this.

PEGBOARD

Holes are drilled in a board. Pegs or clips are attached to models, cut-outs, diagrams or actual objects which may be readily plugged into the board

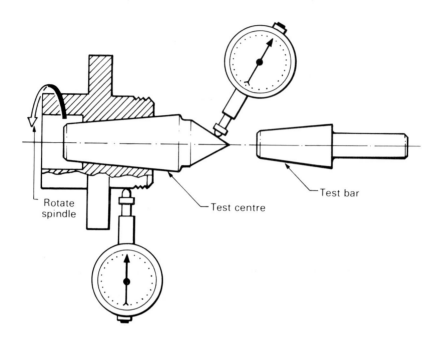

FIG. 9.11 **Alignment testing (A)**

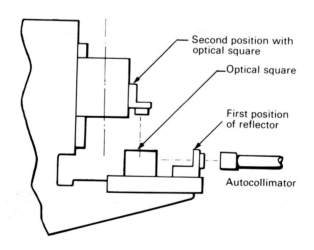

FIG. 9.12 **Alignment testing (B)**

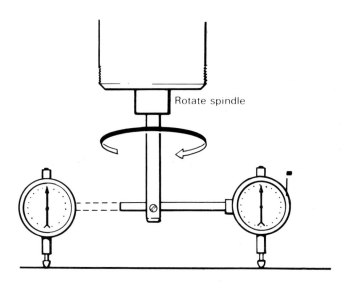

FIG. 9.13 **Alignment testing (C)**

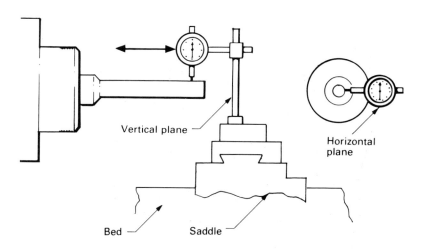

FIG. 9.14 **Alignment testing (D)**

(Source: *T4 Workshop Technology*, by R T Pritchard, reproduced by kind permission of Hodder & Stoughton Educational London)

during the lesson. An example of the use of the aid would be the building up of electrical circuits using actual components.

Projected aids

SLIDES

A remote control 'carousel' type projector or alternatively a back projector may be used to project 35 mm slides (see figure 9.15). Slide/tape programmes may be used in which the tape is electronically pulsed so that slide changes occur at the right place during a tape-recorded commentary. Some back projectors come complete with a tape recorder unit so that the slide/tape package may be used directly. Failing this, a cassette-type recorder fitted with a synchroniser may be linked to a 'carousel' projector.

Slides may be used to stimulate interest, to provide background for a new subject, to summarise the lesson and to present quizzes on the subject-matter. Another important use is the introduction of case studies in the field of human relations, safety and supervisory management.

FILMSTRIP PROJECTORS

These projectors allow for frame by frame projection of a film strip. They are usually manually operated, the instructor winding the film off one reel and on to another, pausing for discussion or explanation at each frame. Commercially produced filmstrips are normally supplied with a set of teaching notes.

LOOP PROJECTORS

Used mainly for presenting facts, teaching skills, forming concepts and presenting problems. A continuous loop of 8 mm film is wound into a cassette. The film is back-projected on to the screen of the projector. The loop may be stopped at any frame for discussion without the risk of burning the film which would occur on most 16 mm conventional projectors. As the loop is continuous, the film may be repeated as many times as is deemed necessary.

EPIDIASCOPE

A useful piece of equipment which is, however, bulky and expensive. It is used to project actual objects, illustrations, pages from books, diagrams, pictures and slides on to a screen in a darkened room. Although it is not in common usage today, it is extremely useful for producing enlargements.

Diagrams or drawings may be projected on to a screen or large sheet of white paper, and the outline traced so that wall charts, posters and other aids may be produced very quickly by relatively inexperienced artists.

It can train a roomful

It can instruct individuals

BELL & HOWELL

It can sell to a few

It always attracts attention

FIG. 9.15

OVERHEAD PROJECTOR

This is an invaluable piece of equipment. It is portable and runs off the mains. Diagrams or written work are prepared on acetate sheet which is then placed upon the glass screen of the projector. Using a bright lamp and a lens system, the image is projected on to a large screen. Perspex mobiles, components and actual specimens may also be projected, while most projectors are fitted with rolls of acetate sheet which may be written upon using felt-tipped pens. After exposure, the sheet may be wound across the glass plate on to a 'take up' roll, thereby exposing a fresh surface.

The whole lesson may be prepared in advance using a permanent marker. The roll is clipped into position and each element projected in sequence simply by winding on to the other roll. The projector should not be moved while switched on. Jarring when the lamp is hot will most probably cause the lamp to fail. Allow to cool down completely before moving.

Audio aids

RECORD PLAYER

Portable players may be used in areas of study such as language training, music, dance and drama. Care should be taken to keep records clean and free of finger marks, chalk dust and scratches. The stylus should be checked at regular intervals.

CASSETTE RECORDERS

Many portable cassette recorders run off either mains or batteries, and utilise tapes of 60, 90 or 120 minute duration. The tapes on which the recording is made consist of acetate, or plastic ribbon coated with magnetic iron oxide. The tape is wound onto a splined reel, with one end connected to a take-up reel. The whole is enclosed in a plastic cassette. With the tape running, recordings may be made using either a built-in microphone or one with a trailing lead; alternatively, wires may be connected to a television set, radio or record player so that the programme is transferred automatically to the tape. The tape may be stopped at any point to allow the instructor to ask questions or emphasise a point. It may also be rewound or advanced by using the appropriate control. Tapes may be used to record lessons and language training sessions, to dramatise incidents or for role-play exercises and case study work. Tapes may be circulated to vast audiences as is done by the Open University so that key learning material may be studied at home.

Tape recordings may be edited by cutting and splicing as required, and may be pulsed and linked to slide projectors so that slide changes occur automatically at the desired point in a commentary. Being relatively small and uniform in size, the tapes are easily catalogued and stored.

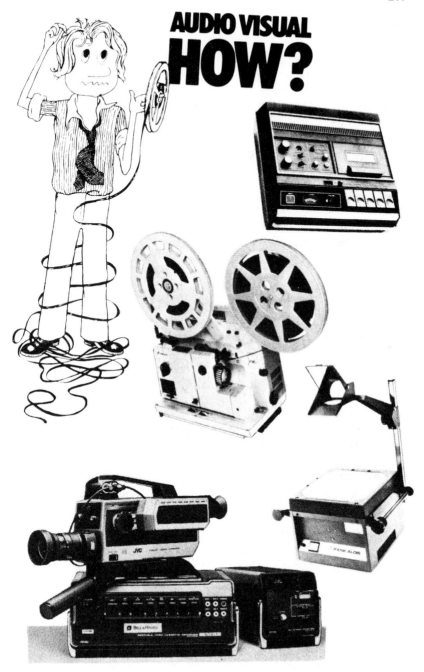

FIG. 9.16

Audio-visual aids

FILMS

16 mm films are available from a number of central agencies and may be purchased or hired as required. Many films are supplied free of hiring charges.

Films present factual information, dramatise events, show processes and illustrate job skills in a very effective manner, thereby motivating learning.

Films should be previewed by the instructor and key points noted. A questionnaire can then be produced and used after the showing to check the effectiveness of the film. The questionnaire acts as a reinforcer. Before showing a film, the instructor should point out to the group what to look for, without going into a full description of the film. Too much detail revealed before showing would have an adverse effect on the viewers' ability to maintain interest.

CLOSED-CIRCUIT TELEVISION (CCTV)

This is a dynamic demonstration technique which uses a CCTV camera and one or more monitors. It may be used in conjunction with a videotape recorder (VTR) to produce a recording of a demonstration while the programme is viewed simultaneously by a large number of people in different rooms. Linking workshop to rooms by coaxial cable is an asset when safety considerations or overcrowding must be allowed for.

Videotapes covering a wide range of subject-matter are produced and marketed by specialist companies and although the cost is relatively high, the tapes are invaluable in the field of skills/operator training.

The videotape recorder is extremely useful in the area of supervisory management training and communications within industry, as it enables participants in role-play exercises to play back the tape and criticise their performances. When the trainee applies it to skills training, he can replay the tape with his instructor, identify his weaknesses and discuss remedies.

Tapes can be wiped clean and re-used many times.

9.4   Preparing transparencies, magnetic aids and slide/tape programmes

As with any piece of information you wish to communicate, planning is essential. Planning should include both design and reasons for using the transparency.

A good visual should be bold, simple and concise. It should be immediately recognisable and should challenge the audience. Visual symbols, lines, shapes and areas of colour should be laid out to use the transparency area effectively.

Colour contrasts such as red and green can be used to give greater impact while some colours have psychological effects, in that they appear to move forward or recede into the screen.

Overlays, revelations and animations should be planned and should be easy to operate. Fumbling can ruin a presentation.

The drawings given on page 282 were designed to illustrate four important factors relating to the subject of 'Ergonomics't namely: heat, noise, light and position. Transparencies are produced from original drawings using a photocopier. The transparency showing a workman is securely taped to an 8″ × 10″ cardboard mount. The other four, to be used as overlays, are numbered and hinged on adhesive tape along the edges of the cutout. By flipping over one overlay at a time each of the four factors represented on the transparencies may be projected.

It is always a good idea to try and evaluate your transparencies when you use them. Try to judge their effect and if you need to re-use them for subsequent presentations, look at them critically to see if you need to modify them before you use them again.

Materials and advice relating to the overhead projector are available from Staedtler UK Ltd, who also run OHP Workshops.

Detailed information on the preparation of transparencies is given in Appendix 9.

Preparing magnetic aids

Many good textbooks and manufacturers' instruction manuals provide sketches illustrating machine construction and principles of operation. These may be used as models from which aids may be developed for classroom instruction. Permission to reproduce illustrations should first be obtained from the publishers concerned, in order to avoid infringing copyright.

†Ergonomics—the scientific study of the relationship between man and his working environment involving the disciplines of applied psychology, functional anatomy and applied physiology.

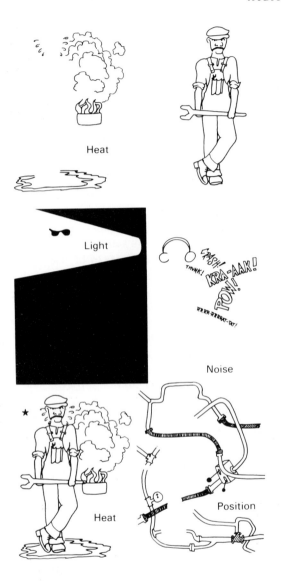

Artist: Brian Snape
Reproduced by kind permission of R Bailey BSc, PhD, Principal, Bournemouth and
Poole College of Further Education.

Please note:
The figure marked thus: * shows the workman with the overlay in position depicting the
effects of heat.

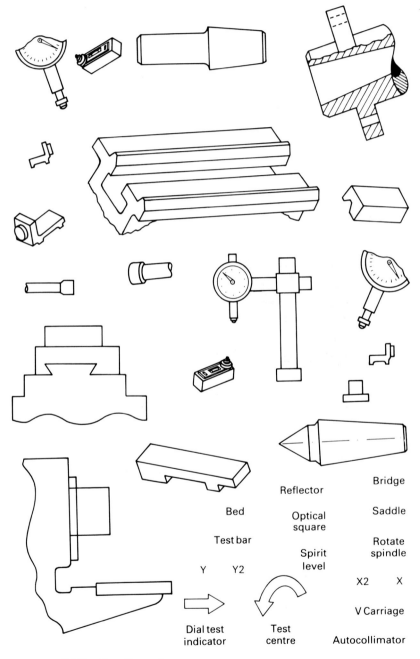

Reflector

Bridge

Bed

Optical
square

Saddle

Test bar

Rotate
spindle

Spirit
level

Y   Y2

X2   X

V Carriage

Dial test
indicator

Test
centre

Autocollimator

FIG. 9.17 **Cardboard cut-outs**

Magnetic aids are very useful in showing how machines are built up and how they work. Before entering the laboratory or workshop, various experiments and tests can be demonstrated using the magnetic board. This saves a great deal of the instructor's time in the laboratory because he can address the whole group and explain what has to be done while in the classroom. On arrival in the laboratory, students are able to get on with the actual experiments without waiting in small groups for instructions or explanations.

Having selected the diagram from which the aid will be developed, identify the number of cut-outs required and the form of each.

The aid must be large enough to be seen by every member of the group; therefore the diagram will need to be magnified. Decide on the magnification factor. Scale each component from the diagram and multiply each dimension by the magnification factor.

Using white paper, draw each component to the magnified dimensions. Cut out each shape and stick to coloured card.

Cut out cardboard components and glue magnets to the back of each.

Assemble on the magnetic board in correct sequence.

Practise several times and if necessary mark each card with the correct sequence of application.

The diagrams in figures 9.18-24 show the range of set-ups which may be obtained using the cardboard cut-outs shown in figure 9.17.

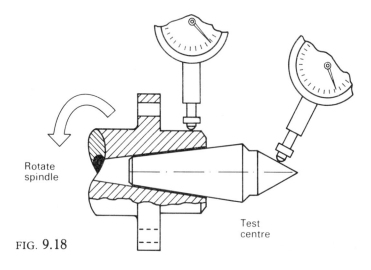

Rotate
spindle

Test
centre

FIG. 9.18

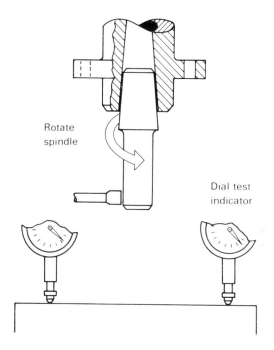

Rotate
spindle

Dial test
indicator

FIG. **9.19**

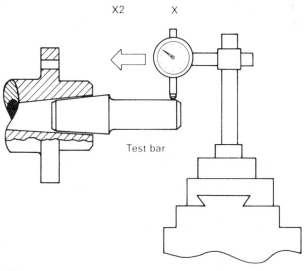

X2   X

Test bar

FIG. **9.20**   Saddle

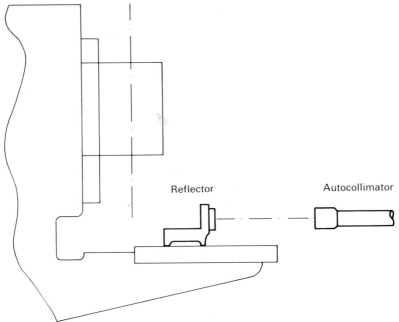

FIG. 9.21

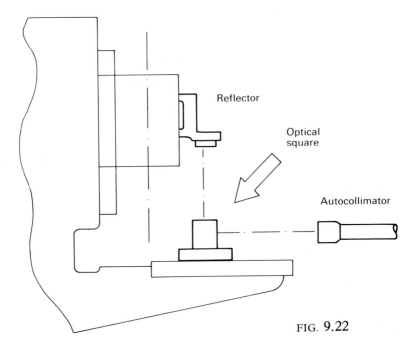

FIG. 9.22

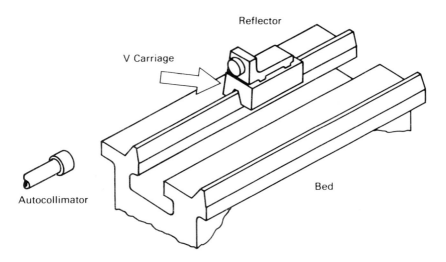

FIG. 9.23

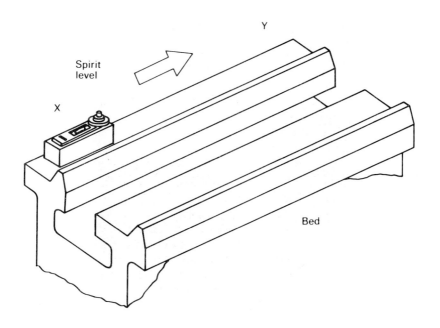

FIG. 9.24

Preparing a slide/tape programme

Using a slide projector such as the Bell and Howell Ringmaster (see figure 9.25), it is not difficult to produce a punchy and convincing programme yourself. The Ringmaster sound-slide projector combines two projectors in one unit. The picture is transferred from the built-in screen to forward projection on an external screen merely by raising a flap at the back. To position the picture precisely, there is an adjustable foot.

All you need is a projector, a camera, some colour film and a blank cassette.

First, draw up a draft script and decide on the pictures that will best illustrate the points you wish to make. Then take appropriate photographs which may include cartoons, diagrams, charts, captions and maps as well as

FIG. 9.25

objects, people and scenes. Special slides, difficult to photograph, are available from libraries. Ready-made sets on such subjects as engineering, science and art can be obtained from the Victoria and Albert and the Science Museums in London, art galleries and museums. The projector takes up to 80 slides in 5×5 cm (2×2 inch) mounts.

An ordinary compact cassette is all you need for your recording which can be up to forty-five minutes long. The cassette pushes into the slot in the projector. For non-stop repetition of a programme, you use a continuous-play cassette with its tape in an endless loop.

Now finalise your script. The best way to lay out a script is to put the commentary/sound on the right-hand side of the paper and brief descriptions of the slides on the left-hand side.

Then make your recording using the microphone supplied with the projector, subsequently using the remote-control/pulsing switch to add the cues that will change the pictures automatically in step with your words. You can change a slide every second—or hold it on the screen as long as you need. Rewind the tape and you are ready to show your programme.

The projector can also be used for quizzes and question and answer sessions, provided that it is equipped with a 'cue stop'. A cue stop enables pre-set pauses to be built into the programme. It is particularly useful for training. A pause can be inserted after a question: after it has been answered, the programme can be restarted at the touch of a button.

9.5 Presenting and evaluating aids

The most effective way of checking the suitability of aids is to present the aids to a group and await their comments.

The aid should be presented in a microtraining exercise on the application of aids to practical teaching. Each group member should write down the assumed objective of the aid as he sees it. The group as a whole should then discuss the impact of the visual message, the design quality and its appropriateness to the presenter's stated objective.

Note: A film and videotape entitled *Don't just tell them* dealing with presentation methods that an instructor can use during a training programme may be hired from Guild Training. For details see Appendix 4.

SUMMARY

- Boredom results from lack of involvement. Audio-visual aids relieve boredom and provide a focal point for attention.

- Audio-visual aids increase the impact of information being passed to the observer.

- Aids should meet the learning objective.

- Use of the aid should be validated and its impact evaluated.

- An aid should be chosen for its function and predicted effect on the audience.

- Visual aids should be large enough to be seen by all and should display the minimum amount of detail required to be effective.

- Line diagrams illustrate essentials and avoid excessive detail.

- Charts representing proportions have visual impact and are more meaningful than lists of figures and percentages.

- Magnetic board displays are versatile aids.

- Slide/tape projectors use electronically pulsed tapes.

QUESTIONS

1. Why are audio-visual aids often used in a learning situation? Summarise the main advantages and disadvantages of using visual aids.

2. Choose a BTEC Objective and select the type of aid which would best be used by an instructor to help trainees attain the objective selected.

3. Produce a pictorial drawing of a sub-assembly suitable for inclusion in a training manual. Enlarge important details and show these inside balloons. Using a photocopier, produce a transparency from the drawing and project this.

4. From a photograph or picture of a machine, produce simple line diagrams to illustrate its construction and principle of operation. Reproduce the diagrams and use them as teaching aids during teaching practice.

5. Observe a process and prepare block diagrams to represent each stage. If you do not have access to a process, show how any commodity of your choice is produced from raw materials.

6. The composition of a certain iron-nickel low-expansion alloy is given in the table below:

Metal	%
Nickel	29
Iron	54
Cobalt	17

On a transparency and using colours construct a 'pie chart' and a '100% bar chart' to represent the information. Project the transparency.

7. The table below gives the melting points of certain metals:

Metal	Melting point °C	Metal	Melting point °C
Aluminium	660	Platinum	1773
Chromium	1890	Silver	960
Copper	1083	Tin	232
Iron	1535	Tungsten	3410
Lead	327	Uranium	1150
Molybdenum	2620	Zinc	420

Represent this information in:
(a) a horizontal bar chart;
(b) a vertical bar chart.

8. From a diagram in a textbook or maker's handbook produce enlarged cardboard cut-outs to represent each component shown. Stick a small magnet or a piece of magnetic tape on the back of each card. Use the cut-outs in conjunction with a magnetic board as an aid to instruction during teaching practice.

9. List the types of projected aids available. State a practical example where each of these could be used to best effect.

10. CCTV is a valuable teaching aid. Give examples of training situations where its use is most applicable.

Note: Aids produced should be presented and evaluated (see section 9.5).

Part 4
Practical Teaching

10

Teaching practice

Each group member will prepare a lesson to last between fifteen and twenty-five minutes and use a check-list to analyse its effectiveness during discussion with the tutor. Additional practice will be undertaken as necessary. (Note: for suitable rating sheets see section 8.4).

Before attempting to teach, the teacher must know what he intends to teach. He must have a clear idea of the objectives around which his teaching plan has been developed. He must also know what the students are already able to do, and pitch his instruction at the right level.

The outcome of the teaching and learning process is that terminal behaviour will reflect what the trainees are now able to do as a result of their participation in the learning experience. Learning will be identified as a relatively permanent change in behaviour brought about by this experience.

The diagram in figure 10.1 shows teaching as a system. The input is a lesson which depends for its success upon effective communication between teacher and students. During the lesson, teacher activity together with student activity, when combined, will hopefully produce a satisfying learning experience for all concerned.

Some practical considerations

MANAGEMENT

A teacher is responsible for the management of instruction and for the deployment of resources to the best effect. His aim should always be to arrange things so that students may learn effectively.

Teaching would be a very simple task if it simply involved pouring knowledge into empty bottles. In the teaching situation—at the chalkface—with real live students, every teacher encounters problems on some occasions. For an inexperienced teacher a lesson can become a nightmare. Good management goes a long way towards avoiding pitfalls.

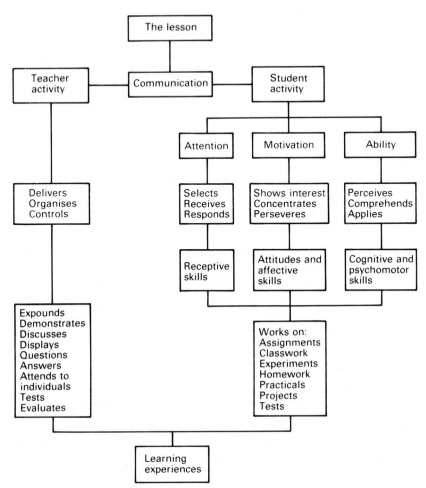

FIG. 10.1   **Class teaching system**

ORGANISATION

In the staffroom or training centre the following comments are often voiced:

'Never use a lesson plan. I teach "off the cuff". It's the best way . . .'

'I use "chalk and talk". I know it's old-fashioned but there's no better way. All these aids are . . .'

'Those blokes who write the turning modules couldn't turn good grub into . . .'

'I don't take a lot of notice of objectives. Never give them to the students. I teach them what I think they ought to know . . .'

'I keep them screwed down. I don't get any discipline problems. If they start "chirping" I dictate a few notes or boot out the troublemakers . . .'

The list is endless.

While there is no one right way to teach a subject, it is advisable to analyse the lesson content before starting the lesson and go to the instructional situation with some sort of plan.

The main task confronting a teacher is the interpretation of syllabus content, and preparation of learning objectives. Once objectives have been written, the teacher will know what must be taught and what the students should be able to do after instruction.

The teacher can then select suitable material, decide on the teaching order and plan the lesson in detail, incorporating such aids as are necessary to enhance the learning process. The aim should be to make it easy for the student to learn and to arrange for maximum student participation.

SUBJECT-MATTER

Learners are quick to spot the bluffer. In any social situation where people meet, those concerned tend to weigh one another up, trying to form opinions on the basis of what is seen and heard. The instructional situation follows the same pattern especially when a group meets for the first time.

The learners expect the instructor to be a subject expert—a fountain of knowledge—who really knows his stuff. In order to match student expectations it is necessary to review lesson content in advance to ensure that important facts and methods of solving problems can be recalled when required. When preparing the lesson it is advisable to make a list of possible questions which may be asked by the learners. Forewarned is forearmed.

Teaching 'off the cuff' is fine some of the time and some teachers prefer to use the method rather than be constrained by rigid lesson plans. But very often, important points are missed completely or the lesson becomes disjointed, following no logical sequence.

STUDENT CAPABILITIES

More often than not, groups are formed randomly rather than by IQ, ability or expertise in certain areas. This is particularly true with mature students and personnel subject to industrial retraining.

All too often the instructor pitches instruction at a given level and works through the subject-matter assuming that everyone understands unless they ask questions. Many learners are reluctant to tell the instructor that they do not understand and will not ask questions. It is embarrassing for them to do so. They fear the prospect of losing face and do not wish to expose themselves to the possibility of ridicule.

The instructor should try to establish individual ability by carefully framing questions, putting them to the group and obtaining responses from each individual during the session. Having established the level, instruction should be pitched accordingly.

MANNER

Instructors and teachers are not all cast from the same mould. Personalities vary from person to person and the list of desirable traits required of a perfect teacher is long. No one person can hope to possess all of the traits required. Perhaps some of the best results are obtained by teachers who are described as sociable, friendly extroverts.

It is important to be enthusiastic about the subject being taught, to be something of a showman, to be knowledgeable and to establish a warm friendly atmosphere. But here the mode of instruction governs to a degree how a teacher behaves and how the students see him.

Above all, a teacher should behave naturally. If a person is normally quiet and reserved, or stern, it would be a mistake to adopt a false identity in front of a group. Sometimes a joke does not go amiss, but this practice is dangerous. If you are not a natural comedian, forget it.

Early efforts should be made to establish rapport. Let the learners see that you are on their side trying to help them. Never talk down to them. Avoid being too familiar but at the same time avoid being a martinet. Try to strike a happy medium. Familiarity breeds contempt and disrespect, while a martinet-type attitude alientates the group. A friendly democratic style usually produces more work and better attitudes.

Approval for good work and prompting or coaxing for the strugglers is better than punishing or showing disapproval. Learners often have several teachers during the same day and compare notes about their methods, attitudes and manner. Teachers tend to forget this and then wonder why they have a hard time when other teachers have no trouble with the same group.

FEEDBACK

Knowledge of results of tests, questionnaires and progress is a very important factor in the learning process. Try to provide feedback as quickly as possible when required, because it is important that the learner knows just how well he is doing—quickly.

MOTIVATION AND ATTENTION

G K Chesterton once wrote: 'There is no such thing on earth as an uninteresting subject; the only thing that can exist is an uninterested person.' If this assumption is correct then a way must be found of arousing interest and maintaining attention so that learning may proceed.

Knowledge of the learners' reasons for attending the instructional session is of great help to the instructor. If the learners can see some personal gain at the end of the course of instruction and the content is relevant to their individual lives, the instructor starts with an advantage. If, however, the learners are present only because they have been told to attend or are under some form of duress, the instructor has problems.

An audience of 'pressed men' is difficult to deal with. In such cases, the concepts to be discussed should, wherever possible, be based upon the learners' practical experiences or on things that are known generally, gradually developing the concept towards the more specific. At all times the instructor should be careful to use appropriate language and terminology.

Regardless of how complex the subject-matter may be, answers to questions put to the group reveal, more often than not, that several members know something about the subject or something closely allied to it. This information can be used to develop the theme and once the group start to contribute, interest is aroused, even to the extent that some start competing to give information.

LEARNERS' NEEDS

Most people want to succeed, both in life generally, and in specific areas of challenge. The learner in an instructional situation shares these common needs.

Learners come to the classroom or training centre with certain needs and expectations which they hope to fulfil. These expectations include social needs, such as taking an active part in group activities and competing with others, and intrinsic needs, such as the need to make progress, to satisfy curiosity and to perform a task well.

The arena is set when the group assembles. The teacher should be aware of the learners' needs and should consider how these may be fulfilled during the time at his disposal in the practical teaching situation.

In conclusion

Having worked through the content of this book, the reader should have acquired a knowledge of the fundamentals involved in teaching. However, as in all things, the proof of the pudding is in the eating. There is no substitute for practice. The best way of learning to teach is to teach, and remember, successful teachers are usually rated highly on warmth, friendliness and enthusiasm.

SUMMARY

A teacher should:
 select, plan, organise and control activity;
 interpret the syllabus;
 define objectives;
 know his subject;
 know his students' capabilities;
 be a good showman;
 be enthusiastic;
 be able to motivate his class;
 maintain attention;
 use audio-visual aids where appropriate;
 ensure that students have practical experience upon which to base concepts;
 use appropriate language and terminology;
 be able to project his voice;
 be seen while speaking;
 be able to establish rapport;
 encourage student talk by prompting, and using questioning techniques;
 provide feedback, knowledge of results and reinforcements;
 express approval and praise or reward rather than punish;
 be able to control the class and maintain discipline.

A teacher should be aware of the learner's need to:
 succeed;
 perform a task well;
 take an active part in group activities;
 compete with others;

make progress;
satisfy curiosity;
obtain satisfaction from classroom interaction.

Part 5
Appendices

1
Check-list of factors affecting output and morale

Accident frequency rate
Achievement motivation
Action training
Adequate motivation
Anomie
Appraisal interviews
Assignment of tasks
Attitudes to supervision and other workers
Boredom
Career advancement
Challenge
Changes in workers' attitudes towards work
Competition and rivalry
Co-operative relationships
Delegation
Drive
Economic motives (wages, bonuses, commissions, gratuities)
Employee participation
Employee attitudes surveys
Fatigue
Flexible working hours
Freedom of movement in the workplace
Fringe benefits
Frustration
Goal setting
Grievance interviews
Group activity/isolated individual
Group consultations

Group dynamics
Group leadership
Group training (Coverdale training)
Hygiene factors (Frederick Herzberg)† (see also page 310)
Incentives
Industrial democracy
Interpersonal relationships
Intrinsic motivation
Job enlargement
Job enrichment
Job instruction and communication training
Job rotation
Job satisfaction
Job security
Joint consultation
Leadership styles
Loyalty
Management attitudes
Monotony
Multi-factor incentive schemes (output, quality and scrap rates)
Nature of task
Open-door policies
Opportunity to create
Participative management
Pessimistic reveries—monotony causing private grief or discontent to surface (Mayo)
Physical environment
Physical health of staff
Power structure
Prestige
Recognition by supervision and management
Refreshment breaks
Relaxation allowances (fatigue and personal needs)
Responsibility
Rest breaks

---

†The 'motivation-hygiene theory' advanced by the American psychologist Frederick Herzberg is discussed in: Herzberg F, Mausner B and Snyderman B, *The Motivation to Work* (Wiley, New York 1959); and Herzberg F, *Work and the Nature of Man* (World Publishing Co, Cleveland, 1966) and (Crosby Lockwood Staples, St Albans 1974).

Scientific management (Taylor, Gilbreth, Grant)
Self-esteem
Social function of work
Staff-development programmes
Status
Teamwork
Training opportunities
Workers' control

2

Murray's list of psychogenic needs†

Needs associated briefly with inanimate objects

Acquisition: the need to gain possessions and property.

Conservation: the need to collect, repair, clean, and preserve things.

Orderliness: the need to arrange, organize, put away objects; to be tidy and clean; to be precise.

Retention: the need to retain possession of things; to hoard; to be frugal, economical, and miserly.

Construction: the need to organize and build.

Needs expressing ambition, will power, desire for accomplishment, and prestige

Superiority: the need to excel, a composite of achievement and recognition.

Achievement: the need to overcome obstacles, to exercise power, to strive to do something difficult as well and as quickly as possible.

Recognition: the need to excite praise and commendation; to demand respect.

Exhibition: the need for self-dramatization; to excite, amuse, stir, shock, thrill others.

Inviolacy: the need to remain inviolate, to prevent a depreciation of self-respect, to preserve one's 'good name'.

Avoidance of inferiority: the need to avoid failure, shame, humiliation, ridicule.

Defensiveness: the need to defend oneself against blame or belittlement; to justify one's actions.

Counteraction: the need to overcome defeat by restriving and rebuffeting.

†'Murray's List of Psychogenic Needs' reprinted from Murray, H A. *Explorations in Personality* by kind permission of John Wiley and Sons, New York.

Needs having to do with human power exerted, resisted, or yielded to

Dominance: the need to influence or control others.
Deference: the need to admire and willingly follow a superior; to serve gladly.
Similance: the need to imitate or emulate others; to agree and to believe.
Autonomy: the need to resist influence, to strive for independence.
Contrariness: the need to act differently from others, to be unique, to take the opposite side.

Needs having to do with injuring others or oneself

Aggression: the need to assault or injure another; to belittle, harm, or maliciously ridicule a person.
Abasement: the need to comply and accept punishment; self-depreciation.
Avoidance of blame: the need to avoid blame, ostracism, or punishment by inhibiting unconventional impulses; to be well behaved and obey the law.

Needs having to do with affection between people

Affiliation: the need to form friendships and associations.
Rejection: the need to be discriminating, to snub, ignore, or exclude another.
Nurturance: the need to nourish, aid, or protect another.
Succourance: the need to seek aid, protection, or sympathy; to be dependen

Additionally socially relevant needs

Play: the need to relax, amuse oneself, seek diversion and entertainment.
Cognizance: the need to explore, to ask questions, to satisfy curiosity.
Exposition: the need to point and demonstrate; to give information, examine, interpret, lecture.

3

Leadership and motivation— films and video available

Films and videotapes on leadership and motivation may be hired or purchased from Guild Training, a Division of Guild Sound and Vision Limited of 6 Royce Road, Peterborough PE1 5YB (Telephone: Customer Service Department on [0733] 3153155)

The art of motivation Running time: 30 minutes
In order to manage people well we need to know how to motivate them. Through the illustrative medium of an artist at work, this programme examines the need for motivational skills and develops this through an exploration of the basic theories of McGregor and Herzberg. An intriguing view of the effects of motivation on employee behaviour, supported by basic behavioural theory.

Common sense motivation Running time: 15 minutes
Understanding the personal goals and objectives of employees enables us to provide the right motivation for them to perform well.

Common sense motivation tells the story of David Rees, a young man who is not interested in work. He arrives late at the office, his work is shoddy and his colleagues usually have to sort out the problems he has created.

Brian, his boss, is a good manager; he has succeeded in providing job satisfaction for other members of his staff but all his attempts to motivate David have failed. Finally, in frustration, Brian seeks out his own boss in order to discuss what he should do about David. It is at this meeting that Brian realises that he has not motivated David as well as the others—Brian is asked to list his own personal objectives and then identify how the same analysis can be applied to David.

Brian constructs a checklist of ways in which he can provide opportunities for David to achieve his goals and thus provide the motivation for David to perform. After some time the results begin to show through.

310

Leadership   Running time: 23 minutes

Understanding the three essentials in leadership—the task, the team, the individual.

What is leadership? In this classic film, Michael Barrett puts the question to Dr John Adair in a documentary-style investigation into the nature and functions of leadership. Not only does Dr Adair review his research into the subject, but he also identifies three major areas the leader must be aware of—the task, the team and the individual.

The film follows a team of unrehearsed managers who are given the simple task of building (with Lego bricks) a tower block within a certain time. As they progress the audience is able to see how the leader responds to the three basic areas of need. The film includes interviews with some well-known personalities in which their personal views of the nature of leadership are expressed.

Leading to the top   Running time: 21 minutes

This is an ideal programme for use on leadership courses and as part of any general management development course.

Chris Bonnington introduces this unique training programme about leadership. Set against his successful ascent of Mount Everest he shows how the leadership techniques employed by him in extreme circumstances on the mountains are the same as those needed to lead effectively in today's exacting and competitive business world.

With dramatic film footage from the Everest expedition, the programme covers: definition of the task; assessing and motivating the individuals; building the team; and the critically important effect of the leader's personal style.

All these leadership skills are effectively related to the everyday tasks of all managers and supervisors who are expected to lead successful teams to achieve their organisation's objectives.

4
Presentation skills—films and video available

Films and videotapes on presentation and training skills may be hired or purchased from Guild Training, a Division of Guild Sound and Vision Limited of 6 Royce Road, Peterborough PE1 5YP. (Telephone (0733) 315395)

The floor is yours—now Running time: 24 minutes
A film or video and package containing a book and training notes. *The Floor is Yours—Now* is the story of Jim, a young manager. Jim has been put in charge of a major research project undertaken by an outside firm of consultants. His boss has given him the job of presenting a paper on the results of the research to a Regional Manager's Meeting—a group of some 15 people, most of whom Jim knows.

At first, confident that he can easily present his report, Jim soon begins to have doubts, to the extent that he has a nightmare about a disastrous presentation whereupon he meets James, his 'alter ego', who gets him into the right attitude of mind. James guides Jim through all the stages of preparation and rehearsal that he needs to undertake in order to deliver a good presentation, and shows him examples of good and bad presentations made by his colleagues. Finally, on the day of presentation Jim is seen opening a well prepared and rehearsed presentation.

Don't just tell them Running time: 20 minutes
In public meetings and presentations audiences learn more through what they see than through what they hear. This film shows how to use visual aids.

About 75% of anything we need to learn or know comes through our sense of sight, against only 15% through hearing. This programme presents a powerful case for the message; 'don't just tell them—show them'.

It demonstrates various types of visual aids and shows how each can be used to maximum effect. It covers chalkboard, drawing board, flipchart, whiteboard, magnetic board, models and overhead and slide projectors. Two case-study examples incorporating visual aids are used to illustrate effective presentation.

The overhead projector   Running time: 25 minutes
In certain circumstances the overhead projector is the best visual aid a presenter can use. However, it needs to be used properly for the best effect.

The overhead projector can be one of the most versatile of presentation aids, but it requires correct use. The programme shows right and wrong ways to go about presenting different types of material on the overhead projector, and illustrates the benefits of the OHP over other aids in certain applications. The techniques of using a base plus coloured highlights, overlays and concealed picture development are illustrated as well as the application of working models and animation.

The programme also shows how the overhead projector can be used at the exact pace chosen by the presenter, and looks at the various accessories such as pens and markers, that can be used with the OHP.

Deskside manner   Running time: 16 minutes
How to question and listen skilfully. Deskside manner is useful for training courses which cover interviewing and questioning skills, particularly when applied to the introduction of new systems and procedures within the company.

It humorously depicts an O & M specialist who, because of his condescending attitude and poor questioning techniques, learns nothing and achieves nothing—except the antagonism of the man whose job he was evaluating.

Who do you think you're talking to?   Running time: 24 minutes
The film deals with understanding transactional analysis and how to achieve better communications.

Michael Reddy, trainer in transactional analysis, works with two actors, Michael Hall and Arthur Whybrow, to demonstrate the particular 'wavelengths', or ego states, which people use to communicate with each other. The programme consists of a series of business scenarios which are acted out using the transactional techniques of the Parent–Child–Adult. Our approaches to personal interaction are discussed by the trainer and actors intermittently throughout the programme.

5

Stages in producing an objective test

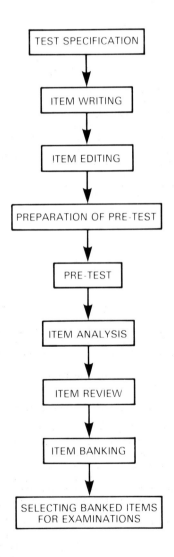

TEST SPECIFICATION

ITEM WRITING

ITEM EDITING

PREPARATION OF PRE-TEST

PRE-TEST

ITEM ANALYSIS

ITEM REVIEW

ITEM BANKING

SELECTING BANKED ITEMS
FOR EXAMINATIONS

OBJECTIVE TESTING
SECTION 1
DEFINITION AND TYPES OF OBJECTIVE ITEMS

An objective test may be defined as a series of items, each of which has a predetermined correct answer so that subjective judgement in the marking of each item is eliminated.

1 There are a number of types of objective item
- multiple-choice
- multiple-response
- matching block
- assertion/reason
- true/false.

The Institute has concentrated on the **four-option multiple-choice item.**

A **multiple-choice** item consists of a *stem* in which a question is either asked directly or implied, followed by four answers called *options*. Three of these are incorrect, called *distractors*, and one is correct, called the *key*. The candidate is required to select the option he believes to be the correct answer. The correct answer must be clearly acceptable to the more able candidates but each distractor must be sufficiently plausible to appeal to a reasonable proportion of the less able candidates. An item of this type is shown in Example 1.

Example 1

The maximum voltage at which one-piece construction on pin-type insulators can be used is

a   11 kV
b   33 kV
c   66 kV
d   132 kV.   (Type of Knowledge – I)

This particular item tests the recall of an important piece of **factual knowledge** (Type of Knowledge I). The same format can also be used, however, to test higher types of knowledge, and the Institute currently deals with two of these, that is

type II – comprehension
type III – application

which require a more thorough understanding on the part of the student.

Test constructors often find that the allocation of a type of knowledge to a particular item is a difficult stage. It may be helpful to remember that
(i)   one should concentrate on deciding what needs to be tested, i.e. forget about the learning steps that lead to it
(ii)   the knowledge categories are hierarchical, i.e. if an item is testing in the application category, it will at the same time be testing in the two lower categories, comprehension and factual knowledge.

Examples of items: testing types of knowledge II and III are given overleaf.

Example 2

The main purpose of the vehicle in a printing ink is to

a   produce properties relating to colour
b   transfer the pigment to the paper
c   control the rate of drying
d   prevent set-off set on the paper.   (Type of Knowledge – II)

Example 3

An exterior architectural subject is to be photographed in colour. The lighting is brilliant sunlight and it is necessary to reduce the image illuminance without affecting colour reproduction or depth of field. Which one of the following filters would do this?

a   Colour correction filter
b   Polarizing filter
c   Suitable contrast filter
d   Graduated sky filter.   (Type of Knowledge   III).

---

2   **Multiple-Response.** A type of multiple-choice item in which one or more than one of the possibilities given below is correct, as in Example 4.

Example 4

Which of the following features should be found in concrete when used for

the construction of a small estate road?
1   Air entrainment
2   Sulphate resisting cement
3   Low to medium workability
4   High cement content (not less than 400 kg/m^3).

a   1 and 2
b   1 and 3
c   2 and 4
d   3 and 4.

---

3   **Matching Block.** This consists of two lists of statements, terms or symbols and the candidate has to match an item in one list, as in Examples 5 and 6. (In these examples the method of answering has been laid out in four-option form for ease of marking, but this format is not the only acceptable method of presentation.)

Example 5

List 1   List 2
A   Permanent wave solution   1   Lawsonia alba
B   Permanent hair dye   2   Magnesium carbonate
C   Red henna   3   Para-phenylene diamine
D   White.   4   Ammonium thioglycollate
                                     5   Azo-dyes.

(Example 5 cont.)

Which one of the following shows the correct order for matching the items in List 1 with those in List 2?

a List
List

1	A	B	C	D
2	4	3	1	2

b List
List

1	A	B	C	D
2	3	4	2	1

c List
List

1	A	B	C	D
2	4	3	5	1

d List
List

1	A	B	C	D
2	3	5	2	4

Example 6

List 1   List 2

A
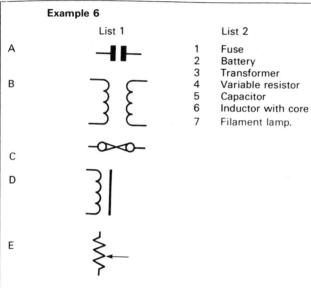

B

C

D

E

1 Fuse
2 Battery
3 Transformer
4 Variable resistor
5 Capacitor
6 Inductor with core
7 Filament lamp.

Which one of the following shows the correct order for matching the items in List 1 with those in List 2?

a List
List

1	A	B	C	D	E
2	5	3	1	7	6

b List
List

1	A	B	C	D	E
2	2	1	3	6	5

c List
List

1	A	B	C	D	E
2	5	3	4	6	7

d List
List

1	A	B	C	D	E
2	2	5	7	6	1

In Examples 5 and 6, the possibility of a candidate getting the last answer correct by a process of elimination has been avoided by making List 2 contain more topics than List 1.

4   Assertion/Reason. This type of question consists of an ASSERTION followed by a REASON and the candidate has to decide whether assertion and reason are individually correct or not, and, if they are correct, whether the 'reason' is a valid explanation of the 'assertion'. The items are usually laid out as in Example 7.

Example 7

Assertion
Metallic or inorganic dyes are often used in a hairdressing salon.

Reason
Metallic or inorganic dyes are progressive dyes and develop slowly by oxidation.

a   Both assertion and reason are true statements and the reason is a correct explanation of the assertion.
b   Both assertion and reason are true statements, but the reason is NOT a correct explanation of the assertion.
c   The assertion is true, but the reason is a false statement.
d   The assertion is false, but the reason is a true statement.

True/False. An item consisting of a statement which has to be judged true or false, as Example 8.

Example 8

Delete either the word 'true' or the word 'false' after each of the following sentences to indicate whether or not they are correct

(i) The coal and shale constituents of true middlings can be liberated by crushing.	TRUE/FALSE
(ii) The calorific value of a middlings is higher than that of its shale constituent.	TRUE/FALSE
(iii) The ash content of a middlings is less than that of its coal constituent.	TRUE/FALSE
(iv) The constituents of true middlings are more intimately mixed together than are those of false middlings.	TRUE/FALSE

This type of question is open to the criticism that, as it requires the candidate to choose only one of two possible answers, it may reward guessing because a candidate has a '50/50' chance of arriving at the correct answer.

CONCLUSION

Although other types of item (multiple-response, matching block, assertion-reason) have advantages for at least some types of subject matter it has generally been found that the four-option multiple-choice is the most useful and flexible of item types.

Institute policy is therefore to concentrate mainly on the four-option multiple-choice type of item, including item groups.

ITEM GROUPS

An 'item group' is a series of items which all relate to a given situation presented at the beginning, either in the form of a sketch or as a description. The item group is a useful method of testing knowledge of laboratory or practical situations as several aspects relating to one job can be tested, and candidates are then asked to apply their knowledge in a realistic manner.

Example of an Item Group Based on a Description (Hairdressing)

The following four items refer to the situation described below.

A client has tinted hair and requires a permanent wave which can be dressed into soft wave movements and loose curls. The hair is thick, abundant and inclined to be porous. In order to obtain the best results, procedure would be as follows:

1   The hair should be prepared for permanent waving by cleansing with

    a   clear soapless shampoo
    b   egg shampoo
    c   beer shampoo
    d   lanolin shampoo.

2   The hair should be cut by

    a   thinning and tapering thoroughly
    b   clubbing all over
    c   layer cutting thoroughly
    d   lightly thinning and tapering.

3   A special reagent should be chosen because tinted hair is likely to

    a   process more quickly
    b   process more slowly
    c   take a loose curl
    d   develop a darker colour.

4   The first test for movement should be made

    a   after winding a few curlers and when half the head is wound
    b   five minutes after winding is completed
    c   when winding is completed
    d   ten minutes after winding is completed.

Further items may follow on similar lines.

Examples of an Item Group Based on a Diagram (Welding Engineering)

Questions 1–4 refer to Fig. 12.

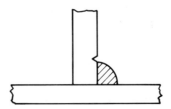

FIG. 12

1   The type of joint in Fig. 12 is a

    a   corner
    b   butt
    c   tee
    d   lap.

2   The defect shown on the weld in Fig. 12 is

    a   undercut
    b   porosity
    c   overlap
    d   cold lap.

3   In Fig. 12, the weld has a face which is

    a   convex
    b   concave
    c   mitred
    d   flat.

4   In Fig. 12, the fusion zone of the weld would lose most of its heat by

    a   convection
    b   conduction
    c   radiation
    d   penetration.

This extract is from the City and Guilds of London Institute *Manual on Objective Testing,* available from the Sales Section of the Institute at 76 Portland Place, London W1N 4AA.

The Institute also publishes an information leaflet 'City and Guilds and Objective Testing' and a 'List of Publications and Candidate's Guide', available free from the above address.

Item writing principles

Choose an item of knowledge **on the syllabus.**

Ensure that the item tests knowledge **important** for the candidate to know and understand.

Ensure that the item is **technically accurate.**

Ensure that the aim of the item is **clearly** presented in the stem.

Ensure that the wording of the item is as **brief** and **clear** as possible.

Use **diagrams** where appropriate.

Ensure that the item has **one** correct answer which appears as one of the options.

The **key** should usually be of about the same **length** as the distractors, not consistently longer or shorter.

All distractors must be **plausible** to the level of candidate being examined.

Avoid giving **clues** in the stem or the distractors.

Avoid **overlapping** options. (Options showing numerical values are particularly prone to this.)

Avoid **negatively** phrased stems. If this is unavoidable **emphasise** the negative.

Avoid the use of **'none of these'** as a distractor.

Avoid the use of the word **'you'**, i.e. what would **you** do...?

Item editing schedule

RELEVANCE
Is the item on the syllabus?
Is it worth asking?
Is it appropriate for the level of candidate?
Is the type of knowledge tested correctly indicated?

TECHNICAL CONTENT
Is the stem technically correct?
Is the key technically correct?
Are the distractors technically plausible?

STEM
Does the stem present a single question?
Note: The stem may be either a direct question or an incomplete statement; in either case is should usually be possible to supply the correct answer without reading the options.
Is the stem clearly and simply worded?

KEY

Is the key the only correct answer to the question presented?

KEY AND DISTRACTORS

Does each option follow grammatically from the stem?

Are there any words or phrases in the options which are also used in the stem and which may serve as clues towards eliminating the distractors or selecting the key?

Is each distractor likely to be plausible to students who have insufficient knowledge of the subject-matter?

6

BTEC objectives and specimen test

A selection of learning objectives extracted from BTEC Standard Unit U76/056 followed by a typical short answer assessment test based upon the objectives is given below. The form of test questions appropriate to the assessment of learning is discussed in Section 3.5.

Section C—Forming and Cutting Processes

3. Recognises the principles of simple press work.
    3.1 Describes the purpose, advantages and limitations of the fly press and the power press.
    3.2 Explains the design and use of punches, dies and bolsters.
    3.3 States the order of procedure for given examples of piercing, blanking and bending.
    3.4 Designs blanking layouts which give maximum economic utilization of material.

4. Appreciates the basic primary forming processes.
    4.1 Describes the form of supply of the raw materials for sand casting rolling, extrusion, drawing and forging.
    4.2 States the special properties required of a raw material used in these processes (4.1), e.g. fluidity, plasticity, ductility, malleability, toughness.
    4.3 Describes with the aid of diagrammatic sketches the basic steps of sand casting, rolling, extrusion, drawing and forging.
    4.4 Lists the main characteristics, advantages and limitations of metals and components produced by the primary forming processes listed in 4.3.
    4.5 Selects a suitable primary process (from the list in 4.3) which might be employed to produce a given simple component.
    4.6 Names the main hazards (including hot metal) in primary process work and the necessary relevant precautions.

5. Recognises the basic principles of the metal cutting process with single pointed tools.

    5.1   States the basic effects of variations in speed, feed, depth of cut and tool geometry on cutting force, power consumption and tool life.

    5.2   Compares the relative merits of positive and negative rake angles (BSS).

    5.3   Compares the advantages and limitations between high speed tool steels, carbides, ceramics and diamonds.

6. Appreciates the role of cutting fluids.

    6.1   States four characteristics of a cutting fluid including cooling and lubricating properties and their effects on the metal cutting process.

    6.2   States and gives reasons for using either straight oil, soluble oil substitute and paraffin as a cutting fluid in a particular application.

    6.3   Selects and gives reasons for the use of a suitable cutting fluid for a particular machining operation.

    6.4   Lists and gives reasons for using the common methods for applying cutting fluid to given metal cutting operations.

Acknowledgement is due to the Business & Technician Education Council for permission to reproduce material from the BTEC Standard Unit U76/056. The Council reserves the right to revise the content of BTEC U76/056 at any time.

BTEC U76/056 Manufacturing Technology II

Test—Section C Forming and Cutting Processes

OBJECTIVES 3.1–6.4

Name: ....

Class: ....

Attempt all questions   *Mark:* ..... %   *Maximum Mark = 100*

	Marks
1. $VT^n = C$ (a) The formula given above has a name. What is it?	1

	Marks
(b) In the above formula	
V represents	1
T represents	1
(c) If the cutting speed on a lathe is increased	
(i) the power consumption	1
(ii) the tool life	1
(d) Write down three factors which affect the metal removal rate when machining a solid round bar on a centre lathe:	
(i)	1
(ii)	1
(iii)	1

2. (a) Identify the forces F_T, F_A and F_R shown in the diagram:

F_T = ...	1
F_A = ...	1
F_R = ...	1
Which of these three forces is the greater?	1

(b) Explain one cutting tool application where one of these forces does not exist: | 2 |

....

....

Marks

(c) Write down a formula used for calculating the power
applied during any cutting operation defining any
symbols used: 3

....

....

....

....

3. (a) Identify the type of cutting tool shown in sketch.

The tool is a .... tool.   1
Angle A is known as the   1
Angle B is known as the   1
Angle C is known as the   1

(b) Write down four requirements of a cutting tool
material:

(i)   1

(ii)   1

(iii) ....

(iv)   1

(c) For each of the following cutting tool materials, state
one advantage A and one limitation L:
High Speed Steel

A   1

L   1

	Marks

Tungsten Carbide

A .... | 1

L .... | 1

Diamond

A .... | 1

L .... | 1

(d) For roughing out M.S. with a Tungsten Carbide Tool the maximum cutting speed should be:

.... | 2

4. (a) State four main requirements of a cutting fluid:

    (i) .... | 1

    (ii) .... | 1

    (iii) .... | 1

    (iv) .... | 1

(b) The choice of a cutting fluid for a given operation depends upon a number of factors. Name four:

    (i) .... | 1

    (ii) .... | 1

    (iii) .... | 1

    (iv) .... | 1

(c) Heat is evolved from two sources during metal cutting. These are:

    (i) .... | 1

    (ii) .... | 1

(d) State three precautions against skin infection:

    (i) .... | 1

    (ii) .... | 1

    (iii) .... | 1

Marks

5. (a) The following statements refer to component parts of a Press Tool. From the statements identify the component:

   (i) 'that portion at the top of the die where the aperture is parallel sided' 2

   (ii) 'bridges the gap between the guide strips and is provided with a hole through which the punch passes' 2

   (iii) 'is spring mounted on the punch assembly and also acts as a progressive clamp on the stock' 2

   (iv) 'small acorn shaped pins projecting from the cutting faces of punches' 2

   (v) 'direct the stock accurately over the die' 2

   (b) Name three hazards experienced in presswork:

   (i) 1
   (ii) 1
   (iii) 1

   (c) Sketch a die with 'double shear' 4

6. (a) Inverted processes may be used in the initial stages of hot forging of cylinder blanks or backward cold extrusion of tubular products. Sketch and label a diagram showing the 'Backward extrusion of cylinder blanks'.

Marks

Show the hot billet loaded ready for the operation and in a separate sketch how the operation is performed.   6

(b) Describe the 'Hot Extrusion' principle: 4

....

....

....

....

(c) Cold extrusion is carried out at room or slightly elevated temperatures. Compare the hot and cold extrusion processes with respect to stress formation: 4

....

....

....

....

....

....

7. (a) List two characteristics of the finished bar in

    (i)   Hot Rolling   1

      1

    (ii) Cold Rolling   1

      1

(b) (i) Sketch an 'Upset' forged bar: 3

	Marks
7. (b) (ii) Name two components produced by this 'upsetting':	
....	1
....	1
(c) Sketch a section through a forged component show-ing how forging improves strength:	3
8. (a) Sketch an 'oddside' or 'false cope' used in casting process:	3
(b) Describe briefly the following terms used in foundry practice:	
(i) Strickle	2
....	
(ii) Drag	2
....	
(iii) Core Print	2
....	
(iv) Riser	2
....	

7

Theories of leadership

'Leadership is not a personal quality, it is a contingent role'

Two main theories of leadership have been put forward in an attempt to describe the nature of the relationship between groups and their leaders. One is known as the 'Great Man' theory of leadership and the other as the 'Situational' theory of leadership.

The 'Great Man' theory holds that a man becomes a leader because of inherent leadership qualities or personality traits which he was born with or has acquired during his lifetime, whilst the 'Situational' theory holds that a person is thrust into leadership by the needs of the moment.

Researchers have attempted to provide a list of desirable leadership qualities based upon studies of famous people who have, in the past, demonstrated their ability to lead in the field of industry and finance, sport, government, war and revolution. As a result of these studies, a long list of personality traits has been drawn up for consideration when choosing a leader. While it is true that many of the qualities set out are highly desirable in a given leader, history has shown that such men as Adolf Hitler have not been endowed with a good number of them.†

The 'Situational' theory maintains that leadership is directly related to the needs of a particular situation, and that if there is a change in need thrown up by a changing situation, it is likely that the leadership will change to satisfy the new need.

The membership and structure of a group are not static. People come and go, and some are more qualified to deal with a given situation or task than others. Initiative in group situations invites leadership. For example, a young inexperienced yachtsman may invite a few friends to join him on a sailing expedition on his father's boat. He naturally assumes leadership of the group. While the weather is fair he is able to maintain this role. However, if the sky clouds over and a gale blows up, creating difficult

†See: Bullock A *Hitler—A Study in Tyranny* (Penguin Books Ltd, Harmondsworth 1972).

handling conditions, it is the person who has the necessary sailing experience who takes over. It is he that the group looks to for leadership. The pressing need to shorten sail and run for the safety of the harbour—the need of the moment—causes the group to reorganise themselves around his leadership.

Examples such as this point to the fact that leadership is an interactive process depending upon the task, the group membership and the circumstances; no one set of characteristics defines the successful leader.

Children at play provide a useful setting for the observation of leadership patterns. Among groups of children playing or engaged in other co-operative activity, some readily adopt the position of group leader and are accepted in this position by the remainder of the group. These leaders are commonly of greater intelligence than the average of the group, although too great a difference is unfavourable to leadership.

In his article: 'Group Leadership and Institutionalisation'† Merei describes how an aggressive young child on joining an existing playgroup uses a range of ploys to gain the leadership. Initially, the newcomer blends in with existing group behaviour, then later he begins to instruct the group to do things the way they are accustomed to doing them, so making his presence felt. After a while he brings small modifications into games or other activities until the group gradually conforms to his wishes after which he soon becomes their recognised leader.

Lewis Yablonsky, in his book *The Violent Gang*,†† suggests that spontaneous leadership is one of the characteristics of a collection of anonymous individuals forming a mob, people in panic or a youth riot. Perhaps the person with the loudest voice, the largest physique, the one who hurls the first brick through a window or he who leads a charge becomes the impromptu leader. He is adopted by the remainder of the group who, in other circumstances, might consider him as a completely nondescript individual.

In W R Bion's book *Experiences in Groups*,††† which relates to his experiences as a member of therapeutic groups, he describes a period of three to four weeks when he was a member of a group of patients, during which time his contributions were ignored and his presence largely

---

†Merei F 'Group Leadership and Institutionalism' in *Human Relations* (1949) pages 22-39.
††Yablonsky L *The Violent Gang* (Penguin, Harmondsworth 1967).
†††Bion W R *Experiences in Groups* (Tavistock, London 1961) pages 41-58.

ineffective. When, suddenly, a patient began to display what the group felt to be symptoms of madness and hallucination, he at once found that he had become the good leader, the master of the situation. He had been accepted by the group as being the only one fully capable of dealing with the crisis—so outstandingly the right man for the job that it would have been presumptuous for any other member of the group to have taken the initiative. A complete contrast to the group's attitude towards Dr Bion immediately before the incident.

In a social group there may or may not be a leader. A leaderless group can survive and operate, but in some cases a group with a leader is more effective, especially when the function of the group is to oppose another organised group. Trade unions, armies and political groups could not function efficiently without appointed leaders, so that the condition for effectiveness in action appears to be a well-organised group with a leader. For the group to be successful, the playing out of roles must be adhered to. A lecturer can only function as a leader if the group remain silent at the right time, remain seated and refrain from dancing and singing. A supervisor in industry can only maintain order if the workers accept his instructions and perform work as specified.

Leadership may change frequently within a social group's life, according to the role required at a given instant, so that these different roles are taken successively by different people. Leadership is then related to events as they happen, and it is these events which control the needs of the group at any given time, and hence, the leader selected.

To observers, the key characteristics of a successful leader are that he should be intelligent, outgoing and adventurous—a kind of sociable, intelligent extrovert—rather than conforming to any long list of desirable traits as suggested by some authors.

It has been said that the basic requirement for successfully attaining group goals is that interaction between qualities of person and task of group is such that neither alone can account for successful leadership.

DISCUSSION TOPICS

1. Make a list of personality traits and leadership qualities which you consider to be important when choosing a leader. Be prepared to justify your selection during a group discussion.

2. Which of the two leadership theories described in the text do you favour? Give reasons.

3. Prepare a discussion plan covering leadership based upon information given in the text.

Recommended reading: Adair J *Action-centred Leadership* (McGraw-Hill, London 1973).

8

Fault Diagnosis

by G Chamberlain, Senior Training Advisor,
Food Drink and Tobacco Industry Training Board
(*Plant Engineer,* volume 24, No. 2, March 1980)

Introduction

The increasing use of high-volume production plants in the food, drink and tobacco industries has placed a heavy emphasis on the importance of good plant utilisation. Achieving effective plant utilisation, ie maximum saleable product at optimum production cost, is a primary objective for production managers.

At the same time, the increasing complexity of plant has made the achievement of effective plant utilisation more difficult. In most food plants there is an urgent need to reduce downtime; relatively small improvements in machine performance can provide large benefits.

To quote one example, a recently installed high volume cake plant operating at 86% on line efficiency was losing an estimated £350,000 of product sales value as a result of the 5% engineering element of the downtime. We are regularly being advised of similar problems and the cost of a lengthy machine breakdown on canning lines designed to operate at 1250 cans per minute is not difficult to imagine.

Since a reduction in the engineering element of plant downtime can result in a major effect on the profitability of a production line, it is evident that it is important to improve diagnostic and general engineering skills among those working closely with the plant. In consequence, the Food Drink and Tobacco Industry Training Board has become increasingly involved in this area of training.

This paper is intended to provide an insight into some of the thinking about diagnostic skills that has gone on within the Board over the years, and contains some of the material used in the diagnostic skills package that is being developed.

Background to Board Work

Some years ago a small group of Board advisers with engineering backgrounds started to respond to requests from industry to provide assistance in designing and carrying out training for maintenance personnel, in an attempt to keep pace with advancing technology and the need to reduce to a minimum the downtime which normally followed a machine malfunction.

These demands have increased considerably in the intervening period, to such an extent that the Board now employs more than twenty advisers with engineering or technical backgrounds. And they could, if desired, spend a large proportion of their time on this one highly significant area of training.

To ensure that we continued to meet the needs of industry in this area of training, it became necessary to collect and evaluate all relevant material currently being used by different advisers within the Board. The collection of this material has now been completed and developed into a package suitable for use by any training specialist, with suitable technical background, in the development of maintenance personnel and of associated job and training aids/systems for the reduction of machine downtime.

The Diagnostic Skills Package

The material which has been developed is

comprehensive and contains tutor's notes, handouts, background material, examples of job and training aids, as well as exercises and overhead projector slides.

Although the package is currently only suitable for use by the Board's own staff it has been compiled in such a way that it can be readily adapted to provide a resource for the company trainer. Subject to internal approval this could be available in 1980.

Diagnostic Skills

Diagnosis is an activity we all engage in every day. The housewife diagnoses what went wrong when food is not cooked correctly; the motorist diagnoses the threat from other traffic when deciding if it is safe to turn right; the doctor diagnoses illness in a patient; the engineer diagnoses faults on plant and equipment.

Little detailed research has taken place into the nature of diagnostic ability and organisations specialising in selection have not defined it. Nevertheless, a number of factors have emerged from studies and discussions with engineers. For instance, one can hypothesise that the expert diagnostician displays a number of characteristics which are part of his skill, for example.

He appears to have a planned strategy in his mind when searching for a fault.

★ Before making any adjustments to the equipment he stands back and weighs up all the available evidence in an attempt to decide what significant action could have been taken previously by machine operatives, supervisors, etc; this is in contrast to the 'muddler' who acts on impulse, making adjustments before mentally sifting through all the available evidence.

★ If working on equipment manned by operatives, there is a rapport between operative and the diagnostician; the operative has confidence in the fitter/ diagnostician's ability to repair the fault rather than make it worse, and thus is willing to discuss openly any action taken and adjustments made before the breakdown.

★ He has an intimate knowledge of the equipment on which he is working; this appears to be knowledge not only of the function and operation of each part of the equipment, but also how each part

relates to every other part-this knowledge is essential when there is cause/ symptom disassociation.

★ He is completely familiar with all of the common faults which occur on the equipment; this is extremely important information since it enables the diagnostician to survey the fault symptoms quickly and decide which, in each particular case, are relevant and which are redundant, and then speedily diagnose and rectify the fault.

Our experience therefore clearly points to the fact that diagnosis is a mental skill, and the traditional craft training which is mainly of a manipulative nature is not directly aimed at developing the attributes required to be a proficient fault finder. This also provides a clear indication that the type of person required to carry out diagnosis needs to have a stronger bias towards thinking skills than in the past.

Some of the components of this mental ability appear to be:

MEMORY

Remembering the machine functions and their interrelations; also the relevant symptoms for each fault situation, and the search strategy and subsequent action. Memory is particularly useful in recalling HOW to approach particular types of problem rather than WHAT was done in terms of specific actions. This is consistent with having an open mind, so avoiding the trap of repeating previous actions irrespective of the true symptoms of previous faults.

LOGICAL THINKING

Based on the clues given in the fault situation. The ability to work out a rational strategy for finding and repair of the fault. However, the component diagnostician will not always follow a totally logical sequence but will think 'heuristically' moving to an immediate solution without apparently following the total sequence.

PERCEPTION

To recognise and interpret the clues given by the equipment and operatives/supervisors so that the correct search and repair strategy can be embarked upon. The maintainer and operator may observe the same situation but, because of their different training and life experiences, they will perceive the situation differently. This can be of significance when an operator explains to a maintainer the events leading to a breakdown.

SPATIAL/MECHANICAL ABILITY
To be able to manipulate parts of the equipment in thought, ie to simulate the working of the machinery to gain an understanding of its action.

SOCIAL SKILLS
To be able to work with supervisors and machine minders, in particular, so that they are willing to discuss faults and hence give valuable information to aid the diagnosis. This is a key ability, and one that requires open minded attitudes and understanding of the total work situation.

PERSISTENCE
With major faults the diagnostician is working in an ambiguous situation, often frustrating and stressful, and hence he must have staying power to keep delving until the cause of the fault is discovered. He must be able to contend with the pressure brought about by the needs of production, and have confidence in his own ability and knowledge.

BACKGROUND KNOWLEDGE
Along with the abilities mentioned above, the diagnostician must have knowledge gained by training and experience. This knowledge is wide ranging and will include product and raw material knowledge, including characteristics of packaging and the processes. This can be used in conjunction with general engineering knowledge and knowledge of the specific machinery. This core of knowledge will enable the diagnostician to behave effectively and, together with understanding of the total factory system, enable him to take appropriate action.

Diagnostic Performance

When considering the reduction of downtime through diagnostic performance, experience tells us that in addition to the training which is necessary to improve the skills of the diagnostician there are other key factors which should be considered. These include, machine and system design, and the availability to the diagnostician of suitable job aids. Indeed, it is generally the case that the better the job aid the less technical training is required. The emphasis on training can then be placed on the correct interpretation and application of these job aids.

Job and Training Aids

If we were opening a new factory and if diagnostic skills were innate and not learnt, we could attempt to recruit the 'born' diagnostician and develop his skills further. The situation most companies find themselves in, however, is different. Evidence suggests that diagnostic skills are neither wholly innate nor learnt, and there would also appear to be a lack of suitable people available. The problem is aggravated further by the fact that many of the jobs which require a high degree of diagnostic ability are already held by tradesmen who served traditional craft apprenticeships and were developed to perform manual rather than mental skills.

This being the case, it is imperative that retraining is carried out and that both new and existing diagnosticians are provided with some basic techniques supported by job aids to assist them in following a systematic search strategy.

There are a number of techniques which have been developed to produce job aids and these all have varying degrees of merit according to the type and complexity of the equipment being considered.

Some of the techniques may also be suitable for use by operatives. Before developing them for any work situation, therefore, it is necessary to consider carefully their many advantages and disadvantages and different situations.

Some of the more common techniques include:

SYMPTOM/FAULT CHARTS
This technique requires a log of faults and their associated symptoms to be compiled. The appropriate action to be taken to remedy the fault can then be added, and the information gathered can then be displayed.

It can be seen from this display that, once symptoms have been identified, they direct the fault finder towards the fault. In some cases there is more than one symptom to a fault, or alternatively the symptom displayed could point to a number of faults. This being the case, we cannot always assume that the symptoms will automatically lead us to the fault. (See below.)

PROBABILITY ANALYSIS CHART
Symptom/Fault charts can be modified, according to experience, to show the *most probable* faults.

Symptom	Possible Causes	Remedy
Fault: ENGINE WILL NOT START		
1 Starter cartridge does not fire	i) Breech indexed on spent cartridge	i) Operate indexing lever
	ii) Barrel not indexing correctly	ii) Change breech
	iii) Defective cartridge	iii) Wait 30 seconds Change cartridge
	iv) Faulty electrical connections	iv) Trace fault, rectify or use emergency battery start
2 Cartridge fires but engine does not run	i) Ruptured safety disc	i) Renew safety disc
	ii) Exhaust valve stuck open	ii) Change starter
	iii) Starter piston stuck	iii) Change starter
3 Engine turns but does not start (ie cartridge fires)	i) No fuel in tank	i) Fill tank
	ii) Air lock in fuel system	ii) Prime fuel system
	iii) Starting accumulator inoperative	iii) Trip accumulator, check racks, prime and change accumulator
Fault: ENGINE WILL NOT RUN		
1 Engine stops soon after starting	i) Defective fuel pump	i) Change pump, prime system
	ii) Air lock in fuel system	ii) Prime system
	iii) Choked fuel filters	iii) Renew elements, prime system
Fault: IRREGULAR RUNNING		
1 Hunting (RPM surge)	i) Air lock in governor	i) Prime governor system
	ii) Worn governor linkage	ii) Renew defective parts
2 Engine races	i) Defective governor	i) Change governor Prime system
	ii) Injection pump linkage stiff or worn	ii) Trace cause Lubricate or adjust linkage

FACERAP

This is a technique built up around the mnemonic FACERAP, which enables us to remember the seven key steps taken in a logical approach to a fault recognition:

Fault — the name of the fault and its classification

Appearance — the description of the fault or symptom relating to it.

Cause — the operational reason for the fault

Effect — the consequential effect of the fault

Responsibility — the correct person to take remedial action

Action — the standard procedure to be adopted to rectify the fault

Prevention — the procedure to avoid repetition of the fault

By using this technique, a logical approach to dealing with all faults can be compiled. Additional advantages include the use of a 'common language' and a clear definition of who is responsible for the appropriate remedial action.

STANDARD TIMING DIAGRAMS

This is a useful technique for displaying information concerning machinery with a common drive, or major sections driven by a common drive. (See diagram 1.)

The movements of the components, reciprocating or rotary, are plotted in relation to the primary drive motion. Alternatively, in the absence of a common drive, they are related to the operational cycle from a base start time.

In many applications timing discs are built on to the machine. This technique is not only useful for the re-tuning of machines but can be used for standard set-up or change over procedures for both operatives and craftsmen.

FUNCTIONAL PHASE DIAGRAMS

This technique can be a useful alternative to

the standard timing diagram. It is a means of examining a dynamic situation by introducing phases of operations which can be related in sequence on a chart. (See diagram 2.)

This technique is particularly useful for rationalising complex pneumatic/hydraulic/electrical circuits.

FUNCTIONALISATION

Possibly the most useful technique as an aid to fault diagnosis is that of Functionalisation.

The commonest means of presenting information about electrical or electronic equipment is the circuit diagram. This provides a symbolic presentation of each component in the circuit, and its physical relationship to the other components. A typical circuit diagram is illustrated in Figure 1.

Each component in this diagram performs a function, and most functions are dependent on other functions for successful operation. Unfortunately, the form of Figure 1 makes it extremely difficult to establish these relationships and to follow them through in particular function sequences.

The same information can be presented in a systematic manner which emphasises these functional relationships, as in Figure 2. By eliminating the crossed linkages and arranging the components so that inputs and outputs flow from left to right in sequence across the diagram, the effect of a malfunction in any component can be easily established.

This now becomes a powerful job aid. Even a relatively inexperienced person would stand a good chance of identifying a malfunction from information presented in this manner. This technique can be applied in all situations where one function relies upon another, and can be readily adapted to pneumatic, hydraulic and mechanical systems in a similar way.

ALGORITHMS

This technique, originally developed for computer programming, is based on binary thinking. It is laid out in a series of logical steps each of which is preceded by a question which will draw an answer of yes or no. This procedure can then be followed until the solution is reached. (See diagram 3.)

This technique is also commonly used for training in switching on or closing down procedures. When considering some of the more complex faults however, algorithms can often be difficult to produce and impracticable. It should also be remembered that algorithms can only be produced for a known or common fault, a factor which can also be applicable when considering the production of Symptom/Fault charts, Probability Analysis chart and FACERAP.

SEARCH STRATEGY

Once the diagnostician has either the skills to visualise a circuit or a machine as a series of functions, or as a job aid to enable him to see it as such, it is then necessary for him to apply a search strategy which will help him to locate the fault in the minimum time.

This can be done by applying a narrowing-down process and splitting the possible area where the fault could lie into two groups, each having an equal probability for containing the fault. Each section can then be tested for inputs and outputs until the fault is progressively isolated (see diagram 4). This is called the 'half split' method.

If there is no power at T1, test at T2. If no power at T2, fault lies before supply divides. (A)

If power is at T2, fault lies in B.

It is apparent that Functional Diagrams are a powerful aid when using the 'half split' method.

Once the attributes of the diagnostician have been developed and he has been trained in a basic search strategy, he may still find it extremely difficult to apply a disciplined approach to all diagnostic situations. It will then be necessary to provide him with an approach which will ensure that he doesn't 'muddle' and destroy whatever evidence is available before the fault is located.

One effective approach which has been used successfully in the past is the 'six step approach'.

The steps are:

1 Collect evidence (stop and think)
2 Analyse evidence (check assumptions)
3 Locate fault (inspect and test)
4 Determine and remove cause (ask why fault occurred)
5 Rectify fault
6 Check system

When carrying out training to develop the discipline required for the successful application of this approach, we have found the film, 'Fault analysis' (produced by Rank Xerox) particularly useful.

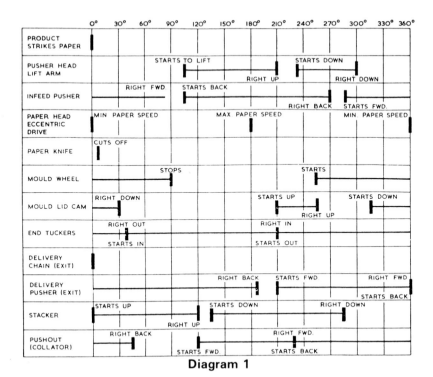

Diagram 1

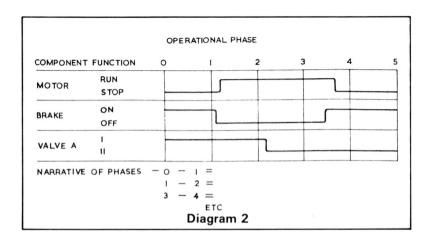

Diagram 2

Functionalisation — Figure 1

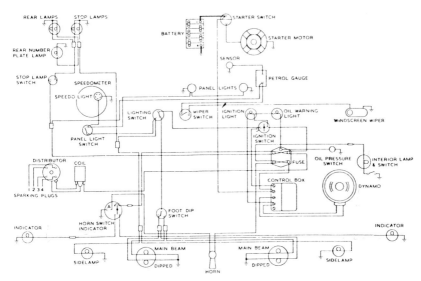

Functionalisation — Figure 2

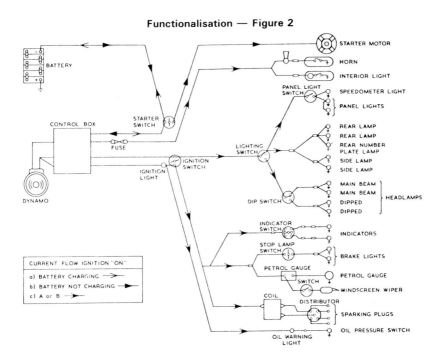

Conclusion

Fault diagnosis is not easy. As technology advances to the extent that machines are becoming increasingly more complex, it is essential that more emphasis is placed on how they are to be maintained to provide maximum utilisation.

There are many aspects to consider when doing this and it is important to consider a wide variety of things which can determine how efficiently fault diagnosis is carried out. These include recruitment and selection, training, systems design and job aids, and how they are all interrelated. Once all of these things have been considered, we can then move more confidently towards reducing machine downtime through improved fault diagnosis.

Diagram 3

Algorithm developed from and for use with Function Flow diagram of car wiring system

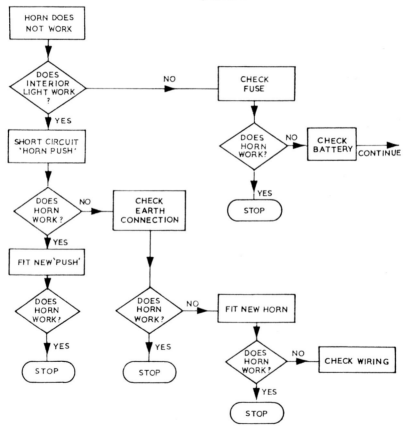

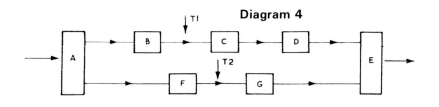

Diagram 4

9

The overhead projector

Prepared by staff of the Department of Educational Resources, Head: C H Teall, BA, Dip Ed Tech, and reproduced by kind permission of K G Lavender, BSc (Eng) (Hons) C Eng, MIEE, M Inst W, Principal, South Thames College.

Your first attempts at transparency making

```
MATERIALS YOU WILL NEED

Squared drafting paper
1 set thin felt tip OHP pens
1 set thick felt tip OHP pens
Box of acetate sheets
Masking tape
OHP Transparency frames
Sheets of transparent selfadhesive
 colour film
Bottle of cleaning fluid
Sharp-pointed knife
```

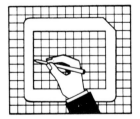

1. *Planning.* This is why you need the squared drafting paper. Lay the transparency frame on a piece of squared paper and draw round the outline of the aperture. Plan the layout of your visual within this boundary.

344

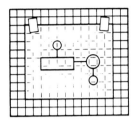

2. Fix a piece of acetate over your draft with small pieces of masking tape. This keeps acetate and paper in register.

3. Using the pens of your choice draw the outlines of your visual. Add colour and lettering as planned.

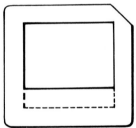

4. Select a frame of the correct size. This will be either 10″×8″ or 10″×10″ aperture. Some 10″×8″ (rectangular) frames have push out sections to make them 10″×10″.

5. Position the Vufoil on the table and place a frame over it so that the cut off corner is to top right.

6. Turn frame and Vufoil over and secure all edges with masking tape.

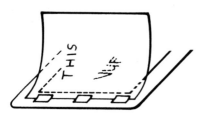

7. If overlays or masks are required they should be positioned correctly and fixed to the top of the frame with self-adhesive aluminium foil hinges (Techinges) or masking tape.

8. Label frame clearly for filing, write notes on frame edge.

This of course is the simplest way of making your visual. Higher quality lettering can be obtained by using dry transfer lettering (Letraset or Letterpress) and large blocks of colour can be added with the self adhesive transparent colour film or transparent coloured tapes (these are very useful for graphs or bar charts).

Applying transpaseal

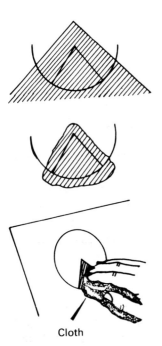

Cloth

1. Select the colour and place the sheet of the Transpaseal over the area to be covered.

2. Using scissors cut out a piece slightly larger than that required.

3. Peel off the backing and carefully apply to the Vufoil surface rubbing with a circular motion from one end so as to exclude all the air bubbles.

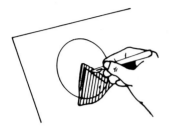

4. Using a sharp knife cut round the true edge lines using the lines in the diagram as guides. Only press hard enough to penetrate the Transpaseal. Do not cut through the Vufoil. Avoid cutting beyond the lines on the diagram as this will leave a scratch line on the acetate which will project as a black line.

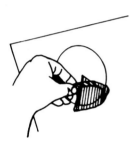

5. Carefully peel off the surplus Transpaseal and discard.

Dry transfer lettering

There are several types on the market. Use Projectatype for OHP work.

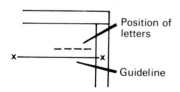

1. Place a sheet of ruled paper under the Vufoil and clearly indicate the base line to be followed. This is to be aligned with the guide lines below the letter.

2. Where positioning of words is left to right start from the first letter.

3. When positioning of words is central, work out the middle letter and start from there. Remember however that not all letters take up the same space. (If 'A' is standard 'I' takes up $\frac{1}{2}$ the space and 'W' $1\frac{1}{2}$ times.)

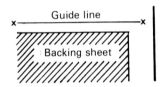

4. To avoid accidental transfer of letters on to other parts of the Vufoil keep the backing sheet between the Projectatype and the Vufoil positioning it to expose the area where the letters are to be transferred.

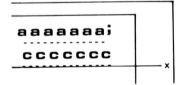

5. Position the guide below the letters on the base line and locate the letter to be transferred.

6. Starting at the top rub down the whole letter with the rounded end of a pen. Start gently at first and increase pressure until the letter separates from the transfer sheet.

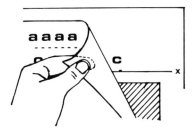

7. Slowly pull the sheet of letters from the Vufoil, leaving the letter adhering to the Vufoil. Hold the sheet in position until you are sure the whole letter has been transferred.

8. Proceed exactly as before to complete the lettering using the spacing marks on the sheet.

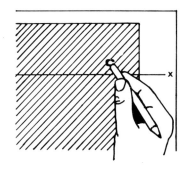

9. When all the letters have been transferred, place the backing sheet over the letters and rub down with a thumbnail or rounded pencil end to ensure transfer.

10. Replace the backing sheet on the sheet of lettering and place in the storage wallet.

Making transparencies using photocopiers

Most offices, educational and training establishments have some type of photocopying equipment. In the majority of cases transparency material is available for these copiers although the range will vary considerably.

Some photocopiers will only take a single sheet—while others will accept a book or other bound material. The most useful copier (and often the cheapest) for making OHP transparencies is the heat copier since a wide range of specially treated acetate is available. By buying different acetates you have a choice of black or coloured lines on a clear background, black lines on a coloured background or white lines on a black background. You can, of course, make your base visual this way and add colour with pens or the transparent self adhesive film.

Heat copiers will only accept single sheets and the original must be drawn in a carbon or metallic based ink or in pencil since they are 'blind' to colour inks.

True photocopiers will produce half tones but usually the quality of a transparency made on these machines is poorer.

SPECIAL HINT

If you have access to both a true photocopier (Xerox, Electrostatic or chemical) and a heat copier you can make a single black and white copy on the photocopier and use this as the original for the heat copier to get much better results.

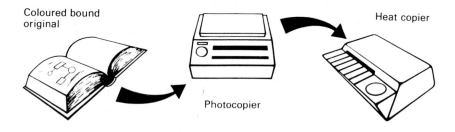

The quality of the result will depend on the type of photocopier you can use and the quality of the intermediate photocopy. Experiment for the best results.

Once again draft your original on squared paper, then draw it carefully – 2B pencil is probably the easiest to use. If the lines on the squared paper are in coloured ink they will not be seen by the heat copier. Do not pass ordinary Letraset through a heat copier – it will lift off destroying your original.

The design of OHP transparencies

The basic rules of design apply but in addition you will find the following useful.

1. Lettering should be large enough to read from the back of the room. Ordinary typeface is too small.

USE THIS SIZE AS THE MINIMUM.

2. Do not try to squeeze too much information onto one transparency.

3.

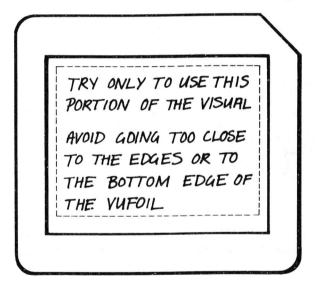

- Do not over-crowd your transparency with too much material or print.
- Get the spacing right.
- Make sure the material is clear and easy to read.
- Try to achieve some visual interest and appeal. Use visual symbols not words.
- Keep it Bold and Simple.

10
A brief account of the results of Piaget's and Kohlberg's investigations of moral development

As adults we tend to assume that the young child's psychological world is just like ours, only in miniature. Well it's not, and the one person above all to show this is Piaget.†

An adult copes with his world in terms of concepts such as mass, time and length, which provide a basis for his thoughts. These concepts are acquired slowly during childhood in fairly predictable stages before attaining the form familiar to adults. Piaget has studied these fundamental concepts.

Piaget stresses the significance of growing up while interacting with the environment and attempts to describe stages through which children gradually acquire knowledge. He places emphasis on the evolution of intelligence over a period of time. His approach stresses the importance of self-direction rather than external punishment and reward.

Piaget's investigations reveal that a child's thinking does not depend upon what it has been told by others, or on answers invented on the spur of the moment. He placed children in stress-free situations and then asked them questions. They had to think for themselves. These sessions included short stories which the child was asked to evaluate. The child was told two stories, one where an act motivated by the intention to deceive resulted in little damage, and another where a well-meant but clumsy act resulted in a lot of damage. The child was then asked whether one was more blameworthy than the other, and if so, why. Piaget was then able to find out whether or not the ' took account of motive in its judgements. He was concerned with the

†Professor D Wright: Television Programme 'Naughty Things' Course D 305 The Open University.

problem of how a child's response to a question should be evaluated. If a child's answer is something overheard from an adult, or the child is saying what it thinks an adult wants to hear, then, it has little value as an indication of the child's own thinking.

In their book *Introduction to Psychology*† Hilgard *et al* outline Piaget's main stages of intellectual development commencing with what he termed the 'sensorimotor' stage. This stage lasts from birth to the age of two, during which time the infant discriminates between itself and objects, gradually becoming aware of the connection between actions and their effects on the environment.

The next—the 'preoperational' stage—covers the age range from two to seven years. During this period the child uses language and can represent objects by images and words. Objects are classified by single prominent features, but towards the end of this stage, the child begins to use numbers and to develop conservation concepts.

Stage three is known as the 'concrete operational' stage from seven to twelve, during which the child becomes capable of logical thought and achieves conservation concepts such as number, mass and force. The child can also classify objects, arrange them in order of size and appreciate statements such as, 'the smallest is lighter than the largest'.

The final stage, Piaget termed the 'formal operational' stage. From the age of twelve, the child becomes capable of thinking in abstract terms and following logical statements forming the solution to a problem or following the stages in a demonstration or experiment. The child is able to identify the essential parts of a problem and to consider feasible solutions; eventually becoming concerned with hypothetical problems and developing a system of ideas relating to or characterising a given topic.

Piaget's work influenced others and in an attempt to discover whether or not there were set stages in moral development applicable to all, Lawrence Kohlberg of Harvard University used Piaget's work on moral reasoning as a basis for further research.

In a study of the moral development of 75 American male adolescents and adults drawn from different social environments and age groups, each participant was told one of a selection of ten stories containing moral dilemmas (see Heinz's Dilemma page 354). Kohlberg then asked them

†Hilgard E, Atkinson R C, Atkinson R L *Introduction to Psychology* 7th edn. (Harcourt Brace Jovanovich, New York 1979) page 71.

questions which were subsequently analysed and as a result proposed six stages of moral development. These were based upon the reasons given for answers to his questions rather than on the basis of whether the answers were considered to be correct.

Level 1, the 'premoral' level, consists of two stages, as do the other two levels. During stage one, the person complies so as to avoid sanctions. During stage two, the person complies for personal gain.

Level 2, the level of 'morality of conventional role conformity', contains stage three, where the person conforms in order to avoid disapprobation and denial by others, and stage four, where the person conforms in order to avoid blame or reproof from those in authority.

Level 3, the level of 'morality of self-accepted moral principles', consists of stage five, where a person conforms in order to retain the respect of others such as neighbours and the public at large, and stage six, where the person conforms in order to avoid self-censure or damnation.

Kohlberg concluded that some people do not reach level 3, the highest level of moral development. This conclusion was based upon the fact that less than one-tenth of his sample were able to frame answers at the highest level of abstract thought, in response to questions such as, 'Should Heinz have stolen the drug?'

Kohlberg's story 'Heinz's Dilemma'†

In Europe a lady was dying because she was very sick. There was one drug that the doctors said might save her. The drug was discovered by a man living in the same town. It cost him 200 dollars to make it but he charged 2000 for just a little of it.

The sick lady's husband, Heinz, tried to borrow enough money to buy the drug. He went to everyone he knew to borrow the money. But he could borrow only half of what he needed. He told the man who made the drug that his wife was dying, and asked him to sell the medicine cheaper or let him pay later. But the man said, 'No, I made the drug and I'm going to make money from it.' So Heinz broke into the store and stole the drug.

---

†Example of a hypothetical moral dilemma presented to Kohlberg's research group. Research results are discussed in Kohlberg L. 'The child as a moral philosopher' in *Psychology Today*, vol. 2, 1968, pages 25-30.

The following response given by a young adolescent illustrates the type of statement that would fall within Kohlberg's highest stage of moral development.

By the law of society he was wrong but by the law of nature or of God, the druggist was wrong and the husband was justified. Human life is above financial gain. Regardless of who was dying, if it was a total stranger, man has a duty to save him from dying.†

In his book *Psychology: Explorations in Behaviour and Experience*†† Sarnoff Mednick says that Kohlberg describes the child as a 'moral philosopher' who develops moral standards of his own, these standards not necessarily coming from parents or peers, but emerging from the interaction of the child with his social environment. Mednick goes on to say that Kohlberg used the term 'stage' in his classification of moral judgement because the sequence is invariable—stage three following stage two and so on. A person always moving in the forward direction and one stage at a time. Although the sequence is invariable, the 'rate of development' is readily affected by environmental circumstances.

Neither Piaget nor Kohlberg offers an adequate explanation of how it is that children come to see lying and injustice as wrong; yet it cannot be merely through their being told so by adults.

Perhaps the most important element in the researches of both Piaget and Kohlberg lies in the possibility that their work on the theory of moral development provides a means of contrasting between other perspectives such as learning theory and psychoanalysis.

†Kohlberg L 'Stage and sequence: the cognitive–developmental approach to socialization', in Goslin D A (ed) *Handbook of socialization theory and research* (Rand McNally, Chicago 1969) page 225.
††Mednick S A, Higgins J and Kirschenbaum J *Psychology: Explorations in Behaviour and Experience* (John Wiley & Sons, New York 1975).

11

The main relationships between social class and educational opportunity and attainment

The backbone of class structure, and indeed of the entire reward system of modern western society, is the occupational order. Other sources of economic and symbolic advantage do co-exist alongside the occupational order, but for the vast majority of the population, these tend, at best, to be secondary to those deriving from the division of labour.†

Primary inequalities in Britain are made up of differences between individuals or groups in the form of income, wealth, class and power from which stem secondary inequalities, including inequality in the areas of health, housing and education.

It follows from this that before considering inequalities within the educational system, it is first necessary to look at the primary sources of inequality.

The most commonly used indicator of social class in Britain and the USA is occupation. Blau and Duncan†† suggest that the occupational structure in modern industrial society not only constitutes an important foundation for social stratification, but also serves as the connecting link between institutions and spheres of social life, and hierarchies of prestige, economic class, political power and authority. They go on to say that the occupational structure is the link between the economy and the family through which the economy affects the family's status and by which the family supplies manpower to the economy.

†Parkin F *Class Inequality and Political Order* (Paladin, St. Albans 1975) page 18. Reprinted by kind permission of Granada Publishing Ltd, St. Albans, Herts.
††Blau P M and Duncan O D *The American Occupational Structure* (Free Press, New York 1978).

Income is, in general, directly linked to occupation, with managers, scientists and professionals receiving higher remuneration than labourers for example. This difference in income and social class deriving from occupation, forms the basis of one of the primary dimensions of inequality and directly affects an individual's education. Educational inequality is therefore essentially a social problem.

Recent psychological knowledge indicates that ability is largely acquired, and that children can become more or less 'intelligent' according to the kind of family they have, together with the social and educational experiences they receive.

Family background and lifestyle play an important part in the development of a child's academic performance, and where home values and norms correspond to those of the school, the child has a greater opportunity to succeed in school-valued tasks. Professor Bernstein's theory of linguistic codes stresses the importance of language and learning, and points to disadvantages in coming from a home where a public language or restricted code is spoken, in view of the fact that schools are essentially middle-class institutions.

If children are labelled 'culturally deprived', teachers will have lower expectations of them—expectations which the children will undoubtedly fulfil. The children will be expected to drop their social identity, way of life and values at the school gate and switch on to a completely different culture more representative of a middle-class lifestyle—supervised by teachers, the majority of whom have either originated from middle-class families or have adopted middle-class values during the course of their education or teacher training.

In an attempt to reduce educational inequalities in the United States and Britain, priority has been given to egalitarian reforms. In Britain, this has been evident in policies to abolish selection, to introduce comprehensive education and to promote positive discrimination in favour of the most disadvantaged groups.

The Plowden Report findings indicated that socially disadvantaged children needed a greater slice of the educational cake in the form of positive discrimination. This was to be in the form of better schools and better teachers who had been trained to teach a curriculum to suit the children's needs and aspirations.

Comprehensives were introduced to reduce some of the inequalities of opportunity existing in society and to eliminate inequalities that go with low income, broken homes or living in difficult conditions in inner city areas.

Political processes for school provision in the form of the variety of schools provided by the state, school-leaving age, buildings, staff/student ratios and political processes at local level, greatly influence the educational opportunities available to children within a given area. The area of residence directly affects educational opportunities depending on range and number of places available.

In his book *The State in Capitalist Society*† Ralph Miliband says that educational institutions at all levels generally fulfil an important conservative role and act, with greater or lesser effectiveness, as legitimising agencies in and for their societies. He goes on to say that today, as in the past, elite schools consciously seek to instil into their charges a conservative philosophy based on tradition, religion, nationalism, authority, hierarchy, together with an exceedingly narrow view of the meaning of democracy, and hostility towards socialist ideas and purposes.

While entry to an elite school is theoretically open to all members of society, a tight selection process operates which works so as to favour children of higher social class parents and those who can afford to pay school fees.

All people are born equal in God's eyes, but from the moment they take their first breath are subjected to inequalities brought about by the social class into which they are born. Also, while innate intelligence is assumed to be randomly distributed, lifestyle and primary inequalities existing in society such as social class, wealth, income and power, tend to work against the poorer classes attaining educationally and developing this intelligence, while favouring the better off.

Non-school factors at the level of the home, local authority and central government affect the life chances of children, while factors such as streaming, selection and type of school attended can contribute to educational inequality. In some cases, schools do no more than train children for future role performance, often as low-paid, low-skilled workers, thereby confirming their class destiny and station in life. For some, the school provides the means of upward mobility, and a few will be creamed off into, perhaps, one class higher than the social class of their fathers. For the majority it will be the means of providing advanced capitalist society with a pool of trained personnel to keep the system going. On the other hand, the school will integrate brighter children into society and help them to escape from their working-class conditions, while assisting the remainder to accept their subordination.

†Miliband R *The State in Capitalist Society* (Quartet Books, London 1976) page 214. First published in UK by Weidenfeld & Nicolson (1969).

This state of affairs is likely to persist unless primary dimensions of inequality in society are eliminated by radical government policy, after which, secondary inequalities such as educational inequality will be alleviated.

In the meantime, differences in learning abilities of young adults and their attitudes toward learning will create problems for the teacher or instructor— problems that demand a sympathetic approach and much resolve on the part of the teacher to help learners overcome the adverse effects of an unfortunate start to their lifetime of learning. However, an equal commitment is needed from the learner if progress is to be made.

12
BTEC Unit DOR/058 Instructional Techniques and Practice

The unit was written by Mervyn F Dadds, of Weymouth College, to form part of the college's submission for a BTEC Diploma Course.

'A technician can be involved in one or both of the following training situations. The appropriate objectives are listed:

(i) Informal training situation—supervising the on-the-job work of an apprentice or trainee.
Objectives: 1.1–1.10, 1.12–1.15, 5.1–5.9, and 6.1–6.8.

(ii) Formal training situation—operating as an off-the-job instructor.
Objectives: all those listed in the unit.

Learning achieved whilst studying the unit will be most effective if planned opportunities to practise the objectives are simultaneously afforded by the technician's employer in actual training situations.'†

The unit has been validated by the Business & Technician Education Council and is suitable for inclusion in both BTEC Certificate and Diploma submissions.

DOR/058 may be adopted as a free-standing supplementary subject which may be studied by BTEC students, training officers, instructors and others engaged in training.

A completed validation form, assessment specification and set of unit objectives is included in the appendix as a guide for college BTEC co-

† Mervyn F Dadds, Weymouth College.

ordinators who may wish to adopt the unit. A specimen test is given at the end of the objectives.

Acknowledgement is due to the Technician Education Council for permission to reproduce the TEC college-designed unit DOR/058. The Council reserves the right to revise the content at any time.

PLEASE READ 'NOTES ON SUBMISSIONS FOR VALIDATION' BEFORE COMPLETING THIS FORM

Sheet

TECHNICIAN   **Programme Code No:**   No. of
EDUCATION | 9 | 9 | 0 | 0 | 4 | 6 | 7 | 9 | 0 | 2 | **VAL IV B : i**
COUNCIL

(Group)

VALIDATION FORM VAL IV B
INFORMATION ON COLLEGE-DEVISED UNITS
(Please use this form with each college devised unit)

1. **Unit Title**   Instructional Techniques and Practice

2. **Unit Code No.**   3. **Unit Level**   Free-standing
   (Form VAL III page ii) | 2 | 6 |

4. **Unit Value**   1.0   5. **Design Length** (hours)   60
   (single unit, half unit)

6. **Prerequisites for Unit**
   General and Communication Studies II

7. **Credit for Unit**
   None

8. **Aims of Unit**
   To enable technicians to develop instructional techniques

TECHNICIAN EDUCATION COUNCIL
COLLEGE DEVISED UNIT

1. **Unit Title:**   Instructional Techniques and Practice
2. **Unit Level:**   Free Standing

3. **Unit Value:**   One   **Design Length**   60 hours

4. **Programme:**   A5 Mechanical and Production Engineering

5. **Prerequisite Units:**
General and Communication Studies II

6. **Credits for Units:**

7. **Aims of the Unit:**
To enable technicians to develop instructional techniques

8. **Special Notes:**

9. **Assessment Specification**
The following gives the unit breakdown, by topic and types of learning, as a key to the production by a College of its assessment specification for this unit.

UNIT TOPIC AREA	TOPIC AS % OF ASSESSMENT	MOTOR SKILLS	Information	Comprehension	Application	Invention
			% of total assessment			
				Intellectual skills		
A	45		3	14	14	14
B	11		1	10		
C	8		1	5		2
D	6	2	1	1		2
E	30	5			15	10
	Percentage of assessment for entire unit	7	6	30	29	28

10. Unit Content

The unit topic areas and the general and specific objectives are set out below, the unit topic areas being prefixed by a capital letter, the general objectives by a non-decimal number, the specific objectives by a decimal number. THE GENERAL OBJECTIVES GIVE THE TEACHING GOALS AND THE SPECIFIC OBJECTIVES THE MEANS BY WHICH THE STUDENT DEMONSTRATES HIS ATTAINMENT OF THEM. Teaching staff should design the learning process to meet the general objectives. The objectives are not intended to be in a particular teaching sequence and do not specify teaching method, but, for example, practical work could be the most appropriate teaching method for the achievement of some objectives.

ALL THE OBJECTIVES SHOULD BE UNDERSTOOD TO BE PREFIXED BY THE WORDS: THE EXPECTED LEARNING OUTCOME IS THAT THE STUDENT:

A. TALKING WITH TRAINEES—COMMUNICATION

1. Develops the techniques of communication.

   1.1 States the psychological needs which motivate people to work.
   1.2 States the reasons why people need to communicate.
   1.3 Explains how communication aims at behaviour change.
   1.4 Explains the importance of non-verbal signals to the instructor.
   1.5 Explains the reasons for nervousness in an instructor.
   1.6 Describes typical mannerisms associated with nervousness.
   1.7 Participates in a microtraining exercise in controlling non-verbal signals.
   1.8 Identifies characteristics which establish rapport.
   1.9 Lists and explains the types of responses required of trainees in order that spoken communication may take place.
   1.10 States that teaching is the art of causing these responses to happen.
   1.11 Explains the three elements of communication and the significance of perception in the communication process.
   1.12 Distinguishes between one-way and two-way communication.
   1.13 Participates in an exercise involving one-way and two-way communication.
   1.14 Appraises a videotaped presentation in terms of its non-verbal support.
   1.15 Participates in a microtraining exercise in establishing rapport.

2. Understands and uses behavioural objectives.

   2.1 Defines an aim and an objective.
   2.2 Writes examples of aims.
   2.3 Explains the meaning of motor, recall, comprehension, application and invention skills.
   2.4 Lists the component parts of a statement of an objective.
   2.5 Recognises the type of skill involved in each of a list of objectives.
   2.6 Writes a set of aims and behavioural objectives for a training programme.
   2.7 Writes a set of behavioural objectives for a short talk to be given to the group.
   2.8 Prepares the closing sentence of the above talk and presents it to the group whilst being videorecorded.
   2.9 Discusses the most successful aspects of other group members' presentations particularly in reference to the supposed objectives.

3. **Understands the value of testing and assessing and designs various tests.**

3.1 States that testing monitors the trainees' progress and measures the terminal effect of the training.
3.2 States that before writing a test one should decide what is:—
(a) critical;
(b) important; and
(c) relevant.
3.3 States that tests should be valid and reliable.
3.4 Explains the terms 'valid' and 'reliable'.
3.5 Describes the form of various test questions appropriate to the assesment of trainees' learning.
3.6 Explains the significance of the normal distribution curve and the grading of test results.
3.7 Prepares an objective type test to measure the effectiveness of a talk.
3.8 Prepares an assessment test to measure the effectiveness of a talk.
3.9 Prepares a verbalised rating scale with· which to give an assessment of the speakers' success in establishing rapport.

4. **Understands and uses the techniques involved in managing a discussion.**

4.1 Defines a discussion and distinguishes it from a debate.
4.2 Describes the feelings which prompt various kinds of responses in a discussion situation.
4.3 Describes the possible influences which participants might be subjected to during discussion.
4.4 States that the discussion should be managed so that each member feels a personal responsibility for every other member.
4.5 States the various useful purposes of discussions.
4.6 Explains the disadvantages of unled discussion groups.
4.7 Recognises the value of the discussion leader having a plan.
4.8 Prepares a plan for a discussion on a given topic.
4.9 Describes the procedure for discussions.
4.10 Presents to the group the opening of the discussion assigned to him.
4.11 Participates in an analysis session of 4.10 and fills in a rating scale for each presentation.
4.12 Analyses a filmed discussion.
4.13 Leads a fifteen minute discussion.

B. **TALKING TO TRAINEES—THE FACTORS WHICH INFLUENCE LEARNING**

5. **Understands the role of perception in the learning process.**

5.1 Recognises that perception is an active response to communication.
5.2 Defines attention.
5.3 Explains the role of attention in the process of perception.
5.4 Describes the effects of excessive detail in the learning process.
5.5 Explains the advantages of using block diagrams.
5.6 Defines perceptual experience.
5.7 Explains the importance of perceptual experience in the learning process.
5.8 Defines motivated experience.
5.9 Describes how motivated perception can be encouraged.

6. Understands behavioural patterns of adolescence.

    6.1 Discusses briefly the physical changes in adolescents.
    6.2 Discusses briefly the social development of adolescents.
    6.3 Discusses briefly the intellectual development of adolescents.
    6.4 Explains the effect of intellectual development on the learning process.
    6.5 Discusses the limitations imposed on intellectual development by a restricted verbal code.
    6.6 Discusses the role of instructor expectation on the progress of a trainee.
    6.7 Discusses the effect of peer group attitudes on the progress of a trainee.
    6.8 Explains the effect of social influence processes on individual behaviour.

C. TEACHING

7. Understands and practises effective lesson preparation.

    7.1 Explains the importance of language in teaching and learning.
    7.2 Discusses the phychological imbalance of superiority between instructor and trainee and explains how to redress it.
    7.3 Lists the questions which need to be asked when designing the training plan.
    7.4 Describes the structure of a lesson.
    7.5 Describes the desirable features to include in a lesson.
    7.6 Describes the methods whereby a student learns.
    7.7 Describes the transfer of training.
    7.8 Describes a learning curve.
    7.9 Designs a lesson plan.
    7.10 Explains how discipline relates to classroom communications.

8. Understands and uses the various teaching methods.

    8.1 Describes the various teaching methods.
    8.2 Describes microtraining.
    8.3 Prepares and presents a five minute lesson on a given single concept or skill in a microtraining exercise.

D. AIDS TO LEARNING

9. Understands the purpose of aids and makes and uses such aids in appropriate learning situations.

    9.1 States the function of an audio-visual message.
    9.2 Identifies the behavioural objectives which might apply to the use of given aids.
    9.3 Describes the different aids available for the various teaching methods.
    9.4 Prepares an OHP tranparency and one other aid to be used in his teaching practice.
    9.5 Presents these aids in a microtraining exercise in which other group members write down the assumed objective of the aid and the group discusses the impact of the visual message, the design quality and the appropriateness.

E. MAIN TEACHING PRACTICE

Each group member will prepare a lesson to last between fifteen and twenty-five minutes and use a check list to analyse its effectiveness during discussion with the tutor.
Additional practice will be undertaken as necessary.

Specimen Test

The specimen test given below would be suitable for assessing how well the learner had achieved the objectives relating to section 2— Behavioural Objectives, the test is based upon a selection of objectives from the BTEC unit DOR/058.

Name_____

MAX MARK = 57

SECTION 2   BEHAVIOURAL OBJECTIVES |Marks

1. Define the following words as applied to the writing of learning objectives:

(a) Aim _____   2

_____

(b) Objectives _____   2

_____

2. Educational objectives have been classified by Bloom, Krathwohl and others into three domains. List the three domains and give a brief explanation of each.

              Domain   *Explanation*

(a) _____ _____ 1   1

_____

(b) _____ _____ 1   1

_____

(c) _____ _____ 1   1

_____

3. For any one of the domains named in Question 2 above list five of the main categories in the taxonomy structure.

(a)_____

(b)_____

(c)_____   5

(d)_____

(e)_____

4. State the three categories which are grouped together to form one known as *invention.*

		Marks
(a)	_____	1
(b)	_____	1
(c)	_____	1

5. Explain the meaning of the following terms:
   (a) Motor skills

   _____
   _____ 2

   (b) Recall

   _____
   _____ 2

   (c) Comprehension

   _____
   _____ 2

   (d) Application

   _____
   _____ 2

   (e) Invention skills

   _____
   _____ 2

6. Write down three examples of correctly written specific educational or training objectives.

   (a) _____
   _____ 2

   (b) _____
   _____ 2

   (c) _____
   _____ 2

7. From the following list, tick those words which would be Marks unsuitable for inclusion in a correctly written behavioural objective. Each is preceded by the word 'To'.

define	comprehend	state	recall
list	know	sketch	appreciate
enumerate	recognise	understand	analyse
draw	evaluate	assess	learn
believe	select	identify	compare

5

8. A list of aims and objectives is given below. Read each statement and classify correctly either as an AIM (A) or OBJECTIVE (O). Enter the appropriate letter in the answer box.

(a) The student shall be able to prepare, cook and present for service a three egg plain omelette.	1
(b) The student shall be a good wine waiter.	1
(c) The student shall have an appreciation of food hygiene.	1
(d) The student shall be able to give an oral translation of selected French menus.	1
(e) The student shall be able to distinguish between facts and inferences.	1

9. Below you will find a stated objective which includes the conditions, standards and performance expected. Complete the section beneath by writing in the word/words which relate to each of the three parts of the objective.

Note: All words should appear somewhere in your answer. "The student shall, without reference to any books or notes, write an essay on the role of the 'housekeeper' in a large hotel, of approximately 500 words in legible handwriting with no more than four spelling mistakes."

Conditions: _____ 2

Standards: _____ 2

Performance: _____ 2

10. The following behavioural objectives were identified as a Marks
prelude to a scheme of assessment. Classify each objective into
one of Bloom's three domains by writing in the name of the correct
domain beside each statement.
The student shall be able to:
   (a) Describe the safety procedure to be followed in the event
       of the fire alarm sounding.
   (b) Wire up correctly a 13 amp three pin domestic plug.
   (c) Calculate the area of a banqueting hall given its length
       and its width.
   (d) Tolerate irrational behaviour from a customer in the
       dining room.
   (e) Develop a technically satisfactory relationship with his
       project group.
   (f) Make a marzipan flower suitable for decoration of a gateau.   6

11. Bloom and his co-workers drew up a hierarchy of the major
categories in the cognitive domain. They considered 'knowledge'
as the lowest level of activity and 'evaluation' as the highest.

(i)   Knowledge: The ability to remember information that
                       has already been learned.
(ii)   Comprehension: The ability to take in the meaning of
                       information.
(iii) Application: The ability to use information that has
                       been learned.
(iv)   Analysis: The ability to break up information and so
                       understand its structure and organisation.
(v)   Synthesis: The ability to link or put together inform-
                       ation to form a whole out of the parts.
(vi)   Evaluation: The ability to judge the value of information
                       for a specific purpose.

Below are six groups of verbs which could be used to describe a
student's ability to act in the above six categories.
Which group of verbs applies to each of the above definitions?
   (a) distinguish, explain, give examples, infer, convert.
   (b) conclude, criticise, appraise, contrast, justify, discriminate,
       interpret, support, decide.
   (c) describe, label, define, list, name, select, reproduce.
   (d) show, solve, manipulate, operate, compute, demonstrate.
   (e) combine, modify, plan, revise, summarise, compile, design.
   (f) conclude, summarise, discriminate, appraise, justify, criticise.

Definition	(i)	(ii)	(iii)	(iv)	(v)	(vi)
Group of verbs						

6

Solutions to problems

Section 3.5—Objective test—Work study BS 3138:1969

1	2	3	4	5	6	7	8	9	10
a	d	b	a	d	c	a	b	c	c

Section 3.5—Statements with key words missing
1. 1895
   1952
   ELIZABETH
   MARGARET
   PHILIP, Duke of Edinburgh
   ANTHONY, Earl of Snowdon
   CHARLES, Prince of Wales
   PRINCESS ANNE
   PRINCE ANDREW
   PRINCE EDWARD
   DAVID VISCOUNT LINLEY
   LADY SARAH ARMSTRONG JONES

2. MILD   0.15   HARD   SOFT   ANNEALING
   NORMALISING   HARDEN AND TEMPERING   COLOUR
   PYROMETERS   THERMO-COUPLE

Section 3.7—Objective test—Mounting of abrasive wheels

1	2	3	4	5	6	7	8	9	10
c	d	b	d	d	a	c	b	c	d

Section 3, Questions relating to U75/004 Physical Science I Unit

1.	P	8.	Q
2.	S	9.	D
3.	L	10.	E
4.	Q	11.	F
5.	G	12.	AD
6.	A	13.	T
7.	D	14.	W

Section 7.1—Task 2

Category	%	Time (minutes)	
Teacher asks questions	10	12	⎫ 72
Other teacher talk	50	60	⎭
Pupils ask questions	5	6	⎫
Other pupil talk	20	24	⎬ 30
Silence or confusion	15	18	⎭

Average time talking/student = $\dfrac{30}{30}$ =1 minute

Section 8.1—Mirrorgrams (Daily Mirror, 1982)
20 January: THE MERRY WIVES OF WINDSOR
25 January: SEBASTIAN COE

Sun Mindbender No. 222

				X			
						X	
		X					
					X		
		X					
X							
			X				
							X

Tartaglia problem

Let C = One cannibal
RC = Rowing cannibal
M = Missionary

	R
C M	I
C M	V
RC M	E
	R

C + RC	——————▶
RC	◀——————
RC + C	——————▶
RC	◀——————
M + M	——————▶
M + C	◀——————
M + RC	——————▶
M + C	◀——————
M + M	——————▶
RC	◀——————
RC + C	——————▶
RC	◀——————
RC + C	——————▶

Index